A WINTER IN ARABIA

Born in Paris on January 31, 1893, Dame Freya Stark is one of this century's great travellers. Her first journey was to the Middle East in 1928, her latest to Nepal in 1981. In more than fifty years of travels in Arabia and the Levant she says that she has made one golden rule: never to make her own coffee or camp-bed. Arab friends called her 'mistress of endurance and fortitude in travel and the suffering of terrors and danger' after she had visited regions where no European woman had ever ventured. *A Winter in Arabia* could be called a sequel to *The Southern Gates of Arabia*, for it describes another journey to the Hadhramaut, that unexplored part of Arabia which in earlier centuries had formed part of the slave route for the lucrative incense trade.

When not travelling Dame Freya lives in Asolo, Italy, where she was brought up. She ascribes her great love of adventure partly to early training in the Dolomites with her parents, who would trek from Asolo across the Pelmo Pass to Cortina, where they caught the train to London. At the age of two, in their trip of 1895 Freya Stark was already showing an extraordinary degree of independence, constantly straying away from her parents, off the beaten track. And that independence has ever since been the secret of her success as a traveller and a writer.

A WINTER
IN ARABIA

FREYA STARK

CENTURY PUBLISHING

LONDON

First published in Great Britain in 1940 by John Murray

This edition published in 1983 by
Century Publishing Co. Ltd,
76 Old Compton Street, London W1V 5PA

ISBN 0 7126 0182 1

To
Doreen and Harold Ingrams
and all those friends in Aden
who made easy the paths of
Hadhramaut

The cover shows a painting from the collection at
The Mathas Gallery, 24 Motcomb Street, London.

Printed in Great Britain by
Richard Clay (The Chaucer Press) Ltd,
Bungay, Suffolk

CONTENTS

Foreword by Sir Kinahan Cornwallis, K.C.M.G.,
C.B.E., D.S.O.

Contents

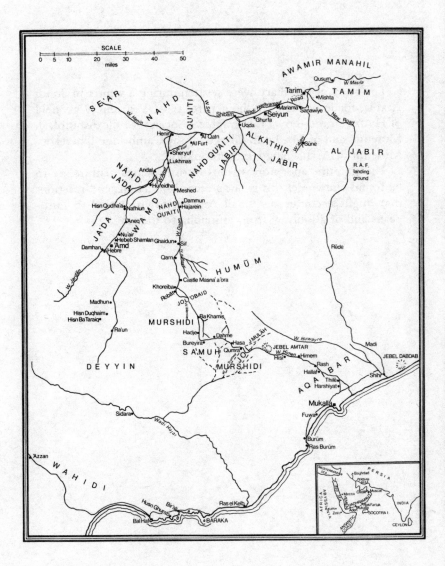

SCALE

0 5 10   20   30   40   50
miles

SE'AR

AWAMIR MANAHIL

Qusum W. Masila

NAHD QU'AITI

Tarim TAMIM

W. Hénin W. Sér Shibam Wadi Hadhramaut Road Mishta

Hénin Mariama Sanawiye New Road

Al Qatn Seiyun

Sheryuf Al Furt Uqda Ghurfa

Lukhmas AL KATHIR JABIR W. Bin Süne

NAHD JADA NAHD QU'AITI JABIR JABIR AL JABIR

Andal

Hufeidha R. A. F.
landing
ground

Meshed

Hisn Qudha'a Nafhiun Dammun
Hajarein

NAHD
QU'AITI

W. AMD W. Du'an

Aneq

Nu'air Rède

Hebeb Shamlan Ghaidun Sif

'Amd Hebre

JA'DA Damhan Qarn

HUMŪM

W. Jardin Castle Masna'a'bra

Madhun Khoreiba
Robât

JOL 'OBAID

Hisn Duqhaim Ra'un Ba Khamis

Hisn Ba Taraiq MURSHIDI Hadje

W. Huwayre Madi

Bureyira Dahme Hasa JEBEL DABOAB

SAMUH Qumra W. Mulāh JEBEL AMTAR

DEYYIN MURSHIDI Hisi W. Himen Himem

AQA BAR

Hallaf Rash

Thile Shihr

Harshiyat

Sidara Mukalla

Fuwa

Wadi Hajr

Burūm
Ras Burūm

'Azzan

WAHIDI

Husn Ghurab Bir'ali Ras el Kelb

Bal Haf BARAKA

The notes of this diary were written during a winter in South Arabia, made possible by the generosity of Viscount Wakefield of Hythe, of the Royal Geographical Society, of the Ashmolean Museum, and of Mr. Louis Clarke, of the Cambridge University Museum of Archaeology and Ethnology.

The scientific and more serious records of this venture are to be found elsewhere: this is but a record of actions and reactions that might occur in any small Arabian town unused to Europeans and of a journey from Hureidha to the sea.

FOREWORD

By Sir Kinahan Cornwallis,
K.C.M.G., C.B.E., D.S.O.

MISS FREYA STARK'S DIARY OF HER EXPEDITION TO ARABIA will afford interest and amusement to many, but it also points a lesson which no traveller in Eastern countries can afford to neglect. With two Englishwomen and unaccompanied by a police escort she set forth into country which, it is true, she had visited before, but which had never been brought under regular administration. The peace of the Ingrams had only recently replaced long years of inter-tribal warfare, and though the Shaikhs remembered her, they and their people were inclined to look upon the visitors and their unusual occupation with suspicion. Here was a situation which, if mishandled, might have led to failure if nothing worse; but Miss Stark is an experienced traveller who has a genuine interest in the Arabs, and her patent friendliness was able to bring success to the expedition and, no doubt, to leave behind pleasant memories which will last.

For several years I had experience of Miss Stark when I was in the Ministry of the Interior in Iraq. The movements of ladies in some of the wilder parts of the country without permission was quite rightly restricted, and unauthorized visits to Persia were strictly forbidden. Miss Stark made light of such bureaucratic red tape; she saved our hair from premature greyness by just going and telling us all about it on her return. She exercised, in fact, on us the same qualities as she showed to the Arabs, and soon built up for herself a privileged position.

The lesson is obvious. The Arab, like most of us, is essentially human; treat him, as he should be treated, as a friend and an equal and you get the best out of him; if you are aloof or superior or patronizing, you will get what you deserve. He is more than ordinarily sensitive and quick to imagine a slight, but he responds in like degree to friendliness and kindness. The value of personal contacts and friendships has been proved over and over again in the Middle East, and the evil effects of aloofness and indifference are clear for all to see. The average Englishman is not blessed with an exaggerated sense of imagination in his dealings with other races, but it is to be hoped that all who read Miss Stark's pages will learn the difference between the right way and the wrong, and profit thereby.

Chapter I

FROM THE AIR

" They shall behold a land of far distances."

(Isaiah.)

ON THE LAST DAY IN THE FIRST WEEK OF NOVEMBER, 1937, WE flew eastward from Aden, in a cool air filled with early sunlight, a honey light over the sandy shore.

We flew with the Indian Ocean on our right, puckered in motionless ripples, and upon it the broad white roadway of the sun. Seen from so high, the triple, lazy, lace-like edge of waves crept slowly; they did not turn all at once, but unrolled from end to end in a spiral motion, as it were the heart of a shell unwinding. Our aeroplane hung over the azure world with silver wings.

We moved eastward even as the great globe below imperceptibly moved, and were gaining on its circular horizon. Sharks far down were dimly visible, so limpid was the water; small black boats, pointed at either end, were out with their fishermen near the shore; a village or two, earth-coloured huts unnoticeable but for the fields around them, took shelter here and there from wind and sand. On our right the unfurrowed ocean, marked like a damascened blade; on our left the gaunt, leopard-coloured lands, equally lonely; and above, or rather around us, joyous, vivid, and infinite, the skyey spaces loud with our engine, which, like many a

3

mechanical mind, listens to its own voice alone in the silence of creation.

Beyond Shuqra, an ancient flood of lava pours to the sea. Heavy as dough, it rolls into deep water; craters with ruined edges are scattered among its folds. Northward, beyond its bleak and pock-marked slope, stands the high level of Kaur, a wall unbroken. The lava stream is past; the shore flattens out again for many miles; we quiver over the bay of the Fish-eaters, whose coasts, if we could see them close, are scattered with empty heaps of shells where their descendants still enjoy an ocean meal. The mountains again approach. A white table-land of limestone meets black volcanic ridges; sand drifts over all the landscape; it piles itself in blinding dunes where the great Meifa'a wadi sweeps to sea; it makes pale foot-hill ranges of its own, and covers with its shifting carpet the ancient floor of lavas. Here somewhere the frankincense road, the Arabian highway, came to the sea and found a crater-built harbour where the volcanic headlands lie, since there is no other commodity for shipping along the shallow strips of shore. We look down eagerly, for we mean later to investigate these inlets. Bal Haf is there, three small square towers on an infinitesimal, hook-like bay facing west. The lava-ridge runs in snouts beyond it; an empty crater, round and perfect, stands like a buttress and forms another inlet. I marvel to see no trace of ruins here, and only find out the reason months later, as I ride along the coast: there is no water.

But a great bay opens beyond, an amphitheatre of volcanoes and drift-sand, and in it another crater-buttress at the water's edge with markings like walls upon it, and the little square town of Bir Ali. Here, I later came to think, is the town of

To Mukalla

Cana: but now, as we fly over, we can take our choice of craters; one of them sticks out to sea like the horns of a crescent moon black in eclipse. Two islands, one black, one white with the droppings of gulls, lie in water misty with sunlight; they are the landmarks for Cana, given by that good mariner who wrote the Periplus nearly two thousand years ago.

And now we have passed Ras Kelb and Ras Burum, the fire-twisted ridges are past. Mukalla is in the distance, gathered at the foot of its hill; and our aeroplane, slowing obliquely, sinks to the landing-ground of Fuwa. Jusuf, who presides over landings, is there to meet us, a Buddha figure suddenly active: the young American who has come to look for oil is there, in a new Dodge, that races us over the sand. The sea makes a gay splashing, as if its solitary fields too were meant to be a playground: a million bubbles shine in the sun at the breaking edge of waves, tossed like lace frills on a petticoat; crabs, innumerable as water drops, slide from before our approaching car; until we come to fishermen, who walk barefoot along the hard wet shore and carry on a yoke their baskets of fish—we come to the camel park near the estuary which now lies full of water; through the pointed stone arch of the gateway, by the guard-house where Yafe'i mercenaries play at dice; to the home of the Resident Adviser.

Chapter II

MUKALLA REVISITED

"What little town by river or sea-shore,
Or mountain built, with peaceful citadel. . . ."

(KEATS "Ode on a Grecian Urn.")

HAROLD AND DOREEN INGRAMS WERE A NEW INSTITUTION IN Mukalla.

When the Italians brought their civilization to Abyssinia, the preoccupied glance of Whitehall, lighting for a moment on those vast shores which fringe the Indian Ocean, noticed that some of them were coloured pink and were, therefore, presumably British. Only presumably, for many maps had omitted to tint them, owing to the absent-minded reticence of Government at the time when the South Arabian treaties were signed. The treaties, however, existed, scattered over various dates that began before 1886. The Hadhramis were anxious for more active protection and restive under what we like to call non-interference and they are apt to think of as neglect. The British Empire decided, out of its immense resources, to grant one man, and discovered Harold and Doreen in Aden. The Italians at that time looked upon our eastern possessions as cheeks turned towards them for perpetual slapping and were annoyed to see Mr. Ingrams in the middle of a landscape which they were beginning to consider as their own. Rumour has it that they paid a visit to the Foreign Office and asked to see the map. Luckily the one on the desk happened to be a pink one: Mr. Ingrams had an indubitable right to be there; and when we reached Mukalla we found him and his wife settled in a white house behind the Sultan's palace, carrying on the business of some thousand miles of country with the help of their own infinite ardour, and half a dozen native clerks.

This country of the Hadhramaut had been to Harold for many years a secret goal of dreams, since first he learned of it from a servant in Zanzibar. He had left Zanzibar and gone to Mauritius, when the offer of work in Aden again brought the Hadhramaut near. And now his dream had become reality, he was alone in the land, striving after its prosperity and peace with a slenderness of resources incredible to anyone unacquainted with our particular methods of empire; and he looked with a mixture of kindness and apprehension on our feminine invasion, a nuisance inferior only to oil.

I am not of those who blame officials for looking upon me with misgiving. Far from it. If they are right in nine cases how should they know, by the mere look of us, that we are that exceptional coincidence, the tenth? And who shall say that in nine cases they are wrong?

> "If nine be bad and one be good,
>   There's yet one good in ten, quoth she,
>   There's yet one good in ten."

One quotes Shakespeare and leaves them to discriminate. My companions, both better educated than I am, rightly took themselves more seriously. They were rather prone to that female superstition which, in a circular world, thinks

7

of Education as "Higher," regardless of the Antipodes just below and the fact that so many people get on well without it. British officials—those easy-going people—they explained to me, are knotted with unsuspected anti-feminist complexes. In this case however we were bound by ties of kindness to co-operate as far as possible with officialdom and Aden. They had welcomed and helped us; they had opened a door which might easily have remained closed—all that they asked was that we follow their advice in a country they knew, and that we give as little trouble as our nature and occupations permitted.

With this in mind, I spent long hours learning from Harold and Doreen and the office papers what had recently been happening among the tribes, the intrigues of our neighbours across the straits, and who in general were enemies or friends. The little room one sat in was cool, open on all four sides, with a lattice-work of coloured glass fitted casually here and there, and such armchairs decayed from former splendour as Mukalla had been able to provide. Doreen would come in from the office where she combined the functions of Treasurer, Private, Political, and Oriental Secretary, and Chief Typist; she would give a passing look to her adopted daughter sitting over its mug of milk in the morning sunshine. This baby, Zahra, had a mop of small yellow curls apparently produced by mere washing from the unpromising oily black locks of the Arab child. In her small and engaging person she represented Education for Women in the Hadhramaut of to-morrow; a delicate future lies before her.

"I am not averse to women's education," a liberal sayyid[1]

[1] The Hadhramaut sayyids are descended from Ahmed bin 'Isa al Muhajir who came from Basra in the tenth century. They form a religious caste.

told me later in Tarim: "so long as it is not *excessive*. If it is carried on to the age of nine and then stops, I do not think it can do any harm?" He looked at me anxiously, afraid that perhaps his modern tendencies were carrying him too far.

From an office below, teeming with every sort of tribesman, a tired Harold would emerge at intervals and, with his blue-eyed expression, which must have given him a misleading and seraphic appearance as a small boy in the choir, would recount the latest cases of murder and brigandage in his lands. They were singularly few, for he had persuaded most of the headmen and Sultans to sign a three years' truce and give to the cause of peace an opportunity denied to it in Europe. This truce made our journey unadventurous and easy; it was known all over the country as the Ingrams or the English Peace: but being a fragile creature and of such tender years, the fear of disturbing or damaging it in any way tended to limit our plans more than the wars of the bad old days, when a casualty more or less could make no odds.

The scientists spent their time in search of prehistoric tools on banks east of Mukalla where they alone could read in letters unknown to others the history of the past. It is one of the greatest allurements of Asia that its nakedness is so clothed with the shreds of departed splendour; like a face lined with age, its joys and its sorrows are furrowed upon it, not so much in human ruins as in the very structure of the continent itself. Its vestiges of fertility, irrevocably lost, make it a world not only dead, but ruined. This must be so, of course, everywhere in some degree; but here the time is vaster, the contrast greater, and the drama of nature more obviously identical with the tragedy of man.

Muskalla Revisited

For this I envy the Geologist. She can see simultaneously before her the past and the present. To her the fan-shaped terraces of gravel, opaque in sunlight, are still tumultuous rivers in whose heart the pebbles have been rolled from pre-historic highlands. Their banks and uplifted estuaries carry, in petrified evidence, plants and shells and creatures that once animated them. Like a staircase receding, the geologic ages climb back into Time; and on their very lowest steps, poignant as toys found on forgotten shelves of childhood, lie the earliest tools of men.

Three of these terraces have been washed near Mukalla from their ancient heights towards the Indian Ocean, and lie in ruins, their flatness gnawed into broken ridges, behind the sand-dunes of the modern shore. The oldest and highest is Pliocene, where human footsteps, if they passed, have left no traces: but on the middle terrace, where still the beduin build their hearthstones and their cairns for burial and for shade, one can pick up flints brown, black or amber, notched into triangular blunt instruments or sharp flat-pointed blades. The Archæologist, with a precision which would have sur-prised their former owners, called them Levalloisian. With unhesitating fingers she picked their different kinds from promiscuous heaps we brought her. As by some Ariadne-thread invisible to others, these two were able to trace their way through the labyrinths of time, moving at large among these vast compelling facts with awe-inspiring ease.

The present, too, was pleasant in Mukalla, and especially the never-ending delight of its shore. Acres of small flat silver fish with blue backs, laid out in rows like bedded plants, were strewn there in the sun: they dry for six days and are then stacked in heaps for the camels to feed on. They are

The sea

caught in a circular net of small meshes, about 1 cm. square, thrown by a man who stands submerged to the waist beyond the breaking waves. Each morning the *huris* came full sail, their bodies low on the water, filled with fish to the brim. They looked as if they meant to ram the shore; but the square sail dropped, the lovely movement was suddenly arrested, and the crew came wading out of the sea with fish bulging in nets on their shoulders.

And in the evening the American car would carry us towards the sunset, when a rising tide slowly devoured the sands. Between rows of breakers the shallow wave water shone pink and brilliant as its cold smooth shells. Amethyst mountain ranges ran out to their wild capes. Grey cranes with ragged wings rose in slow flight above the tossing water. On the shore some black quick-moving figure of beduin stirred among the rushes like an incarnation of the night. And once, as we came back in the dusk, four small humped cows impeded us: they wandered unattended to the water's edge, dipped their noses in the breaking waves, and appeared to be drinking the sea.

Chapter III

TRANSPORT AND THE COOK

"Le monde inconnu nous enveloppe, c'est tout ce qui est hors de nous."
(ANATOLE FRANCE. *Le Petit Pierre.*)

QASIM, TOGETHER WITH MOST OF OUR EIGHTY-ONE PACKAGES, arrived by boat, dressed in a check loincloth, white shirt and white and yellow turban whose end stuck up like a plume in the Aden way. The Master of Belhaven, who kindly lent him, unjustly said that he could produce nothing edible beyond stew and tea, but that he enjoyed beduin raids and early rising. He possessed a limited intelligence and a tender heart; his love affairs ruined many of our dinners. But he had that personal capacity for devotion nearly always found in Arab servants, and was ever ready to neglect a household duty for a classic poem, an endearing though inconvenient trait. He brought his bed, which was a blanket, and a small box to hold all worldly necessities inside it; and being sent out to market to buy our kitchen utensils for the winter, returned with a solitary curved dagger whose culinary advantages he pointed out to me with a guileless enthusiasm I found disarming.

Apart from Qasim, we engaged one other man only, an ex-bankrupt chauffeur who had wound himself round the heart of our experts by the deft way in which he handled their instruments. He was a man with cringing manners and one of those townee faces ravaged by emotions mostly bad. Doreen and I, who know good Arabs when we see them, disliked him at once, but took him, anxious to please the experts and convinced that his duration would be short. I gave him ten rupees to buy a bed and to console his family. But when the lorry actually came that was to transport us far from the green electric light and single boulevard of Mukalla into the dangers of the north, the creature's chauffeur heart misgave him; the ten rupees, he presumably reflected, were anyway safely spent; he stood with his bedding clasped to his chest, deprecating, obstinate and dishonest, and—to my relief—watched us depart. Doreen, I am glad to say, eventually retrieved most of his ill-gotten capital by making him work it out in her kitchen.

We meanwhile, like full-blown roses clustered round the driver on the front seat of a lorry, sped ponderously along the new motor road towards Shihr and Tarim.

In the middle of the morning we rested on mats under dark trees in one of the royal gardens, a solitary oasis kept by a friendly African family of slaves[1] : and at noon launched again into the ocean of the sun.

Low ridges with watch-towers, now decayed, are scattered in the valley at whose wide end lie Shihr and the sea. A ruinous fortress stands there with round towers above a pink sandstone ravine. Leaving that on the east, you reach the gate of Shihr, whitewashed, with new-looking walls, recessed with buttresses inside in a small Babylonian way. Here in the lorry company's office, we waited on mattresses on the floor among rows of cash boxes, whose clerks were all asleep for

---

[1] Slaves are, of course, no longer imported into the country, but a certain number still remain, gradually disappearing.

Ramadhan; until finally our crew was ready—a driver, four assistants and a comic called Bakhbukh. Dressed in somebody's discarded tweeds, he seemed like a small dried nut in a large nutshell, his sad negroid face framed in an airman's helmet. Two sayyids returning to their homes added themselves with bundles at the city gate.

Our lorry retraced its way along the trough of the valley and soon began to climb long broken ridges that lead to the tilted plateau of the jōl,[1] which soon sloped behind us, green after rain, in gentle headlands to the vaporous sea. Strings of camels burdened with rushes, descending, took the short zigzags while we took the long. In the sunset, on the western lip of a wadi that dropped to a shadow-filled bowl, we set up our beds and slept, among creeping wild gooseberry and flowering solanum that make the stones thorny and gay.

A curious thing happens on the jōl—a constant bird-like twitter in the moonlight, a pleasant and companionable noise. Qasim said it was birds "who praise God," especially towards morning, and we saw wings flit between us and the moon. But the voices sounded like crickets only more melodious, and went on continuous through the windless night. The moon was full quarter, the Pleiades and Taurus just above us. At about 3 a.m. the Great Bear appeared for half an hour, wheeling low over the horizon and the Polar star. My companions murmured that they heard footsteps; they made a small clatter of stones, unlike a wild animal. We lay for a long time and listened, watching the thorns and hill against whose silhouetted outline the low moon rested, for whose setting the prowler would wait. I blamed myself for a camp so defencelessly scattered, but nothing happened,

[1] Jōl—waterless steppe plateau.

except the hysteric yapping of a fox in the depth below; and when we next awoke there was an orange band of sunrise, the greater stars were fading into the gulfs where the daylight hides them, and the footsteps, which still pattered and paused on the hill about us, turned out to belong to four donkeys pacifically browsing.

At seven-thirty we left and took with us a bedu wounded in the foot by stones, one of the tribe that in three months' time was to be at war with government, but cordial now. His friends, swaying from their camels, shouted greetings as we climbed to the empty topmost level of the jōl.

*   *   *

Here all looked dead; the coral-like euphorbia called *deni* had not put forth its young green stars of leaf, though it was out already on the lower shelves we came from. The plain lay like a stripped athlete, streaked yellow and glistening in the sun. On the horizon, scarce emerging, lay the ridge of Kor Saiban and my former journey. Regretfully I remembered it, thinking how much is taken from the tenuous charm of the jōl by rapid travel; its delicate and barren gradations, dependent on the slow transience of light, vanish into drabness under the strident wheels of cars. Even as I lamented, Providence sent a puncture, and gave us ten minutes in the heat of the morning, which the Archæologist improved to an hour by wandering after flints.

I was at that time enthusiastic enough to think nothing of even ten hours in the sun on behalf of a reasonably interesting Paleolithic object, and Alinur, the other Scientist, is the most unselfish of human beings: but the chauffeur and his five were not interested in stones. They had not been told to wait: all they knew was that the Archæologist,

Transport and the Cook

Edwardian and exotic in Arabia, had vanished in the brownness of the distance. Bakhbukh, with splayed gesticulating fingers, appeared at intervals as a delegate from the protesting lorry, which blistered slowly in a landscape devoid of shade. But what could we do? Even the rupee trick—by which Bakhbukh can turn one rupee into two if given the first one—is useless for finding Archæologists. With one to begin with, one might possibly produce a second? I put it to him and he looked at me with the sad eyes of a monkey who is being laughed at. In her own good time the lost one reappeared, a flint in her gloved hand. She gave no softening word. The crew, baffled by anything so monosyllabic, tumbled into the travelling-pen in which they lived. Bakhbukh made one Rienzi-like effort to express general disapproval from the rostrum that held our packing-cases, but the gears gave a jerk and precipitated him, with a last wave of his long splayed fingers, among his comrades, while the target of invective sat innocent below.

* * *

In the late light of the sun, when even the flatness of the jōl throws long shadows from its truncated mounds, we were still racing like a toy train tied by the force of mechanics to the curves and caprices of our road. And we were still far from the Tarim 'aqaba or cliff, a zigzag affair which our driver preferred not to negotiate in the dark. Reluctantly, for he had brought no food for a second night, he began to look about for a place to camp in, and ran meanwhile through a naked land which he peopled with robbers. "They shoot from there," he said, pointing to a circular mound arranged by nature like a butt at a sportsmanlike distance from the road.

"Behold! two of them," he added, as we passed a man and a boy in the dusk. Their fringed shawls were wrapped about them; they were leaning on guns, and looked far more like Italian opera than anything in the genuine brigand line has a right to do.

"Do they always shoot from the same place?" I asked.

"Always."

"And when was the last time?"

"They looted a lorry in the month of Sha'ban a year ago."

"Indeed," said I reassured. "How many came to loot it?"

"Three beduin."

"Well, we are six men and three women and two sayyids. Couldn't we deal with three beduin?"

"The sayyids are no good. The beduin only believe in their own mansabs" (religious heads of the tribes). "And we have no guns." Our female presence, I regret to say, he brushed aside as being of no consequence one way or the other. He was bent on pessimism.

"Allah will protect us," was all that one could say. For this particular night no supernatural exertion seemed to be required. But every good driver tries to see to it that, as far as his car and the beduin are concerned, it is "Never the time and the place, and the loved one all together," and we agreed to drive on till we came to some open place away from the ravines where, just under the surface of the jōl, these people live like their Stone Age ancestors in caves. And presently, sure enough, in the last of the daylight, we saw one of them—a little shepherdess trailing her black gown along the limestone ledges, walking home to her cave with her white goats behind her, as innocent and pastoral a vision as ever was distorted by the eyes of fear.

17

We for our part chose a shallow pleasant little ditch made to keep the floods from the road. There was no green thing visible on the floor of stones, no wind, no damp, the air was dry after Mukalla. Our lorry crew and the two sayyids sat subdued by the fact that they had no supper, while the Scientists busied themselves with the making of their beds. I always felt ashamed, for I never made my bed, but left that to Qasim who had, I thought, too little else to do and was humiliated if he stood idle while we worked. It made him happier to work and it made me happier not to; and saved me from that strange passion, akin to suttee, which soothes the hearts of women who do unnecessary household jobs and spoil their servants. All the same, it seemed horrid to stand by while my companions struggled with straps and pillows; I offered the idle Qasim; and then strolled despondently to our two sayyids, who sat by themselves near the crew of the lorry—for we were travelling on the assumption that East is East and West is West, in two separate worlds, of Ishmael and Isaac. It is regrettable, I reflected, that my heart is always with the Ishmaelites: and yet who else can ever live in comfort in Arabia? The sayyids were patient and pleasant people, not roused to petulance by the want of supper or by the fact that they had only a cotton shawl between them and the rigours of the night. One was an old man in a green turban, who had been away in Java for a year, and now spoke with charming happiness of three little sons and one daughter he would see after the year's journey: the other was a gross bull-necked sayyid from Tarim, of the kind Chaucer disliked. He it must have been who lunched, for when I asked Qasim if the sayyids had eaten during the day (it was still Ramadhan) he answered that: "One did and one didn't." Our own tinned supper they refused, probably owing to the fact that a piece of lard had been discovered in the beans. Qasim had an infallible eye for pork. When Alinur was collecting geological specimens, he came up with a piece of striated limestone, curved in alternate pink and white, and handed it to me saying: "This is bacon."

Next morning we woke to the sight of the sayyids at prayer, one behind the other in white gowns on the stones in the sunrise, and left at eight-thirty with the far rim of the Tarim wadi, a thin blue horizon, in sight.

Looking idly out as we travelled on the sea-like flatness, I suddenly saw a glitter in the sun, the shine that distinguishes a polished flint from natural stones that have known no human labour. For ages it lies where the man of the Stone Age dropped it, and still preserves intact that "old-world polish." The lorry stopped, I tumbled out, and we found that indeed it was true; the black plain was strewn with flints, duskily shining where an artificial surface caught the sun; some were cores, some were flakes—the Archæologist explained how one can know them by the bulge where the flake came off; some were mere blocks, perhaps the raw material to which Paleolithic men climbed to fashion their tools when they lived in the shepherd caves below. They were all blackish, some quite black with a wind-made patina; they lay thick in clusters, pressed down by the fierce weathers of the jōl, and covered the ledge we were on between two wadis; when we descended to a lower level we found only a few, possibly washed down from above.

In the elation of this discovery we reached the top of the Tarim 'aqaba, preceded, as 'aqabas are, by a cairn of white-washed stones. The road at our feet laced it in diagonal patterns remarkably perpendicular, and the great wadi below, tawny and winding, lay filled with light and lifeless, with markings of palm trees upon it, as a snake asleep in the sun.

The driver fixed his brake, the crew crouched to turn the wheels by hand at the hairpin bends; the two sayyids and the Archæologist, equally mistrustful of Predestination, got out and walked. At the narrow corners the crew demolished the parapet of boulders to let the wheels get round: I wondered no longer that we paid one rupee each for the privilege of cutting up the road. Our engine made strange noises, due, we found when we reached the bottom, to a yard of copper wire that had lost itself inside. All went well: but, as often happens, though the operation was successful, the patient expired soon after: in the wadi bed, where it was easy going we stuck and had to unload ourselves in sand.

Here we were in the outskirts of Tarim; a hot and fertile world of crops. The children and the peasants gathered with questions. Why is our Arabic so bad? And why do we drink water in Ramadhan? An old woman came in a green garment with a sheaf of maize stalks on her shoulders whose leaves were the same colour as her gown. She had seen me when I was there before. Would we take a picture of her, to send to her son in Java? He had left twenty-four years ago, a small boy—and there he was. He never wrote, but now and then she heard that he was well and hoped he would come back some day, for she had no other, and her husband was dead. She thanked us for our poor wishes with a gratitude for the kindness of words alone, which one is apt to forget after an absence from Arabia, and went her ways uncomplaining, a sad and gentle soul.

Chapter IV

THE TOWNS OF THE KATHIRI

"Our towns are copied fragments from our breast."

(F. THOMPSON.)

AN ANCIENT CAR CALLED A RUGBY WAS PROVIDED FOR OUR pleasure in Tarim. It must have vanished long since from the markets of Europe and its continued capacity to go was so unscientific a miracle that it troubled the reasonable mind of Alinur. "It isn't *possible*," she would repeat at intervals, while the tomato tin that closed the radiator was shot off or jammed hard on to keep the boiling water down. But the little Rugby went, its wheels on either bank of a goat-path that meandered independently below it: "Über Stock und über Steine, Pferdchen brich dich nicht die Beine," free apparently of all mechanic laws. A goatskin full of water hung beside us, from which small quantities were poured at intervals into its panting lungs. "You like antiquities," said Sayyid Mehdar, our host. "Why not this car?"

He was a mild and kind little man, half Malay in looks, with a large underlip and a gentle expression. He had a good story about a tribe into whose wadi the R.A.F. dropped bombs some months before. One of these failed to explode: the tribe lifted it carefully, placed it against the gate of their enemies and neighbours, shot away the detonator from a safe distance, and enjoyed the result. Malaya, he said, was a

21

more restful country but the Hadhramaut pleasanter, because
so full of relations—a strange thing to prefer to a quiet
life.

With him one afternoon I went to look for the ruins of
Nujair, the last refuge of the Apostates when they fought in
the early years of the Hejra against 'Ikrima and the forces of
Islam.   Nujair had not been identified, but I heard about it
in the neighbourhood of Tarim, and we went in search of it
eastwards, past the landing-ground and the crumbling four-
towered fort where "the guardians of the aeroplanes" live,
by a track beyond any capacities except those of the little
Rugby, through Roghà and a ruined village east of it to
Mishta, where Nujair was supposed to be.   The whole village
turned out to help.   It was only one row of houses, with the
seil-bed on the other side and a minaret white and charming
against the background of wadi Mishta which leads to the
jōl.   No one there knew of Nujair till an old white-haired
man came up and said he remembered it years ago, and
climbed into the car to guide us to a mud heap almost washed
away from a base of what looked like pre-Islamic stone on a
spur between Roghà and Hubaya, about forty feet above the
track.   It looks no more than a watch-tower, but, such as it
is, the tradition and the name are there, though none but the
last greybeard still remembers.

*   *   *

Three women were almost more than the holy city of
Tarim could bear, and the sayyids kept away when we all
drove out together.   But they made things easy with village
headmen and the drivers of donkeys and cars, who took us
to Sūne and to Husn al-'Urr, led by tourist curiosity, since
they are places visited and described.   There was a charm

especially in the latter, our most easterly point in the Hadhramaut, for it is country that has obviously been falling back
to wildness. North of Eināt we went through Qusum's
dilapidated square, where an old wool carder sat in the sun;
by the castle where the governor was sleeping "between four
grey walls and four grey towers" piled like inverted tumblers
at each corner, with overlapping decorations at the rims.
The wadi narrows then, green with rāk (*salvadora persica*),
and grey with thorns; among the rāk bushes the white goats
feed, and run when frightened to their shepherdess who,
under her high conical hat, a new-born kid in the crook
of her arm, a sickle-knife in her girdle, her black dress and
strips of coloured finery dim with rough wear, stands among
them like a small and early goddess of their Arcadian world.

  We came suddenly into the dip of Wadi Khun and saw it
with the rarity of flowing water among weed-clogged
shallows, full of frogs whose nostrils floated on the surface,
their eye-slits powdered with gold. Minute fish, colourless
as glass, rushed up and down like lines of London traffic;
toads with black stained backs lay with closed lids on damp
earth pretending to be stones. The river here is Life, and
nourishes with the same fervid kindness the creeping weeds
and small creatures and the half-naked Tamimi who live in
huts on its banks and plant a few patches of millet and a thin
fringe of palms round the well where they draw their goatskins full of water. Security must still be too recent for
agriculture, for the river flows almost in solitude, wasting its
blessing on unused lands, visited only by shepherds and
fishermen who find here a surprising and excellent fish called
sulaib, as much as two feet long. There was a time, however
when it fed fields and gardens, and the traces of its irrigation

lie over several miles of sand round the ruins of 'Urr. The castle emerges on a rocky mound, with the width of about half a mile of wadi on either side of it, so that from it, as Qasim said, "one can shoot at everything." Van der Meulen has described it, and Harold Ingrams had just discovered a pre-Islamic inscription on the eastern wall which still stands, finely built. It was inhabited by Arabs and finally ruined and abandoned in A.H. 657 (A.D. 1298). Alinur and I, freed by ignorance from labour, watched the small figure of the Archæologist as she toiled in the sun below, round sandy bases where potsherds are found, picking up objects here and there. We wondered at her sure and clever way with stones, the product of knowledge, and at the long learning that alone can give such effortless familiar ease.

We pushed on beyond 'Urr to Sōm, last village of the Tamimi, who live there with the Manahil in uneasy fellowship. It was the boundary of the well-ordered lands. A demand for blackmail, half-heartedly pressed, showed that we were coming to the edge of Harold's truces. As we drove back, a bedu waved his gun to ask for news of the world. "No news," said our Somali. "No murders, no news," he turned towards me to explain. He had the journalistic mind.

* * *

The little Rugby succumbed under the insertion of a new radiator which its constitution was not strong enough to bear: it was the parable of the new wine in old bottles: but after five days in Tarim we were given a handsome car, with green and yellow tassels draped over the speedometer to obscure all useful information, and Abdulillah, an old Somali friend, to drive us to Seiyun.

Sanahīye

On the way we stopped at a ruin-crowned spur on our left called Sanahīye, a heap of crumbled mud with pieces of stucco still left in roofless rooms; the walls had been rounded at their base as is still the fashion in the primitive houses of Du'an. While the Archæologist examined them, Alinur and I did our best to lure the more noisy part of the population from interference with her labours. They were 'Awamir beduin, and had a bad reputation when I was there before, but now, thanks to the "English Peace," were ready to show how pleasant criminals are when not engaged in crime, and took us to their well, a circular shaft dry-walled as deep as one could see. It was sunk to water-level on the plain, a hundred feet below. These immense wells are characteristic of the Hadhramaut which, even in ancient times, seems to have got its constant supply of water from underground, and to have reserved the canalizing works mainly for the preservation and distribution of flood waters in spring.

When we had looked over the crumbling edge, the population took us to their mosque, in whose ruin a wooden minbar with date carved upon it gave the presumable age of Sanahīye's prosperity. It belonged to the year A.H. 693 (1293 A.D.). The script was not completely clear and the schoolmaster came to help, an ancient man nearly blind and all grey to his sparse chisel beard and formless shirt, and the agate bead or Sawwama he wore round his neck against toothache. The population looked at him with affectionate veneration while he pronounced the words after me, pretending to be reading them himself: indeed, he was almost too blind to read anything at all, but doubtless knew enough of the Quran by heart to keep his flock in their appointed ways. They evidently loved him for himself and murmured with pleasure when I pressed half a dollar into his unexpectant hand. They were an agreable nest of robbers.

With only two more antiquarian pauses, one at the town of Mariama, a late and uninteresting ruin, and the other at a valleyside spur, we reached Seiyun. Here the splendours of Sayyid Abu Bekr's new house, which I had seen beginning, had blossomed into what their owner must feel sadly now and then is almost a hotel. All travelling Europeans, including every member of the Air Force, stay there, except Harold, who prefers, when he can, to live with the sayyid in his old and less sophisticated home. Here we too spent some days enjoying ash-trays and velvet chairs, mosquito-netted beds, and the hours of Big Ben on the wireless, with electric light splashed round us in a regardless way—till nine o'clock, when it went out. A row of little bulbs runs round the court, each one supported on a pseudo-Greek column, as it were Atlas with a pingpong ball upon his shoulder. Gone is the Eastern charm of Seiyun and its pleasant conversations with Leisure all around. Only the bath, an Eastern institution by birth, has retained its oriental delights; the white tiles are gently tilted so that soap and water, used to wash with, pour away, and one steps, clean and happy, into a tepid jade-green lake, eight feet by eight and almost to the neck; and splashing there, looks at oleographs of Adam and Eve and Aphrodite, arranged to meet the level of the eye, the composite efforts of the Ancient and Modern worlds.

Sayyid Abu Bekr, with his fine and gentle manners, came to see us, and in the evening I would take one or the other of my companions, plaintive because they "did not like parties," to the harims I knew, to meet again the sayyid's lovely wife, and the singers from Ghurfa, and the Learned Sherifa, affectionate as ever and very pretty with her full red lips and dark eyebrows, in spite of enormous black-rimmed spectacles on the very tip of her nose. Her plump little hands still waved about in explanation of such exciting things as the difference between a noun and verb, or the relations of the heart to the five senses, of which she probably knew more than most theologians: and in her own house she showed us, reverently and without touching it, for she had not washed her hands, a page from the Quran copied on parchment ("the skin of a gazelle") in beautiful Cufic, written—and who would contradict her?—by the hand of 'Ali Abu Talib himself, and sent as a present to her brother by the Imam Iahya of Yemen.

One more thing we did which I remember with pleasure, for I had meant to do it and been prevented by illness before, so that it came in the nature of a victory over accident and Fate. There was a rumour that reservoirs of water existed in the side valley that runs to the jōl between Seiyun and Mariama. Here, after the date harvest, people of both places go, with kids or sheep to roast, and spend the day fulfilling some dim rite whose meaning is forgotten. For they have no saint'or tomb to worship in this valley, merely the enduring presence of water, active there since the landscape first was made. When we climbed to it, an hour or so above the flood-swept gravels of the plain, we found no cisterns, but three pools scooped in the high limestone valley by the action of time alone; a few plants grew there, rushes and tufts of grass with feathery plumes, and lithab trees (*ficus salicifolia*) against the smooth white boulders. The limestone shelves lean, eaten away, long and narrow, above the upper pool; the higher shaly slopes lie thick with flint tools, polished yellow or black or iridescent, or curdled white like milk when they happen to have fallen and have never moved from the spot on which they fell. Cliffs surrounded this place in columns, like great piers. The stones were still cold to touch in the sun—the earth had not yet warmed itself though it was ten o'clock in the morning: over the motionless water there was a humming of small flies. "La voix aigue des insectes s'élevait dans le silence de l'univers." Hearths of the beduin were scattered on the shelves, and little cairns built by pilgrims at their annual feast. They sit in the shade, and kill a hundred sheep or more in the day, and shoot off their guns at sunset and return, binding the ages of their world unconsciously together. The Scientists climbed on, while I wandered to the lower pool and paddled, watching the struggle of curiosity in the hearts of newts and frogs. They came with small movements to see the pale feet in their pond. The newts had Humpty Dumpty bodies with eyes near together at the top; immense tummies and two tiny legs, like financiers in need of exercise, and brown-black tails: but the frogs were handsome like medieval pages, with stripes round their legs, and vague black speckles on their backs. There were other creatures too—a tiny violent ribbon worm wriggling emotionally from its tail, and crimson dragon-flies. Into this antique world unchanged and peaceful a bedu came walking along the rocks above. Almost naked, his shawl thrown like a scarf on his shoulder, a white wand horizontal in his hand, he walked uphill without effort on bare feet, and when I called stood stock still like an animal surprised. Then he moved on furtively and swiftly, and lifted his arm in greeting as he vanished.

On the 25th of November we left for Shibam.

THE DIARY

November 25, 1937.   "*Wer sich behaglich mitzuteilen weiss,*
Den wird des Volkes Laune nicht erbittern."

(Faust.)

No one in their senses would say, "I have spent ten years
in Holland and therefore I know all about Bulgaria"; but
it is a fact that seven people out of ten will assume that a
visit to Morocco opens out the secrets of Samarkand. The
East is just East in their minds, a homogeneous lump, and I
take it that the fault lies with the printers of maps, who give
to almost every state in Europe a page to itself, while they
separate the infinite variety of Asia only by faint lines of pink
and green and yellow. Perhaps it is for this reason that our
archæologist, who has spent years in Egypt, is disappointed to
find Arabia different, and wishes to see as little of its natives
as she can. In the happier deserts of Egypt one sits, she says,
in one's tent through solitary evenings in a silence broken
only by the cook, who, in elastic-sided boots, announces
dinner at the punctual time provided with a clock. But
this, alas, is far from the deserts of Egypt. Qasim has no
clock, though he does possess a pair of tennis shoes for smart
occasions; and as for tents, there is no place here where in
fifteen minutes they would not be crowded to overflowing.
Nor can one shoo these people away and still be welcome
among them; the very corner-stone of their democracy is a

29

general accessibility. Officials who visit here know this and act upon it, and how should we—unofficial guests on a new venture—not bow to the customs of the land? We are but a pioneering expedition in a country where the habits of archæology are unknown. We cannot indulge that theoretic benevolence toward natives that takes no personal trouble and stands no wear of contact.

* * *

Poor Alinur is ill. On the day of our departure from Seiyun she appeared with a septic throat swathed in scarves and a pathetic look in her eyes, brown and guileless like those of a retriever. She is the unselfish member of our party, and sits in the uncomfortable middle of the car, submerged in bundles. By the time we reached the piled-up houses of Shibam she was nearly speechless. Here Harold was supposed to have arranged for our reception. No visible sign of his effotts appeared, but this meant nothing at all in a country as casual as the Hadhramaut. Harold is trying to avoid bombing the Se'ar tribesmen, who have stolen forty-two camels; being very busy, he had in fact omitted to write to the owners of my former bungalow, who presently appeared with hurt feelings and distant manners, only after being sent for.

We sat cross-legged in a small columned room washed by the sunlight of the wadi, high on the city walls, in the house of Ba Obaid[1] the same active, kind, unshaven little man I had left lying at death's door with a large gall-stone three years before. He had refused the assistance of the R.A.F., who offered to transport him to Aden, but was instead rubbed by his family with ground glass and butter till the stone came out. Alinur, rather sick, listened without

---

[1] Ba Obaid is M. A. Besse's agent whose services were kindly lent us.

enthusiasm to this medical epic. While he told the story his brother bustled about to prepare their own house in the suburbs, and I wondered uneasily which of the many delicate causes that ruin eastern relationships could possibly have wrecked my friendship with those other two, Sa'id and Husain. Lunch came—eggs and bread and honey: they brought us mattresses and pillows, and left us alone with the flies. When the afternoon was cool, our house stood ready: they trailed us towards it across the sandy wadi, tumultuously assistant with lamps and carpets and every sort of oddment one could need. Before two hours were out Alinur was installed in an upper room, a supply of drinking water in goatskins from the far side of the wadi had been ordered from Sa'd the donkey man below, and most of our host's retainers were tactfully evicted. The Archæologist, under this first shock of genuine Arabia, is outraged to the very depth of her well-regulated heart. I have promised to keep her, as far as possible, separate from the inhabitants of this land; but alas! what will she make of a country whose chief if not only charm lies in its people? We cannot be completely isolated, like European delicacy in cold storage.

November 26.   *" Tot congesta manu praeruptis oppida saxis."*
(*Georgic Bk. II.*)

The best of our house is its view. From it we see the whole of Shibam just opposite, the Sultan's palace striped white and brown, the minaret, and the whitewashed gateway on a rise busy in the sun all day with its medieval traffic. It is an entrancing view, a Memling or a Dürer come to life, with nothing yet to mar its slow-built harmony since, by a merciful law of nature, we are debarred from seeing our own selves walking about in it. It is less of a fortress town than when I last saw it, partly because the gates are open and the houses lit at night for Ramadhan. Through the dark, sounds of feasting and laughter come out to us from its walls: figures pass behind the lighted lattice-work: our sleep is broken by bands of visitors across the sandy stretch below, or by the drummers who walk beating their tattoo to tell the population that the dawn is near.

The house itself is a little mud-built castle, full of sudden steps and with a balustrade terrace to every floor, and stands alone in a small suburb of detached residences under the cliff

> "Whose high and bending head
> Looks fearfully on the confined deep"

towering above us in white tiers in the moonlight. The ground floor is a small family mosque, where our hosts come of an afternoon to pray, spread their carpets on the terrace, and sit with a few old servants to wait for the sunset gun and their hookah. They are too busy, they tell me, to live here for more than a fortnight in the year: one would hardly have imagined the business of Shibam, going in and out of its gateway on slow strings of camels, to be of so city-like a nature. But this morning I have been watching, from the windowless twilight of Ba Obaid's shop, the figures of the buyers silhouetted against the door among comestibles in baskets. Three hooded women were helping with advice while a rough bedu from Hureidha bought ginger, coffee husks and dark molasses, and poured them mixed and without wrappings into his indigo shawl; and the operation, branching off into various discussions on politics and the prices of food, must have taken twenty minutes. Ba Obaid is a quick and nervous little man: his expeditious dealings held up at every moment by the leisurely customer, whose day was all before him to do with as he liked, were amusing to watch, like an ox and a polo pony yoked together in one team. One wonders how his impatience can have survived the wear and tear of fifty years or so of Arabian commerce.

On the second floor, Qasim's kitchen and my bedroom are installed. The Scientists are alone in the two best rooms above, with carved lattice-windows which, like most beautiful things, exact their price, for they let in the mosquitoes. The beauty of our moonlight, too, is mixed with a concentrated smell of donkey from the stable below; it seems to grow in potency with the advancing hours of night, and reminds them of typhoid, which is a pity, for it might just as well awaken happier associations, such as the beginning of the Christian religion. The donkey smell, if they only knew it, is one of the best of the Hadhramaut smells.

Meanwhile we sacrifice ourselves on the altar of hygiene by drinking boiled water. It comes from a well under the northern wadi cliff, far from any habitation, and is safely enclosed in a goatskin, so that I secretly think the boiling unnecessary, especially as it causes the salt to precipitate: what that means exactly I do not know, but the effect on our tea is loathsome.

There are two schools of health in these countries. To my mind, with so many microbes about, and of so unknown and violent a character, it seems a waste of time to try to avoid meeting them. The thing to do is to disinfect oneself at frequent intervals in order to make oneself less acceptable to them than the many other lodgings they can find. This I do with care, pouring iodine

on cuts, inhaling menthol before going to sleep, and swallow-
ing things like kaolin and charcoal after a more than usually
picturesque meal: I cannot help hoping that by this means I
make myself almost as disagreeable to a microbe as the smells
of its own native Shibam are disagreeable to us. It cannot
enjoy living in a constant reek of menthol any more than one
does onself. But as for not eating, or drinking or touching
things, when every dusty mouthful of air we breathe is full
of disease anyway, the psychological result would be
so demoralizing that almost any risk is preferable. I am not
a very good advocate, having had most diseases at one time
or another, but the wisdom of the Arabs is concentrated in
the old story of King Solomon and the Angel of Death.
This is the story as Sir Sydney Cockerell told it me, who
first heard it from Wilfrid Blunt: it is found in one form or
another all over the insanitary East.

A man, walking in the streets of Jerusalem, saw the Angel
of Death staring at him in a pointed way, as he thought.
Having gone to King Solomon, to ask his advice, he decided
to absent himself from the Angel's vicinity, and departed for
India. Now the Angel used to come at intervals to visit the
king, and on his next appearance, when they had spoken for
a time on this and that, King Solomon said:

"I should be much obliged if, when you walk about in the
streets of my city, you would take a little care how you look
at my people: they are apt to recognize you and to feel
discomposed." And he told him of the man who had been
afraid.

"Indeed," said the Angel of Death, "I will remember what
you say. But as for that man, I was looking at him with no
unlucky intention. I was merely surprised to see him in

Jerusalem, for I have been ordered to fetch him from India in three weeks' time."

* * *

Alinur, whose throat I have been wrapping round with fomentations, is convalescent.

November 27.   *"Greift nur hinein ins's volle menschen leben!*
Ein jeder lebt's : nicht vielen ist's bekannt
Und wenn ihr's packt, da ist's interessant."

(Faust.)

There is little sleep to be had in our small house. A bat flits through the carved lattices, a child cries with a voice that never stops: Qasim says he can tell by the sound that its pain is in its left side, which is very clever of him. The nights are watchful anyway in the latter end of Ramadhan. We have decided to stay a week in Shibam, since no work can be begun till the fasting month is over. Its moon has shrunk to a white shred in the sky, and all men's thoughts now turn to it: if they long to drink or eat or smoke they lift their eyes towards it and say: "Only eight days more to the end of the moon." Nobody is quite sure whether it is eight days, or nine, or ten. And in my heart I find it rather pleasant to depend on anything so unregulated.

* * *

This night I dined with Husain and Sa'id. The cloud between us has been happily removed by diplomatic questioning of Iuslim, my old servant, and Husain comes in again as he used to do and sits cross-legged on the floor helping with Arabic letters, one knee as a rest for the paper and his bare toes wriggling in the agony of composition. He is all curves, spotlessly clean and smart, with an embroidered scarf flung

35

over one shoulder and several gold teeth flashing in his smile. Iuslim comes too, either with him or alone. When the sunset gun goes off, Qasim appears holding a bowl of dates and shares a mouthful with the assembled company, to keep them all going till their evening meal is ready. Salim too has been, who nursed me in my illness. I went to take a present to him, in a tenement house of our suburb which he shares with many other families. He is a butcher, and very poor, and the houses of his street are all mud, unadorned with whitewash: I climbed through a dingy entrance up many invisible dark steps with small landings: until Salim's door opened, and we stood in a tiny room swept and carpeted, with a coffee hearth, and a mortar and two or three cups upon it. Little else in the room, except a pretty wife and a blind sister and a quilt to rest on, but it opens on to a terrace balustraded so that the women may be there invisible and sleep on its coolness in summer: the wadi lies open below, and the beehive panorama of Shibam; and if I had to live on Salim's income I would rather be there than in London. He was pleased to receive me, with the selfless hospitality of this land, and he had asked a neighbour in to share the occasion, a hideous man like the Barber in the Arabian Nights, who gave to our little party an eighteenth-century touch of the grotesque.

But to-night I have been among the rich with Husain, who came to fetch me after sunset in his car. It cannot get into Shibam, because all the streets are too narrow, but he has built a white garage with stucco columns just inside the gate of the town. The night had fallen, and lights were lit; the houses leaned away from each other towards the stars; at Husain's door, reached by winding ways, a servant waited with a lantern, and led up many steps to a white room with

green niches, a Venetian mirror on the wall. Here Husain
and his three brothers settled for a few moments in avid
silence to their hookah, after the day's fast; and presently took
me to the harim above, where the wives and sisters dallied
with samovar and tea things spread about them on the floor.
They are pretty, all with full under-lip,

> "As if a bee had stung it newly."

Husain's wife, her loose and flowery pink brocade tucked in
a silver girdle, looked like one of those Egyptian heads
painted on mummy cases as she sat with one knee up
and one flat on the ground, attending to the tea. Her
mass of small plaits was divided by a parting down
the middle, and two subsidiary partings at right angles
to it, one at the front and one at the back: from the
front, one or two ringlets, not plaited, fall over her ears.
I have counted 212 plaits on the head of a small girl. The
whole effect looks very like the mummy headdress; but
Husain's wife is pretty and alive and spends half a day every
fortnight arranging and oiling her curls. Her eyes are
brilliant and strange: when she is interested she opens them
so that the iris shows in a full semi-circle against the white.
When she rises, the trailing gown, short in front and gathered
to the girdle, gives a slanting effect of quick motion; it is
charming to see the women come in and greet the company
assembled on the floor: they do not straighten themselves
between one greeting and the next, but walk very gracefully
in a stooping position from hand to hand as it reaches up to
them, trailing their gowns among the teacups which, like
small coracles in the wake of a steamer, have to do the best
they can. If the person to be greeted happens to be absorbed

in conversation, the newcomer, still stooping, snaps her fingers as noisily as she can to draw attention, and having obtained her hand-kiss, moves on. The ceremony goes all round the room, until the circle of the slaves is reached—a rather difficult boundary for the ignorant foreigner to be aware of: her business is not to kiss hands to the slaves, but, when she is seated, to let them in their turn come and snap their fingers to kiss their hands to her.

I felt happy in this friendly atmosphere. They invited me to stay, and showed me the room where Doreen slept when she came, in a brass bedstead netted with pink tulle and decorated with ribbons. The brothers and I sat round a central dish of rice with eleven planets of excellent dishes round it. After I had climbed to another feast of cake and tea with the ladies upstairs, I walked back with Husain in the darkness. The tall houses were all lit up: a whispering and a gaiety goes on behind their high illuminated lattices through the sleepless nights of Ramadhan. As in a well the medieval streets lie silent in the stench of their open gutters: no tread makes an echo in their dust. A moan of prayer came from the lighted mosque as we passed it; camels and donkeys were couching in the square; a soldier sat at the gate, wide open in the moonlight. It is kept open late in Ramadhan. When we reached our home across the wadi, Husain followed me in to chat, for the night was still young: he walked straight upstairs to the Scientists, who greeted him coldly, for they had just thought of going to bed. I led him away, puzzled, to my room where Qasim makes tea. In the few moments at his disposal he too had been puzzling Alinur by explaining that sore throats in the Hadhramaut are due to "the changing of the stars."

38

Potters and dyers

November 28. *" There are two causes, it seems, of deterioration of art.*
And what are they ?
Wealth and poverty . . ."

(PLATO. *The Republic.*)

To-day I spent happily but dustily photographing the carved doors and windows of Shibam, and incidentally discovering its industries. They are poor enough, for a city of this size. The making of pots, the dyeing of cottons, the traffic of the lime-kilns comprises the whole. And the pots are still made here without the potter's wheel.

They are made in a village nearby called Hazm, under the southern cliff from which the petrified red earth is taken that the potter likes; he mixes it with straw and uses a bit of waste ground by the village to set up his *zirs* or water-jars, which are built in tiers from their base. Each tier must dry before the next is built above it, and there are about eight to a *zir* and each takes half an hour to fashion; the old man goes round backwards at a semi-run smoothing the wet earth between the palms of his hands. One can see his pots standing there parti-coloured, drying a few days in the sun before he stands them in his oven, an open place with a mud wall round it and a few holes for a dung fire below. Apart from the *zirs*, the pottery is rough as can be, and rudely painted— not so good, they told me, as the produce of Sif and Tarim, the only other places in the country where pottery is made.

The dyeing is a more elaborate industry and was important in Shibam before the development of foreign trade. It used to be done with *hawir* (wild indigo), a shrub of the jōl ravines which needs no boiling. Some beduin still use and prefer it, because they say it is warm to wear while foreign indigo is cold; but the latter has now been adopted by the towns,

39

and is the only dye in Shibam. The whole industry centres in one tall house where the dyer and his womenfolk, who assist him, live. They were busy to-day polishing their tall cups and dishes for the approaching feast of Ramadhan; tinned cups like chalices, most beautiful in shape, were shining in the sun. The paraphernalia of their work is one brass cauldron, two feet or so across, decorated in ribs of metal that run alternate ways: here all the stuffs of Shibam are dipped, and dried on the roof high over the murmuring shadow of streets below; and then sent to be pounded by the pounders who sit, naked to the waist with mallets of wood, in a little house built for them outside the gates. They blow water on to the stuff at this stage to give it a shiny surface, and it is then brought back to the dyer for the *roq* or polishing, which makes it glossy by rubbing between smooth stones. So prepared, it is the foundation of all the peasant and beduin gowns, the men's shawls and the women's black overdress of Sif, Hajarein, and Hureidha. I cannot say that I like it. All the trouble that goes to its making only results in an appearance like the cheapest Manchester cotton made shiny with gum, and the blue comes off on everything it touches.

As for the lime-kilns, that is a cheerful business which goes on everywhere. The lime is burnt in small mud huts with dung fires in the lower compartment. When it is ready, the labourers mix it with water and beat it with poles. They work in gangs of ten or twenty, beating from alternate sides and singing as they whack it, a mess like bad rice pudding on the ground.

Visitors and mercenaries

November 29.   *"Che fan qui tante pellegrine spade?"*

(PETRARCH.)

The most amusing people come to my lower room. I have made friends with the mercenaries who garrison the square watch-tower of the jōl. Three of them at a time live· there to guard the town. They are dependent on Sultan 'Ali of Qatn, now reinstated as governor of Shibam. When they are not on duty—and they very rarely are—they lounge with a gay Renaissance air, their ringlets out round the edge of their turbans, their daggers decorated with cornelians, their garments striped and gay, a sprig of the scented *rihan* stuck over one ear or a twig or two of *rak*, which they use as tooth-picks at odd moments, straight up in their turbans.

I happened to admire a silver armlet one of them was wearing as he sat in the gate of Shibam, engaged with a pointed stick stuck into a cartridge-case, like a Lacedemonian, in combing out his hair. Pleased to have anything about him admired, he came back with me to bargain for the sale of the armlet, and since then hardly a day has passed without a visit from one or other of these rather disreputable acquaint-ances whom Qasim disapproves of. They are handsome and fearless, and give a great deal of trouble. They are quite a different type from any that one sees about here, and one can tell them by their slim and snaky grace, their thin mouths and long faces, often lengthened still further by a small.tuft on the chin, their handsome eyes and swaggering carriage. When I leave my room, I find three or more squatting round the door. They have come either to "look," or simply to complain of the toothache which, I have to explain, is due to a worm inside which only doctors can kill. They like to talk of their home in the hills, a ten days' journey away.

There is a house, they say, not far from a place called 'Afifa, on the door of which is written the Unity of God. In it is a table of brass. It is guarded by soldiers, and when the old year joins the new, the table begins to hum.

Qasim, who is helping to explain, quivers all his ten fingers to illustrate the noise.

"When this happens, all of us who hear it go to the house and sacrifice some animal—any sort of animal. We eat the sacrifices," say the Yafe'i, "for the table only requires that blood should flow. Then it stops buzzing. If it does not stop, it is a sign of trouble all over the world." It sounds Totalitarian. This year it went on for three days without stopping, until the world-situation was relieved by their united sacrifices.

These mercenaries, who are scattered all over the Qu'aiti lands, have been a thorn in the side of quiet people for years, and now they look with anxiety on the local police that Harold is recruiting. They themselves are enlisted through headmen of their own, who pocket most of their wages and encourage them to make up the loss on the population of their district. It is only a matter of time, till the local troops are formed, for them to be returned to their own highlands. Qasim, with the natural feeling of an Arab of one district for an Arab of any other, has no good word to say for them.

*　　　*　　　*

Qasim appeared to-day in the new *futah* (loincloth) I have given him for the feast, arranged like a ballet skirt with butterfly wings under his naked young torso, a sprig of sweet-smelling *rihan* in his turban. He looked like an apparition of Youth in the frame of our dark stair.

He has a cheerful nature and an engaging liveliness in his

opinions. The delicate shades of distance, whereby a servant is kept as a servant and not a family friend, are wasted on him: he emerges buoyant from every snub, with mere pity in his heart for us elderly irrational females. But Alinur he considers with affection, since she alone has some notions of cookery. On modern commodities such as camp-beds, he looks with scorn—"comfortable for the dead," he says.

This is my week for housekeeping, and I usually find him and his assistant in a far corner of the kitchen squatting over a book of qasidas while the meat, boiling itself to toughness, bubbles in the middle of the floor. A servant in England would be abashed when surprised in literature, but Qasim leaps up delighted to show his poems, beautiful in red and black script. To have him and us in the same house, is like the Orient and Occident under one roof. The Orient does not get much done: it looks upon work as a part only—and not too important a part at that—of its varied existence, but enjoys with a free mind whatever happens besides. The Occident, busily building, has its eyes rigidly fixed on the future: Being and Doing, and civilization, a compromise, between them. There is too little of the compromise now. Too much machinery in the West, too little in the East, have made a gap between the active and contemplative; they drift ever more apart. Woman hitherto has inclined to the eastern idea—the stress being laid on what she *is* rather than on what she does; and if we are going to change this, taking for our sole pattern the active energies of men, we are in danger of destroying a principle which contains one-half the ingredients of civilization. Before ceasing to *be*, it is to be hoped that our sex will at least make sure that what it *does* is worth the sacrifice.

The Diary, Shibam

Meanwhile I have just found Qasim straining the soup through an ancient turban that has seen better days. He says he washed it first.

November 30. "*We all dwell in one country, O stranger, the world; one Chaos brought all mortals to birth.*"

(MELEAGER. *Greek Anthology.*)

Sometimes, struggling here between Scylla and Charybdis, East and West, I cannot avoid a small occasional feeling that the red tape of archæology is being treated too much like vestments of the church by a churchman. Our archæologist is a ritualist. But I can think of her also in happier moments —far from this alien background—when in stillness of museums, walking along the careful paths of learning, she traces with honest ardour elusive footprints of facts; climbing, laden with honours that come of long fruitful devotion, from the theory of yesterday to that of to-morrow. Her qualities are trained in formal ways; how should she not be offended by casual methods which Arabs understand; but how could they understand her constant silent disapproval?

We are in a proud country still new to Europeans, the first foreigners to live in its outlying districts for any length of time; and the hope that I cherish is that we may leave it uncorrupted, its charm of independence intact. I think there is no way to do this and to keep alive the Arab's happiness in his own virtues except to live his life in certain measure. One may differ in material ways; one may sit on chairs and use forks and gramophones; but on no account dare one put before these people, so easily beguiled, a set of values different from their own. Discontent with their standards is the first step in the degradation of the East. Surrounded by our

44

mechanical glamour, the virtues wrung out of the hardness of their lives easily come to appear poor and useless in their eyes; their spirit loses its dignity in this world, its belief in the next. That this unhappy change may come here as elsewhere is only too probable; but it will be no small winter's achievement if it does not come through *us*.

December 1. "*Breathe music, O Pan that goest on the mountains, with thy sweet lips, breathe delight into thy pastoral reed. . . .*"

(Alcaeus of Messene. *Greek Anthology*.)

Iuslim last evening brought a singer of Qasidas.[1] He was a self-conscious little man, followed by a huge piper with a squashed hook nose, by a tall negro in a green *futah* with a drum, and a small negro boy. These all filed in to where I lay in bed with sciatica, as it happened. They squatted in a row and wrapped their shawls round knees and shoulders— they call this the "Arab chair": and a small audience of Iuslim, Qasim and the gardener's family gathered to listen too.

The piper is an expert both with the single pipe, the *madruf*, a plain reed from the coast with four stops on one side and one on the other, bound with metal at both ends, and with the double pipe or *mizmar*, a lovely little instrument made of the inner tubes of an eagle's feathers. The whole thing is about seven inches long and one wide: the parallel tubes are bound together with gilt wire between each of their five stops, and there is a sort of joint at the top made of the wrappings of a leather thong, where two smaller reed pipes are fitted in, about two inches long. The feather tubes are semi-transparent, like old horn. The small reed pipes give

[1] Qasida roughly corresponds to our Ode.

45

a great deal of trouble to fit and try and take out. Pieces of paper must be chewed and inserted, and thin rods, which are kept ready tied on with string, are used for poking through when they are clogged—and even in the middle of the song the piper stops to fiddle with his reeds, leaving the song to carry on solo. But otherwise he led the singer with his melody, and, playing all the time, bent his head towards him to show when the tune changed; while the singer, holding his ear shut on the side of the drum, listened to the pipe, his hand curled round his left ear to hear better, his face puckered in agony on the long-drawn note which falls to a low refrain. When the verse is ended the pipe goes on; the singer bows his head between his arms, joins his hands above as if in prayer, and marks the time with fingers opening and shutting gently. The piper's cheeks swell out and show the length of his Arab face, for even when he blows hard as he can the face does not get round but only pear-shaped. The tall negro sits cross-legged, the little round drum carelessly balanced on his knee, one slim leg and beautiful foot and ankle projecting from his *futah*. He looks like a ballet negro, far too big for the drum, which he beats nonchalantly, with the tips of his fingers and the lower cushion of the thumb alternately, looking round at us meanwhile with an amused good-natured face. The little negro boy, hunched and absent-minded between him and the singer, makes it look more like a ballet than ever.

But the songs are charming, with none of the whining Egyptian twang about them. The notes hang poised and steady in the air like the eagle's feathers they are made of. Some are songs of Musiffer, a poet of Shibam, or of Bedr Mutawairiq, prince of the Tamim, long dead but still famous in Seiyun; some are from the Ba'Atwah, who call themselves descendants of the Beni Hillal, and are still singers in the Hadhramaut. One song came from Hyderabad, sent by Salah Ahmed, and one from 'Abd al Haqq of Dammun.

"How do you get hold of them?" I asked.

The singer smiled, and scratched the air with his hand; it is his business to steal them as quickly as he can.

Qasim, whose long lashes had been quivering to the music as he clasped and unclasped his hands in time, got up to make tea. The piper told me how he had helped carry me to the aeroplane when I was ill three years ago. In the doorway there suddenly stood a boyish apparition grey as dust, with big untidy turban, a staff in his hand. He brought a letter of welcome from Sultan 'Ali. There is always something dramatic in a letter that comes by a messenger: even in London it has a special charm: here, on the open threshold of night and the lighted room, the dusty figure seemed a very incarnation of the Unknown.

* * *

My last effort yesterday, before taking to my bed, was to go into the town to see about rice, sugar, paraffin, etc., for our approaching journey. But I found Ba Obaid far too busy to attend. Every merchant distributes $2\frac{1}{2}$ per cent of his ready money to the poor at the end of Ramadhan. Ba Obaid's shop was closed, and the poor, incredibly old and ragged, stood all about his stairs. So I went instead by the earliest mosque, which lies west beyond the walls, and made the circuit of Shibam among deep ditches and gardens from which it emerges, towering like a liner above the waves of palms. The east side is rubbish heaps, dotted over with stooping figures of the miserably poor who scavenge there:

and thence one again reaches our southern slope, of open sandy wadi and the well below the gate.

In the seil,[1] Shibam becomes an island on a river that lasts a day or two, or even as much as a fortnight—an enchanted city imprisoned in water. As it is, it is lovely enough, with the loveliness possible only to things that die. In my bed I lie for hours watching the gate and all who pass. Caravans, dancers, soldiers lounging, the female water-carriers in trousers, herds of goats, little bright-gowned girls, women in white robes for prayer, sayyids in white overcoats taking their sunset walk, and never a wheel except on rare occasions when one of Shibam's five motor cars goes in or out. There *is* no wheel in this country, except the clumsy pulley of the wells. The white of the city is gold when the daylight plays upon it. In the low morning sun the shadows show the batter of its walls, its long horizontal streaks of gutters, the oldness and crookedness of houses still beautiful in their crumbling and decay.

I lie contentedly enough, and amuse myself with a book which Qasim, seeing me in pain, has brought me in his kindness. It is his most treasured possession, a life of the Prophet in big lettering on rough paper, brown-black on brown-white, with flowered borders and headlines with the name of Allah, the author's name in a lunette at the top of every page, and the number of the page in a little flowered frame of its own on the margin. It gives one pleasure to handle anything done, even by mechanical means, with so much loving care.

The book itself is written guilelessly, and tells the legends of Muhammad; how Amina, his mother, bore him without

---

[1] Seil is the spring flood.

weight or discomfort, and in sleep saw the prophets month by month in turn, and in the last month the Prophet Jesus— for the substance of Muhammad, a drop from the River of Paradise, had been in the bodies of all the Prophets before him, beginning with Adam. And he was born already circumcised and with a rim of kohl round his eyes.

I had got so far in my reading when an invasion of two neighbours, an old woman, and all our staff brought me back to the affair of my rings, which began a day or two ago.

The old woman began it. She came while I was upstairs, and had to be shooed away, murmuring angrily that "she had only wanted to see us." If I could have let her sit for five minutes and look at us from the corner of the room, she would have been a guest of the house and nothing would have happened: as it was she went muttering downstairs, saw my door open, walked in, and stole my rings. The one I most valued she left, because it has animals engraved upon it and is a talisman that saves one from the Jinn, but she took three others that I always wear.

I was annoyed, for I hardly ever have things stolen. I asked the household, and Ba Obaid, and Husain what to do about it. They advised me to apply to a sayyid in Hazm whose business it is to retrieve what is lost. I sent Iuslim to see him. Iuslim, when he returned, told me that the sayyid had written on a piece of paper, and that the thief would become so unhappy, the rings would return of their own accord. Nothing further occurred for two days.

I was then told that it might be advisable to supplement the sayyid's talisman with a mention of the police. "It must be the old woman," said Ba Obaid, "because she seemed agitated." I was not so very sure, because in her place I should have felt agitated whether I had stolen the rings or not. But people know their own countries best; the old woman was sent for.

She appeared, dressed for the feast, with finger-joints and palms yellow with henna and festal ringlets round her wizened old face. A stranger with a beard came too, to see fair play, and Sa'd the gardener to look on. The mention of the police left her indifferent. She had taken no rings, she said.

"Well then," said Qasim, "you will have to drink the talisman that the sayyid has prepared for you, and if you are speaking the truth nothing will happen, but if you took the rings you will swell out like this"—he made a balloon-like gesture in front of his own slim tummy.

The floodgates of eloquence were now loosened. She stood with upraised hands, her rust-coloured dress and blue cloak draped about her like some Mater Dolorosa of a rather florid period, her voice rising in squeaks equally inspired by injured innocence and the prospect of drinking the sayyid's charm.

"It can't do you any harm," I said at last. "It is words of the Quran, and they only harm the wicked. I will drink too, so that you may not fear."

"Iuslim was in the house," said the Impartial Bearded Man. "He might have taken the rings. He should drink."

"And I'll drink," said Qasim of his own accord. "We will have it all ready by to-morrow morning."

The old lady was drawn away, still protesting with raised arms. This was half an hour ago. Now Qasim and Iuslim have appeared from my terrace, the rings, tied with a twist of red rag, in their hands. The old lady threw them up as she passed through the garden below.

A decalogue for travel

December 2. "*It is private life that governs the world.*"

(LORD BEACONSFIELD.)

This morning, in pity for Alinur, I remarked that sickness is a woman's difficulty in Arabia; there are microbes ever ready to fall on moments of weakness.

"It may be so for some," said the Archæologist in her limpid way. "I myself am never ill": but she did not say it in the tone of gratitude such a dispensation deserves in this country —rather as if a head cold were a portion of Original Sin. In spite of being crushed by this Olympian attitude to weakness, I cannot help wondering *why* we should so often look upon health as a creation of our own, considering that we accept beauty as a gift from heaven: the same hand presumably fashioned our inner and outer tissues. But I did not say so, for there is something frightening about the very robust woman. I merely sent up a little prayer, that I might not fall ill first.

Anyway it is, I believe, a fallacy to think of travellers' qualities as physical. If I had to write a decalogue for journeys, eight out of the ten virtues should be moral, and I should put first of all a temper as serene at the end as at the beginning of the day.

Then would come the capacity to accept values and to judge by standards other than our own. The rapid judgement of character; and a love of nature which must include human nature also. The power to dissociate oneself from one's own bodily sensations. A knowledge of the local history and language. A leisurely and uncensorious mind. A tolerable constitution and the capacity to eat and sleep at any moment. And lastly, and especially here, a ready quickness in repartee.

*   *   *

51

The Diary, Shibam

In the evenings, if I have no one below, I climb upstairs to sit in comfort except for mosquitoes—enormous creatures with white rings round their legs—that infest this region. Alinur, now recovered, is by the table with a book, in a comfortable domestic atmosphere; the Archæologist is on a terrace in the distance, with *Time and Tide* and the *Spectator* (very old) strewn about her. A lantern on her right hand and the moon on her left illuminate the neat blouse, and grey hair whose brushed waves still keep a faint rebellious grace of girlhood.

December 3. "*Politeness fell out of use as it always does in times of feminine emancipation.*"
> (JAMES LAVER. *Taste and Fashion from the French Revolution until To-day.*)

"Learning," an old tribesman has been saying to me, "is wider than all things except the excellence of God."

This surely does not apply to our female education, too often founded on arrogance and spurred by jealousy of sex! It cannot be wise so to despise all grace of living that we attain a learning whose highest boast is merely that it rivals the learning of men! Far pleasanter is it to achieve wisdom for its own sake; to fill our pitchers, without this miserable rivalry, at elemental rivers where, in sight of a supermasculine infinity, we may remember humility and praise.

To the Arab, manners are everything; he will forgive any amount of extortion so long as "your speech is good." To us, since the end of the eighteenth century, they have become dangerously unimportant.

Alinur, who spends her life among intellectual females, preserved by a love of flowers and her own natural kindness, has been saying that they are better than they seem. I am sure this is true, but what a poor sort of praise it is. There is some merit in seeming better than you are, an improvement induced by Art on the raw material of Nature; to be better than you seem is merely to inflict on fellow creatures shortcomings which do not even exist.

*   *   *

The fast of Ramadhan is over, and the feast has begun.

The gun went off after dark last night, and the new moon must have been visible at least an hour before, but its appearance has to be verified and confirmed by various elders. Sometimes it has been seen on three different days in the towns of Tarim, Shibam, and Hureidha, and the day of the feast has varied in each. The Archæologist, when I told her that the date was not yet certain at sunset last evening, looked cold disbelief: there is no denying it, the Hadhramaut calendar is quite unscientific. But who cares about that? The very steps of the servants are rejoicing through the house. Everyone has blossomed with lanterns or songs. Even from this distance the town has a festiveness smothered in its shadows. A bee-like hum of gladness surrounds it; the valley sand-bed is walking with lights. They cluster like fireflies through the gate and dance in dim shafts upon it; they throw tall shadows on the city walls. The houses are swathed in a dim luminous halo, except in windows where small bright spots move swiftly. From Sultan 'Ali's palace, a pool of darkness, rifles flash reddish and green. The sound takes a second or two to reach us, while already its light has faded: and each dull explosion is greeted by thin voices of invisible people cheering in the town.

The Diary, Shibam

December 4. "*Behind him march the halberdiers; before him sound the drums.*"
(LORD MACAULAY.)

Yesterday I fulfilled the obligation of the feast by visiting Sultan 'Ali of Qatn in his palace; he had arrived the night before, and appointed the inconvenient hour of sunrise for a call. Abdulillah the chauffeur, who brought his message, was so concerned to find me in bed that he rushed up to seize my two hands, and touched me by this unexpected kindness: but in the night the sciatica got better and I was able to go with Qasim across the pink morning sands of the wadi, cold to sandalled feet. It is convenient to wear sandals when visiting, for one can slip in and out of them easily on the threshold of carpeted rooms.

The governor's palace rises in white and brown tiers above the space within the gateway of Shibam. It has archaic carvings on its doors, and long bare passages, and parapets that overlook the square; and is an old-fashioned place. At its gate the drummers and the banners were preparing, for the Sultan and all notables visit the mosque in state on this day of Zina, the first day of the feast.

Nothing was yet happening, however. I found Sultan 'Ali alone with a few retainers, a hennaed beggar woman pouring blessings upon him from where she squatted in a corner of the room. He was browner and better than when I saw him last, dressed in a long brown surplice coat. We drank tea and presently left him to prepare for prayers, and I asked for a chair on the shelf that runs from the palace doorway so that I might spend the morning there and photograph the town.

This was a pleasant, idle, festal morning. The drummers sat on their heels by the door and drummed incessantly from sunrise onward till the Sultan came: they had two little drums called *mirwas*; a big tambourine-shape beaten with small sticks, and called *marfa'*; two shallow wooden *tasa* drums, like bowls with skins drawn over the top, and a big pale-blue barrel called *hajir* or *tabla*. The drummers relieved each other; their chief, an old man, sat by trying on his own hands the fine flexible strips of palm with which he beats his tunes, reserved for the important moment. The mercenaries began to arrive in ones and twos with their rifles on their shoulders, and smiled at me as they went in, for they all know me by now; so do the children—who are worse than the drains of Shibam, since they stir up microbes and dust around one in a perpetual whirlwind. Now, however, they promise to keep the rest of the crowd from the centre of my lens; they try their little best to remember, but creep slowly nearer like meeting waves till my camera and I are submerged and a soldier removes them with a switch on their bare toes. Two banners are brought, green and red, one on each side of the door: and now there is a stir, the Sultan emerges, walking swiftly with eyes downcast, and dignified: the banners are seized and move behind him; elders follow, in white with Mekka skull-caps, multi-coloured; the soldiers come in a bunch, shooting their rifles in a promiscuous way; the drums and the crowd all move across the square till the narrow street opposite swallows them in shadow, and the infant population and I remain to await their return.

Few pleasures give as much constant satisfaction as the inactive one of sitting quietly while the shows of life go by; it adds to the delight of contemplation the subtle satisfaction that others are fussing about things that leave us personally calm—the feeling that one has after poking an anthill with a stick. This morning even the ants were absent: all of us who were left in the square shared the contemplative life. Hadhramaut has a theory that if two people are late together they cease to be late at all: it seems to bear out the mathematical rule that two negatives make a positive. Women, hurrying for prayers, trailing gowns white or blue against the round windowless buttress where the dark street ends, met other women equally late: it would have been inhuman not to linger and talk it over. The little girls came out now, in tiny trousers under their silks—orange or magenta, trimmed with lace green or blue, and necklaces from waist to neck and patterns on cheeks and foreheads, green arabesques done with *rang*—a Persian word; they came like butterflies, their silver anklets frilled with bells, or golden circlets askew over their insteps. The women began to group themselves on the rising bank of a well, like a shadow-splashed bed of delphiniums against the buff and whitewashed houses in the sun. A dazzling minaret shot into the sky above them. A flower-bed of children sat at their feet. The crowd began to return: the Sultan passed with drums and banners through his door. Below his palace the soldiers danced; the square filled with the returning crowd. It wedged itself so close that the soldiers with difficulty kept their circle clear; above the heads of the people their triangular daggers flashed and caught the light. They were all in bright colours to-day like ruffling birds, their turbans high at the back and low over the forehead, clean *futahs* tucked into belts full of cartridges, and zip-fastened vests above. They danced their highland dance in groups of three, advancing to the centre of the circle or following each other at a jog-trot round the edge, bare feet and neat ankles active on the stones, their arms and crooked knives uplifted. They have danced all through the afternoon, and look pale with fatigue, the black kohl heavy round their eyes, their long strange profiles rather like those one sees on Etruscan tombs.

Towards sunset I left them, and found the young boys of Shibam outside the walls preparing to play football, beside the well where the goatskins are filled.

★ ★ ★

The Archæologist is ill, with what looks like sandfly fever, and our departure in two days' time must be put off.

December 5. "*Thy cheeks are comely with rows of jewels, thy neck with chains of gold.*"

(Song of Songs.)

The feast is a fatiguing time, for while it lasts it would be very impolite not to visit every harim of one's acquaintance and they are all crowded and buzzing with conversation and finery. I have been doing my round, and have amused myself by counting the trinkets and adornments on one small bride of twelve years old in the house of Ba Obaid, beginning at her head, where she wore gold acorns and an amulet on either side of her parting, and ending at her feet, festooned with a lacework of henna, painted to look like a sandal an inch up from the ground, with a gold anklet aslant over her instep. On her neck she has three rows of small gold beads above a sort of collar called a *m'labba*. Below this came a necklace of perforated gold beads alternate with old Greek coins and a British pound among them: a necklace of big round gold beads below; a necklace of amber, a gold necklace rather like an order, with cases for charms and big coins alternate, the coins specially minted by a philanthropic society

57

for the unemployed in Egypt; another necklace to hold up the great square amulet in front and a longer one for the large crescent moon in gold. European earrings and rings in quantity: lion-bracelets made by Chinese jewellers in Singapore, and a golden girdle. Her hands were done delicately in an intricate wheel pattern of blue henna, a wheel in the middle and a small one on the two finger joints, a palm branch, a red star and red crescent in the inside of her palm. Her eyebrows were painted dark so as to join each other. She sat incommoded but pleased with all this weight upon her, twisting her side curls which, being almost the only thing about her not made of solid metal, could not be trusted to keep their perfect symmetry. She was almost too stiff with decoration to smile.

December 6. "*Sunt quos curriculo pulverem Olympicum collegisse iuvat.*"

(HORACE. *Ode.*)

I meant to spend this day in bed, for I, too, am now sickening for a fever of some sort; but Husain had taken trouble to prepare for us a house belonging to an uncle of his at the village of Hauta where to-day all the district goes in pilgrimage to the tomb of an early sayyid, Ahmed bin Zaid.

"You will like it," said Husain. "There will be horse-racing. It is a pity you were not here last year, for then there were three horses, but now two have died."

"Then who does the racing?" said I.

"The one that is left," said Husain, evidently surprised at so obvious a question.

I felt I could not miss this spectacle, and Alinur said she would go in the afternoon if Husain would fetch her in his car. He and his brother Ahmed and Iuslim came for me in

the morning and took me to a little house full on the pilgrims'
way. From it I could see the road and all that went on upon
it; the sunlight fell pleasantly on its whitewashed walls through
the lattice of the windows and palm trees outside; cushions
and a rug were spread, a samovar was brought for tea, I spent
the morning happily watching the road and its traffic, careful
not to show myself, for this instantly gathered an animated
crowd, until the procession, rolling by with banners in its
centre and a few camels like islands about it here and there,
gathered and carried along with it all stray thoughts and
people of the little town.

Husain who, like any Englishman, disliked being too
conspicuous, had dumped me in this unobtrusive spot with
the evident hope that I should stay there. But I had no idea
of missing the rites of the pilgrimage and the visit to the tomb.
It was only a few minutes down the road, the egg-coloured
domes were visible in their bare waste of graves. The cliffs
of a side wadi embrace them with shallow open arms. Iuslim
and I joined the women, whose bright blue now trailed in
that limestone whiteness. I have been noticing all these
days what great increase of dignity is given to any public
function when people dress more or less alike; some quality
of the sculptured frieze falls upon them; the mere fact of
repetition gives them a reticent and sober splendour.

This crowd, save for the women's blue, was dark in colour,
for the beduin of all the neighbouring country had gathered
to the shrine. About seven thousand must have been there
assembled, an immense concourse whose long line repeated
the line of the cliffs behind it. The sun shone upon them,
their four banners, like the ark of the Israelites, rocked in their
midst; the tomb under its dome was dimly visible in shadow

against an open door behind it. For a minute or two I saw it all, small, detailed and hard like a miniature; then the crowd noticed and engulfed us.

Iuslim vanished, though we kept fairly near each other and made for home. A stranger took my hand and led me. Wave after wave of beduin surged towards us and above, struggling for a glimpse of the stranger. They were friendly but terrifying by sheer numbers. Volunteers appeared to beat at them with sticks; like the air in the Ancient Mariner, the human mass "opens from before and closes from behind"; a strange wild head with hair parted down the middle in long locks like Charles I appeared and reappeared persistent as a dream before me, tossed on the living waves. When we reached the doors of the little house, the wooden key, of course, would do nothing in a hurry. Three men held the crowd while a knife with a crooked blade was tried. Iuslim now emerged worried and dishevelled. When the key turned we made a rush; our three assistants held the onslaught for a second with their arms, and the door was closed behind us. I showed myself like royalty from the terrace, and was greeted with cheers or their Arabian equivalent by the mass of people which now stretched almost out of sight below.

After this it was scarcely surprising that Husain should not appear in the afternoon to take me to the "races." I did not expect it for I know by long experience what a nuisance I am. But Iuslim came and explained that his master had a slight temperature which prevented him from fetching Alinur as he had intended, or coming for me in his car. Iuslim and I would walk; the mosque round which the people gather is only a short distance west of the town.

It is, as a matter of fact, about three-quarters of a mile, and long before we got there we reached the crowd, all going that way. Iuslim strode on with a dogged look, quite useless as far as I was concerned. But I saw a donkey with two small friendly boys upon it; they gave it me; I thanked God for my divided skirt, leaped on by the one and only stirrup to accompanying cheers, took some friendly stranger's proffered stick and, escorted by about five hundred people, turned the affair into a sort of progress. Iuslim with very dusty eye-lashes walked beside me, his pale blue turban slightly disarrayed, his manner glum.

When we reached the wide bay of the races, a lovely but anxious landscape appeared, for it too was filled with people, the concourse of the morning. The solitary mosque, mud-walled and yellow-brown, was crowded on every balustrade with the blue draperies of women. I thought we were going into some room there, but Iuslim seemed surprised.

"Where is Husain?" I asked.

"Here," said he, looking round at the five thousand human beings now making for us as fast as they could from every point of the compass.

Round the base of the mosque was a shallow platform about a yard wide and equally high, and crowded with women. I made straight and quickly for it, averted a female panic by speaking Arabic just in time, and scrambled as it were on to an island among them. Iuslim sat at my feet. Two volunteers threw people off as fast as they mounted on either side. Men below kept a small free space with sticks: one drew his sword, but put it back again in answer to my signal. Those who got a foothold, I dealt with: I found that by seizing their arm, looking them in the eyes, and saying firmly "Get down," I could make myself obeyed.

61

As I was the sight of the afternoon, a sort of whirlpool went on below. Small boys lost their feet and flew about like footballs. They were all in holiday mood and cheerful, and when I looked up from my photography and smiled, the phenomenon was greeted with shouts of joy. The horse-race was practically forgotten: I could see the solitary racer, a tiny Java pony, careering in a circle far away. Aloof and above the turmoil, five or six camels stood out of range of trouble, and I wished I were on one. Beyond them were the four banners: their gilt crescents glittered in the sun against the cliffs behind them, their pink and red silk rounded itself like rose-leaves in the sky. In the half-naked beduin crowd, I was suddenly surprised to see a camera bracketed upon me; it belonged to the portly Aulaki commandant of police in Seiyun. He struggled to within shouting distance and called out in English: "Is everything O.K.?" and left me to my fate.

But now the banners began to move away, and the crowd with them. When they had broken into groups and thinned, Husain was discovered and asked in no dilatory way to bring his car. We drove back through the young palm plantations in a golden twilight, overtaking home-going parties, the beduin on camels with their women pillion behind them, the sayyids sideways on donkeys or walking, the edges of their long white coats flapping from them at every step. Iuslim was almost speechless, white even to his moustache with the dust of battle; he began gradually to laugh.

"This year," he said, "you and not the blessed Ahmed bin Zaid have been the centre of the pilgrimage."

By air to Aden

> "*Ah, to touch in the track*
> *Where the pine learnt to roam*
> *Cold girdles and crowns of the sea-gods, cool blossoms of water*
> *and foam.*"

> (SWINBURNE. *Atlanta in Calydon.*)

The people of the Hadhramaut all say that, in spite of the great heat, the summer is their healthy time. In winter they suffer from a cough which settles with fever on their lungs and is as widespread as influenza in London. We all have suffered, and continue to suffer from it. When I returned from my pilgrimage I, too, went down, and as the aeroplane was leaving, decided to hasten matters as I hoped by a week in Aden hospital. Alinur was now well again, and the Archæologist better; they preferred to convalesce in Seiyun, where Harold and the R.A.F. were temporarily installed, negotiating with the Se'ar in the north. It would be a little while before the Archæologist was fit to begin her work: I hoped to be with them, or very soon after them, in Hureidha.

But who can predict the course of events, even with the help of mechanics? The hospital refused to relinquish me when the week was up: the aeroplane left alone, and crashed while joy-riding in Tarim, luckily with no damage except to its own machinery and the nerves of the pilot: the Hadhramaut was suddenly removed as it were from the Home Counties to the Antipodes. The kind and pleasant hospital still wished to keep me, but I was naturally anxious to rejoin the marooned expedition, from which of course no news was coming through. So I left in a 4,000-ton pilgrim boat touching at Mukalla.

All day we ploughed along the Arabian coast, watching the

63

changing colour of the sea. From the morning's sapphire to the afternoon, shot silk like a kingfisher's wing and barred with luminous shafts, it grew white in the sunset, its underlying darkness showing only in smooth and oily shadows. The tossing flecks of foam in mid-ocean, like tritons suddenly diving, all subsided. The detail of the coast grew clear of haze, the west a stair of gold. Inland ranges with sharpening tops showed thin as paper above their misty flanks. The seagulls' crescent wings against the west were unfathomably dark. The ocean, too, darkened like old black cloth gone green with age.

In the morning at seven we wakened off Mukalla, grey and dove-like in the dawn, to a sea alive with fishing porpoises: their sharp perpendicular fins make the small sudden splashes of foam. Gulls flying low above their heads were fishing too; and so were the men in huris, paddling their round oars. Man here is happy; he joins in the activities of his universe: he lives in a pleasant companionship with the porpoises and gulls. The sailor in his ship is happy too among the gulfs and islands of his round world, whose weathers and vicissitudes he shares; his inventions have not outstripped his mind. But we are now companionless in a universe in which we are unique; our pressing need is to find some harmony which once more may include us with forces equal to our own, greater than those our science has outrun.

There seemed to be no chance of finding a motor car from Mukalla for at least a week. It was Christmas. I had accepted with happy resignation a necessity which obliged me to eat a holiday dinner with my friends, when a small aeroplane appeared making for the landing-ground of Fuwa: the postmaster, the mail-bags and I packed ourselves into a car and found the still nerve-shattered pilot and a small spare plane ready to take us on. The rest of Christmas morning I spent with the surface of the jōl below me, intricate and gnawed by water like a sponge. I lunched at Seiyun, and dined at Qatn, talked about Arab history with Sultan 'Ali, met there my old patriarchal friend, the Mansab of Meshed, and continued the day after for Hureidha.

In this part of the wadi, the stretches of corn are almost continuous on the south, because of the nearness of water in the ground. The sunshine lay upon the green like a yellow garment; the houses stood solitary, peaceful and far apart. The land belongs to the tribes.

We came to the openness of Wadi Kasr, which I remembered. It is an ancient name, descended from pre-Islamic times, for it exists in an inscription. In the spring, said Abdulillah, the driver, the whole space from cliff to cliff is a wide green sea: now there was nothing but dry grass which showed on the reddish sand like tow-coloured hair on a fair complexion.

Our company grew gradually. We started with only one man with meeting eyebrows who said he came from Shabwa and was helping with the car. The new Seiyun postmaster, from Zanzibar, then climbed in with an immense and charming smile and a book of the Sunna in his hand. The Mansab of Meshed's son added himself at Qatn, and then the Hureidha postman whom we overtook riding with gun and turban on a donkey almost invisible below him. He tied his gun to our door and the Shabwa man made room for him by sitting on the bonnet. When we broke down, which we did three times that morning, Abdulillah peered into the interior of the bonnet. "Nothing," he would say, in a detached manner.

The Diary, Hureidha

"It is only dirt." He polished various small objects with a duster, and the car went on. In the fullness of time and in the heat of noon we reached Hureidha.

HUREIDHA. *December 27.*

> *"J'avouerai que j'ai eu l'hardiesse de laisser aux personnages les aspérités de leur caractères."*

(LA CHARTREUSE DE PARME.)

The first news I had of my party was from a Nahdi tribesman, a nearly naked man with, on his head, one of the knitted sports caps which the Italians across the sea have made unhappily popular. He strode up during the breakdown of our car and, having barely greeted us in a truculent way, said: "These two women, what do they want? They shut themselves up and see no one. I have been twice to call and have not seen them. Do they dig up gold?"

Qasim came running to meet me down the hill where houses are piled one above the other. Our own, a small brown one, grânted by the Mansab or Religious Head of Hureidha, is near the top, in the last row on the southern edge, and looks south over a wadi about a mile wide. A mosque and a well stand in the stony flat below. The ladies were out: they had arrived some days before, and found a site and begun to excavate. I had hardly settled my things about me before a message came from the Mansab Hasan asking me to lunch.

He is the religious ruler of this place, a descendant of the Converter of the Hadhramaut, of the tribe of Qureish. When he walks abroad, people kiss his hand as he passes. He has a manner of authority, and looks handsome, his green turban wrapped round a grey skull-cap that matches his grey gown. He leaves behind him a scent of sandal-wood. His feet and

66

finger-nails are dyed with henna, and he winds an amber
rosary six times round his wrist. When he lifts his turban,
which he does absent-mindedly in conversation, the top of his
head shows bald with a fringe of black curls round it, like that
of a medieval monk. His mild eyes, darkened on the lower
lid with kohl, his mouth sensitive and rather full, his beautiful
hands with long fingers, give him an almost feminine elegance.

When I was here before I met two brothers, 'Ali and
Muhammad, but the Mansab was away, for he travels in India,
Somaliland, and Egypt. He was here now, he said, only because of the message sent through Sultan 'Ali of our coming,
and because his brothers had spoken of me; and he watched,
pleased, as I dipped my fingers in his rice and enjoyed the
"asit," a pudding made of pounded dates, sesame oil and sugar.
His brother 'Ali the Qadhi sat on one side and did not
eat with us, for the respect paid to the Mansab is very great.
The Italians entertain him when he travels in their lands,
and, as I happened to know one of them, we talked of mutual
friends.

"I have been waiting till you came," the Mansab said
presently, "to decide whether to allow you to dig here, and
meanwhile I have given those ladies four men. They asked
for eight. I thought four was enough."

Amused by this attitude towards female emancipation, I
agreed with the Mansab's prudence, but suggested that the
ratio might now be raised. The giving of labour would increase his prestige with the tribes around. The tribes are the
perpetual thorn in the flesh of the Mansabs of Hureidha.

Female emancipation as a means of propaganda became
comprehensible in his eyes and we parted friends. The
Mansab, like any ordinary Englishman, appears to be afraid

of the Strong-Minded Woman (whose mind, I sometimes think, is apt to be her weakest point). He had obviously imagined alarming things about us.

"I am glad," he said, "to find that you are Arabs like myself."

*　　*　　*

Many people came to call in the afternoon, and at sunset the experts returned, pleased with their day's work on the mound of a castle or temple on the north side of the wadi, an hour's ride from here. The whole valley floor over an area of miles is strewn with undistinguished mounds, and to have discovered an important one so soon shows the excellence of our Archæologist.

But all her charms in my eyes are momentarily destroyed by the fact that she has established Qasim's kitchen in the W.C. just by my bedroom. It is quite a pleasant little apartment in itself and the sun and air have rendered it outwardly innocuous since the last inhabitants were there, but still . . . it has never even been whitewashed since. Qasim showed me over it in an embarrassed way and finally asked if I thought it nice to cook meals in a W.C.? I did not tell him what I thought, but said that he had better take himself and his traps to the shed below. Apart from other things it would shock Hureidha if I slept like Cinderella among the servants.

But for one night there was no help for it, the shed could not be prepared in time; my bedroom, which opens on to the terrace without a door, was the only way for Qasim to go in and out. Tired and vexed, I sat waiting for him to finish while the last saucepan was being polished with what seemed unnecessary care; and next morning in the uncharitable hour

Hygiene : the dig

before dawn, dressing so that Qasim could get in to cook the breakfast, wondered at the curious vagaries of people's attitude to hygiene. Qasim and the scientists are equally shocked by each other. One is always coming upon these mutual and identical criticisms from East and West. Meanwhile, being still weak from hospital and the nights and dawns extremely cold, I am ill again, and so annoyed that I can scarcely indulge the harmless pleasure of picturing to myself the surprise to European feeling if Qasim's uncivilized opinions on Western sanitation were disclosed.

December 28. *"Verily fire is kindled by two sticks, and verily words are the beginning of warfare."*

(NASR IBN SAYYAR.)

I had one day's interval to visit the "dig" before this catastrophe of my relapse became complete. It is on a mound, an hour's ride or so away, above a hollow which must once have been an artificial basin, still called Karif ath-Thabit, or The Steadfast Pond.

The flat and yellow wadi lies around it, threaded by the canal and by the seil bed, a dazzle of white stones. Ancient débris lie there, hummocks surmounted by grey boulders, wavelets in the sea of sand and time. In this bare and pleasant space, where the horizon cliffs melt into the western distance like an avenue of sphinxes tawny in the sun, a little crowd was gathered, of workers, sightseers and volunteers, and Sayyid 'Ali, an old friend, in their midst. He is, as it were, our liaison officer. His turban floats unwound in the heat of argument; his mind is far too busy with all his small corruptions to let him be of any use as a director of labour. He is a little man and when he walks uses his arms like flippers through the air to push himself along. Politics are the passion of his life. In his breast-pocket (when he wears one) he keeps a dingy much-folded piece of newspaper with the portrait of Mr. Anthony Eden. He scrambles through life avoiding or haranguing creditors, and seizes any money that lies handy, to distribute "for the honour of his name": his honesty is peculiar to himself; but he is an idealist in his way, caring more for the shapes of his fancy than for material things ; a born comedian and a mimic, delighted with a joke; an avoider of work and lover of words; fond enough of adventure to join in it without a thought of gain; and ready always in the magnanimity of his small soul to appreciate those virtues which he himself does not possess.

The Archæologist calls him "that little cur," and has difficulties with him over the men's pay, which 'Ali, in the innocence of his heart, thought of as a small gold-mine of his own. He has a plan, too, to find new workmen every day, "so that all the countryside may benefit." What would not benefit, I have been pointing out at some length, is the work of excavation. The matter of the pay I have taken over since 'Ali knows me and I can do it without unpleasantness. He is a native of the Ja'da country, and an indispensable man, and is our only go-between with the tribes, who pay very little attention to what the sayyids of Hureidha may say. The daily feeding of the men has started in his hands and will lead to difficulties, but there is nothing to be done about it till trouble actually arises.

Our house in Hureidha

December 29.   *"If this born body of my bones*
                    The beggared soul so barely owns,
                    What money passed from hand to hand,
                    What creeping custom of the land,
                    What deed of author or assign
                    Can make a house a thing of mine?"
                                        (R. L. STEVENSON.)

A serious problem lay waiting for me in the matter of our house. It is a small brown house on the edge of the town, and slants at a steep angle down the hillside below the cliff. It looks past the solitary castle of the Children of Muhsin to a palm-fringed wadi below. We can settle here very happily. But our landlord has received letters, asking him how he can bring himself to allow Christians inside it? Whatever happens, it would not do to be ousted on a point of religion. The landlord is an old man, and absent; he lives in Du'an: personal influence cannot reach him. All that can be done is to start a rumour on its way to say that we think of paying rent, an unusual proceeding here for visitors, and I have asked his nephew, who lives next door and manages his affairs, to come and see me.

It is fortunate that it is possible to attend to these matters in bed. I lie under a mosquito net in comfort: three of the twelve openings in my room have been boarded up and the Archæologist has compensated for the unfortunate episode of the W.C. by kindly draping her rug over my door. The two come here to breakfast and to sup on a packing-case table, and I spend their hours of absence dealing with the endless negotiations that Arab life requires, with Qasim to help when medicines or money are wanted from the chest. One has to know a lot of religion to be a doctor. A man came in with a poisoned foot which I bound up with Antiphlogistine. He

71

was a handsome creature, slim-waisted, with the small regular nose and well-shaped chin of many of these western tribesmen, and he had just shaved and had his hair cut and bound it with a coloured scarf. He was going back to his wadi, worried by the thought of the bandage which would keep him from washing for prayers.

"You can wash all round the place—your five toes and your heel and your instep. Won't that do?"

"No," he said, "it isn't enough."

"But don't you know that you are dispensed when you are ill from washing altogether? If you are *very* ill, you are allowed to pray by just flickering your eyelids as you lie."

The Ja'da man looked unconvinced. Qasim had to be called to corroborate. He hobbled off dubiously, and I am sure took off the bandage. Perhaps it may be counted him for merit and his foot may cure itself.

A more difficult matter has been that of Mubarak the Slave who is one of our workmen, and to whose wife I have given medicine. She has been ill for a year, and he came to-day for a new dose. He is fond of her, and would take her to Aden, or even to the doctor in Mukalla, but the sayyids tell him he is a slave belonging to this earth and cannot move.

"I know," he said, "that I am free by law, but what is the good of that?"

I have advised him to wait for Harold's next visit, who has only too many of these matters on his hands. It appears that there are a number of such slaves in Hureidha, and their freedom only becomes effective when some British official is near enough to be applied to in cases such as these.

*   *   *

My pleasantest visitors are the children, who remember me

with favour from last time, when I told the chauffeur to give them a ride in the car—an event still unforgotten. They rushed down in a little cluster even before I reached the house and have never left me since. They are most delightful children, friendly and unselfconscious and affectionate, and sit, half a dozen or so at a time, round the bed, looking at my oddments, a fairyland for them. I have a mechanical donkey, which puts its ears back and wags its tail and is so popular that I lend it to be kept for a day and a night. It is brought back honestly in the morning, carried with loving care, a little grubbier each time, and it is amusing to watch the older boys pretend to take no interest, and gradually fall and ask for it just as they are leaving. Qasim too cannot resist playing with it, and is going to ruin the machinery.

I had four crackers too, with whistles and paper caps inside them. Salim, my particular friend, pulled the last one; he stood in a sort of ecstasy, smoothing the red-and-gold paper in his dirty blunt little hands, smiling to himself. His cousin Ahmed, who came late, could only be accommodated with a paper cap in which he stood in stricken silence, with dusty eyelashes sucking up tears like blotting-paper, till Qasim lifted him to see in my mirror the vision of himself crowned with green tissue-paper and sent him away happy too.

Salim is a darling, minute for his eleven years. His features are beautiful, rather pointed and very fine, and he has that rare thing in this country, a well-shaped head. He has the most charming feelings. When I offered a biscuit he refused.

"Oh, now why not?" I asked, surprised.

"One must not *covet* things," he said.

When I am tired and ask to sleep, they leave at once. "We

exhaust you with our chitter-chatter," they say politely, and file
downstairs to Qasim's shed which is always full of a small
babbling crowd.

The poem of welcome that 'Ali the Qadhi wrote for me in
their school three years ago is now sung all over the country,
the children say. But alas, the school itself is closed for want
of funds. The scattered sayyids who kept it going have
ceased their contributions, and the house in Java whose rent
was its mainstay is empty because of the slump.

December 30. "*Il ne s'emporte jamais, ne prononce pas de paroles injurieuses,
est incapable de lâcheté ou d'avarice, ne frappe aucun subordonné,
ne repousse aucun quémandeur, et ne s'est pas une seule fois
révolté contre Allah.*"

(Praise of his uncle by 'Umara the Yemeni—12th
century.)

The ruin on the mound appears to be a temple with two
flights of steps, and inscriptions taken from older temples are
inserted promiscuously about its walls and pavements. Yesterday a hideous little idol with head roughly chopped out of
the end of a brick was found in an annexe, with three incense
burners and two broken pots before it. Ugliness never
seems to have hindered the worshipping instincts of men.
It is strange to think of the smoke curling up from those three
burners in that place so long ago; the smoke that still arose
the other day from the sea-front of Mukalla, when they lit
fires of incense in honour of King George's coronation. The
idol looks exactly like the rag dolls the little girls here make
and play with, except that these are dressed in coloured bridal
garments, provided with strips of black rag for hair, decorated
with necklaces and green festive patches on their faces, and
loved tenderly. I asked for one and a quite repulsive collection

appeared, carried secretly by the little girls in the big blouse sleeves of their gowns. This playing with dolls is a pagan affair, not approved of by their brothers.

*   *   *

There has been a fearful shindy at the dig. The Archæologist, whose Arabic is scanty, is apt in moments of excitement to push the uncomprehending worker silently aside. This is understandable, for they can misplace things in the twinkling of an eye, but there are ways and ways of pushing. There is your sociable push of comradely eagerness, which no one minds, and there is your gesture of aloofness with its unconscious racial innuendo which the Arab visibly dislikes. I noticed a push or two myself, and, like Cassandra, foresaw trouble coming; but, unlike her, said nothing about it, having learnt that much wisdom out of three thousand years. It has come now over the finding of the idol, which meant a little *bakhshish* to the two lads who discovered it. One of them had been the recipient of one of these pushes of which the perpetrator was quite unconscious, unaware probably that the hands of women are anyway degrading. The victim, pleased with his find, did not mind in the least: "She can hit me if she likes," he said, misjudging our Anglo-Saxon pleasures: "it is only the remarks that I mind."

A man who had seen the idol and found nothing himself shouted out: "Ha, you who let a woman beat you!" The boy said: "She is a better woman than your mother!"

The angry man heaved a stone and cut the lad's head open: he then brandished his dagger and foamed at the mouth: whereupon the Archæologist put herself in the line of fire, which is a dangerous thing to do, and 'Ali, by his own account, which I am sure is not true, clasped the wild man to his breast and prevented murder. They all eventually arrived at my bedside, the Archæologist still blissfully unconscious of being the unwitting cause of violence.

All three men are dismissed, which is the way of the world. The injured one proposes to go to the Mansab for a trial; in Yemen, Qasim tells me, they have a schedule assessed for wounds in every part of the body, but I do not know how it is done here. The Mansab has sent me a little note to ask if we would mind not hitting our workmen, and 'Ali has begged me to prevail on the ladies to be moderate—one would think they were Bacchantes liable to frenzies by the fuss it has caused.

*　　*　　*

There is violence of a more serious kind in Wadi 'Amd, where a man asleep in his house has been shot. Rumour has it that it was done by his daughter, so that we do not appear to be the only energetic women in the district. There are no soldiers and no police in this Arcadia, and Sultan 'Ali of Qatn has been written to, being the nearest man with an army. He will have to send to Harold, and in course of time the wheel of justice may revolve, but there is some fear that the tribesmen may do something in their own quicker way first.

December 31, 1937. "*She went out but little and then always veiled, either to excite and then disappoint curiosity, or because she knew it suited her.*"

(TACITUS.)

The Mansab visited us yesterday.

He came with the sayyid who acts as our landlord, a bitter-faced old man who tried to slip away without drinking tea. This is a slur I had no intention of putting up with, and had him forcibly recalled by Qasim, for it is a mistake to overlook any social carelessness; and the old man returned full of amiability, while the Mansab, smiling, clicked his rosary slowly.

Alinur came down and sat with us, spreading biscuits with cherry jam and explaining the temple, altar and inscriptions; while he, equally anxious to tell the "real" history of antiquities about here, interrupted with the news of *three* temples, two Zoroastrian and one Burmese! and a treasure of lead beneath one of them. (It is curious that a legend about a treasure of lead wanders throughout this region.) The Mansab won, and held the field, partly because Alinur was busy with the biscuits.

*　　*　　*

The Mansab's two handsome sisters, Rahiya and Fatima, have also called.

These sayyid ladies come in the evening, when the streets are dark and empty so that—even veiled as they are and covered in sheet-like white—they may not be seen. Qasim lets them in, and then clears the kitchen and even the street for them when they leave. "In the day-time," says Fatima, "there are *men* about," in a voice in which one might talk of a plague of locusts.

"How happy you are unmarried," she told me. "Allah alone is above you."

She is a handsome matronly creature with great eyes, pleasant to talk to, for she has a lively wit and speaks in images. When she describes a fat man she pats herself all over and says: "Such a lot of meat to carry." When I first came here three years ago and European women were unknown, she had been afraid, she said, to meet me. She beat her breast with little taps to show the fluttering of her

77

heart. "And then," she said, "I saw that you were smiling, and I felt that anyone who smiles must be like us."

She is the mother of the little boy Ahmed, the one of the paper cap, and it was his favourable report which brought her down to see us. With that small boy and his sister she lives alone in a house on our opposite ridge, and gets small sums at long intervals from a husband in Batavia, and asked me rather sadly if I had any medicine to make a man love his wife. But she is devoted to the Mansab, her brother, who consults her in many matters, for she is clever and strong, with an affectionate heart.

Her sister Rahiya is the wife of the long-faced sayyid next door, and we have now made friends, so that I hope the house problem may settle itself without a hitch; the harim is usually the quickest way for diplomacy.

The women here all use expressive but inaccurate gestures to explain their feelings, and it is very difficult to diagnose a pain described, for instance, by the slow closing and opening of all five fingers. "It does *that*," they say, fixing me with anxious eyes and waiting for a cure.

They come in clusters with little presents of dates or salted melon seeds and keep their veils on, for Qasim is in attendance, and all one can see of their heads, tight-bound in black, are brown soft eyes in the silver-threaded eyelet holes, and a little bit of varnished yellow cheek. It would be the greatest blessing in the world if a doctor could tour these valleys even once in a year. There is a perpetual sickness in winter, of the kind that I am suffering from, coughing and aching in every limb: and as at least a dozen sick people cough in my face every day, I suppose I shall never get well. Little Salim has an attack of it and I have taught him to turn away during the

Qasim in love

paroxysms, and have given him a breast-plate of cotton wool to wear; but his family have taken it away from him because they think it is a Christian amulet and not safe. He always refers to us as Unbelievers and is abashed when I correct him.

January 1, 1938.   *"Il lui était reconnaissant d'être aimable et de laisser traîner après elle un parfum d'amour."*
(Le Mannequin d'Osier.)

Qasim is falling in love.

The sayyids next door lend us their maidservant, a pretty round creature from Rakhiya in the next valley. Her name is Ne'ma (the same name as Naomi) and her face is like a very cheerful diminutive moon. Her voice has a lilt in it, a petulant little note of song, and she has small quick gestures and something funnily French about her. She is quite wealthy, chiefly in the ownership of girdles, of which she has gradually collected two, all studded with silver and coral beads, with amulet cases round the lower edge. The buckles are brass and come from Hajarein, and they are taken off when a woman is bearing a child, for every stage of life here has its appropriate clothes. Ne'ma has a husband somewhere or other, but I think he is going to divorce her, and anyway he does not count; and her pretty sing-song voice goes on in the shed with Qasim long after the rooms are swept. She is not allowed in the Archæologist's room, which is locked with a European key, but she tidies Alinur upstairs, and Qasim usually helps her, and the whole proceeding takes a very long time. She is a great authority on everything that has to do with clothes or cosmetics. The fashion for painting the face green, she tells me, is going out. She can explain the uses of herbs, of the white-flowered harmal that grows everywhere and is squeezed into kohl as a strengthener of eyes, or its leaves ground fine and mixed with cardamom and oil and a cowrie shell for luck, and smeared daily for forty days on the faces of new-born babies and their mothers. It is called murr, or Bitterness, and must be a horrid introduction to life for the baby. She tells me also that the birth of a girl here is welcomed in a household just as much as that of a boy—a great difference from North Arabian lands. Indeed, the people are charming with all their children, whose noisy little congregation is the swiftest way through the hearts of the harim to the friendship of its masters.

In the Castle of the Sons of Muhsin south of us lives Sayyid 'Aluwi's beduin bride, whom he married for love. He is the friend from Woking of my former journey, and I was just able to call on his bride before taking to my bed, and found her shy and pretty, a daughter of a headman of the Ja'da. 'Aluwi is away, but his brother Husain was there, though he had to retreat hastily from the room because his recently divorced wife appeared on a visit. He comes almost daily to see me, speaking Arabic slowly, for his native language is Malayan and he has only recently come from Singapore. He likes Singapore better, but the religion of the Hadhramaut is purer, he says. He is a good-natured, wide-eyed, curly-headed creature, with a taste for rather frequent marriages which his family deplores. In our talk yesterday we fell upon the subject of courage and he told me that a man once asked the Prophet what it was; the Prophet answered thus: "Courage is Patience." It is, at any rate, what with one thing and another, a virtue much in demand here; and it is very exhausting.

*　　　*　　　*

Visitors : news of the valley

In the afternoon the Mansab of Meshed's son, the same who drove with me from Qatn, came to say goodbye. I bought his silver knife from him, for we are all collecting them; they are made in a delicate pattern of flutings and balls. He turned it round in his hands, dubious whether to part with it or not, while Mubarak the Slave who was standing by, murmured at intervals: "Make it easy for her. She is a guest." The slave cannot take his wife to an Aden doctor, but he can give advice to his masters.

Having obtained the little object I presented the young man with a pocket-knife made for the Coronation, with a picture of King George upon it, sitting on his throne, and sent him away happy, for none of the presents I have brought are as successful as this one.

Januury 2. "Clientum longa negotia." . . .
                                    (HORACE.)

Out of bed, with a fluttering heart, I sat on my terrace to-day, small and mud-walled, and looked over the wadi, its sand-coloured villages and warm cliffs, and the palm trees burnished in the sun; and drank at the loveliness and fragility of life, as one does in the first days of convalescence, when the body lies lazy, as a snake that has shed its skin. From the stony slope below, the children playing with their native dust caught sight of me, and their voices, small but persistent, have been calling: "Freya, Freya, let me in," ever since. One has to pay for popularity!

I have ended the day as usual with a talk with 'Ali, who comes after work (a euphemism as far as he is concerned), to sit with his mug of tea at my bedside, and spit melon seeds over my carpet, and give me the valley's news. He has had a secret letter from the village where the man was murdered in his sleep. It is signed by some of the Elders and designates the three whom they suspect to be the guilty men—a curious insight into methods of justice. This affair is causing uneasiness, for the tribes are no longer supposed to be in authority and there is no government visibly able to take their place: and the family of the murdered man are clamouring.

*   *   *

The Mansab came this morning, and brought a very precious possession, a manuscript copied by his grandfather from earlier histories, a sort of commonplace book of all that was thought worth preserving at that time. It has the fascination of old and treasured things, gathered for someone's private joy. Among a great deal of religion, there is a medieval chronicle, which as far as I can tell is more or less unknown: so I have been sitting on my terrace, copying it out, after the Mansab's departure.

He came to tell me that he had been in person to the old sayyid who thought to turn us out of this house, and that the matter is quietly settled. And then he sat, drinking tea and clicking his amber rosary, and talked of history and battles long remembered. We discussed the route which the Rasulid Sultan Muzaffar took to Dhufar. This is not specified in Khazraji, the only local history of the fourteenth century known to us, but the Mansab seemed to have no doubt about it, and assured me it was by Redet ed-Deyyin (from Bir 'Ali therefore), by Ghaidun down the 'Aqaba Ghar Sudan, by Hajarein, Haura (at the opening of this valley) to Hedye near Qatn (which is older than Shibam), and thence by the usual road to Seihut and the coast. The Mansab's ancestors went to Sultan Muzaffar in Haura on this occasion and offered fealty,

and were given the sovereignty of their lands. He spoke of
his fourteenth-century gossip with the same interest as if it
had been a matter of yesterday; like a Persian miniature, there
is no perspective in the historical mind of Asia.

After this, little Salim appeared, slinking through the door
between one visitor and another. He sat in a corner and
looked at *Country Life* and recognized the Adam fireplace in
the great drawing-room of Corsham as "the place where
they cook the dinners." He was very happy and came to
ask in a whisper if I would give him a notebook and write
his name inside, which was done, both in Arabic and English.
The asking for a gift is always done in a whisper in one's
ear!

Then the Mansab's servant came. He had brought me
yesterday a present from his master, a necklace of variegated
stones, agate, cornelian and many others, a beautiful coloured
thing from Yemen, and now he came gently to remind me
that the customary present to the bearer of gifts had been
forgotten. He did this in a delicate way, by saying that he
had a small son, three years old.

Then my old friend Jamila called, loving, dark and capable
as ever, after a nine days' journey from Mukalla on a camel.
When I asked after her mother, who is her love and care in
this world, she smiled and put her five fingers close together
and her head on one side in a tender little gesture, as if to show
the smallness, and sweetness, and helplessness of age.

After Jamila came Husain, with an old sayyid who has an
antique carved incense-burner to sell, cut in black stone. He
was a charming old man with a fringe of hennaed whisker
and a fine green cashmere shawl, and placid, beautiful manners
produced by the consciousness of religious superiority. At

the beginning he did not wish to drink tea or sit in this unbelieving house, but went away friendly after a time, though I did not buy his relic.

Then came the man whose head had been cut open, then the carpenter to make a cover for the W.C., another man with a wounded hand; the washerman; five affectionate children; and Sayyid 'Ali to end up with. By this time the morning had gone.

In the afternoon came Salim again, asking with concern as ever how I was. He felt my hands, and said:

"Hot, hot, the sun is in them."

He is the only one of the children who comes to talk to me first and only afterwards looks into the waste-paper basket, which is the children's permitted hunting-ground, full of treasure such as empty film cases.

To-day he turned his attention to my electric torch, and asked if it had a heart. He meant the bulb inside.

"Yes, it has a heart," I said.

"Everything has a heart," he observed after a moment's reflection. "Men, women, lamps, everything—and if it stops they die, may God be praised."

He has a busy, quick way of talking, and tosses out his hands as he does so.

"Have you ever been away from Hureidha, Salim?" I asked.

"No." He said it with a moment's wistfulness, but added stoutly: "It is the best place in the world, and later on I shall travel and go to Meshed like everyone else."

"Oh," I said, "you will go further than that; you will go to Mekka: that is half-way to me. You will come to see me."

A question of taste

Salim gave me one of his smiles, very sad and sweet.

When the sun had set and I was in bed again, the Mansab's brother, the Qadhi, came to help with explanatory notes for the names of places in the manuscript. We discussed Maqrizi, who says that the Se'ar tribe can change themselves into wolves. The Se'ar have stolen forty-two camels and are probably going to be bombed by the R.A.F., so that it might be a useful accomplishment just now.

"It is not true, however," said the Qadhi seriously. "It is a pure fairy tale of Maqrizi's. But it is quite true of the Beni Shabib near Qatn."

January 3.   *"We stroll to our box and look down on the pit,*
               And if it weren't low should be tempted to spit."
                                    (CLOUGH. *Dipsychus.*)

I have in my room an old yellow-and-pink carpet full of holes.

I was horrified when first I reached Hureidha to find that nearly every woman I talked to spat on it when she mentioned my companions. Alinur's kindliness is now winning its way; she has made friends by coming down when the mother of Ahmed called, and the word goes round. But the Archæologist does not talk to anyone and continues at present to be unpopular and my carpet to suffer, though all they find to say is that the corners of her mouth turn down. It has made me notice that corners of mouths in the Hadhramaut do, as a matter of fact, hardly ever turn down. The expression of their faces is amiable; hatred is common, but bad temper is scarcely known. The faces of the men are often spoiled by theology, or by being puckered for years in the sun; but the women keep into old age an expression of

85

calmness and sweetness, and the lines that are common in Europe are hardly to be found in these harims. This comes, I think, because, living always together and under a rigid code of courtesy, the feelings which create these lines are never allowed free play. Better than self-control, they have that true serenity which begins at the very source, eliminating those feelings for which self-control is required. I think it is because of this inner quietude that the faces of nuns, of Quakers, and of Arab women have, as they settle into age, the same look of peaceful acceptance and repose.

This nun-like appearance does not, however, interfere with the habit of spitting, which develops at the earliest age and at present seems to concentrate on the Archæologist and my carpet. The small Ahmed this morning sat quietly in his corner, turning the pages of *Punch* with a running commentary—for these are the first images of human beings the children have ever seen on paper, and to them they are living people. "That man is smiling, God be merciful to him" (an advertisement for cigarettes): "That surely is not one of the children of Adam, I take refuge with God, it is a Jinn" (a lady in corsets): "And that is the Madame who digs"—he put his small finger on the image of a man and began to spit, hitting the page two feet or so away with remarkable accuracy, and inspired, I begin to hope, only by a dislike for trousers.

I dislike them too, and so does Doreen, foreseeing the day when the ladies of the country in their turn will adopt this peculiar Western ugliness; we have suggested in vain to the Archæologist a loose, light coat to cover them. The question of dress is indeed very difficult. But I think one should avoid what to the Arab himself appears indecent and

also what, when copied, as it inevitably will be, will look
discordant against the background of these towns. For we
cannot very well complain of the ugliness of the East
when we ourselves have introduced it. Trousers are, I think,
generally ugly on the female figure, where everything is round
that the tailor intended to be straight; they do not, however, appear indecent to the Hadhramaut Arab, because they
are not as yet particularly masculine. The comfortable
sarong of the country is worn both by Harold and by the
oil expedition, who have made themselves extremely popular
by this adoption. If their precedent is continued, trousers
in the Hadhramaut will soon come to be considered as
exclusively intended for female wear!

January 4. "*It is naught, it is naught, saith the buyer; but when he is gone
his way, then he boasteth.*"

(Prov. 20. v. 14.)

Husain brought his old friend to-day, for a second round
in the affair of the incense burner, which it is obviously
intended that we shall buy. We approached it in the classic
manner of diplomacy, beginning with the life of Husain's
grandfather, who ran away as a boy to Australia. There he
spent all his fortune, and returned in contented poverty to his
Java home. He had a passion for music, so that he would rise
from bed in his last illness to hear a celebrated singer; he must
have had something of Husain's own easy-going nature. By
the time we had done with him, and discussed a little philosophy by the way, and heard how the old sayyid was the
builder of the new mosque in Hureidha, in whose floor the
two pre-Islamic inscriptions are uncompromisingly buried—
by the time all this was said, the sayyid's price had descended

to forty dollars and my offer had risen to fifteen. We left it at that and took friendly farewells: but Husain soon came hurrying back alone and suggested a compromise of twenty-five as a favour to himself. Reasons for buying here are not mere commercial ones of supply and demand, they are weighted by the social standing of the seller: it is scarcely nice to refuse to buy something you do not want from a *sherif* of noble birth. So we compromised on twenty-five dollars.

I had barely settled to my manuscript again, when an elderly bedu woman came with a bag of melon seeds, an offering, in her hand. She had a tattooed chin, and her kind face, full of lines, was dyed yellow with turmeric, together with her arms. Her eyebrows were plucked in a thin straight line as if she came from Bond Street. She is the wife of the Nahdi tribesman who lives in a cave in the hillside and guards our excavations at night, and came with a message to say that he would like to see me.

"Why does he want to see me?" said I, in our clumsy utilitarian way.

"He would like to talk Arabic," she explained. "And then," she said, "one day we would like you all to eat with us, if you do not mind our cave."

This I promised to do, and, having talked a little about the pleasure of being a grandmother, which is the same in Arabia as elsewhere, had again settled to my manuscript when the Mansab came, extraordinarily handsome in white skirt with green edge, white coat, green turban, and his amber beads.

He came to tell of a plot arranged against us by the Sultan of Qatn and some sayyids of Meshed in the hope of extracting large sums if we dig there; he has been asked to join, but has written his disapproval, and as we do not mean to dig in

The Qu'aitis and the Kathiris

Meshed the matter has no importance, except in so far as it shows the pitfalls that lie about one. It is unkind of the Sultan, who is supposed to be a friend, but a political tangle is now threatening to ruin all his British relations. Sitting here, we can watch these things arise, lifting their modern heads out of unsuspected avenues of time. There is a feud, generations old, between the Qu'aitis of Qatn and the Kathiris of Seiyun, nominally bridged over by the recent peace. But the feeling remains, and the fact that British headquarters have come to be Seiyun is sufficient to identify us with the enemies of Qatn, whose ear is hence inclined to foreign voices: nor will the matter, when it comes to its inevitable head, ever be thought of as what it is, a reincarnation of the undying medieval feud, but will figure in the enthusiastic Press of various countries with whatever label of rebellion or crusade may happen to be in fashion at the time. So we live in our cave, watching the shadows of things distorted between us and the sun.

*　　*　　*

The Archæologist came back last night with fever and is in bed to-day, but it is apparently dwindling quickly. It is a strange endemic sort of disease, and lies in wait for any moment of weakness, nor do I suppose we shall recover from it completely till we go. The people here are nearly all affected in a lesser manner, and in many women it seems to bring almost a paralysis of their lower bodies so that they can hardly drag themselves about, probably due to sitting, when the illness is upon them, with only one garment in the draught of their low windows. Salim has been coughing badly, and I rub his chest with camphor.

*　　*　　*

Meanwhile we are marooned from Europe . . . we have no news and no letters; the aeroplane that brought me has never come again; of Harold and the R.A.F. in Seiyun we have no word; and the oil people have vanished into air or possibly gas. Alinur is out all day, and I, well or ill, have my work to do indoors, so that it does not matter, but it is hard on the Archæologist, immured upstairs in sickness and seclusion.

January 5. *"Thou should'st see the merchants of Alexandria : three table-cloths, forty dishes, to each soul seven plates of all sorts, seven knives and seven forks and seven spoons, large and small, and seven different glasses for wine and beer and water."*

"It is the will of God," replied the Effendi; "but it must be a dreadful fatigue to them to eat their dinner."

(LUCIE DUFF GORDON.)

The Mansab sent a message this morning to invite himself to dinner. Qasim brought it, together with a white kid, frisking in ignorance, which he got from our neighbours as part of the menu. I am still in bed after sunset, and the other invalid secluded upstairs, but it did not matter, for we arranged rugs on the floor by my bedside, where I could reach the food, and Alinur, with the Mansab and Qadhi like Van Dyck pictures come to life, sat round, while Qasim and Sayyid 'Ali squatted, offering conversation from the doorway. They have gradually learnt of themselves that they can talk in the presence of Alinur.

We had an international meal of tinned soup and fruit salad, and Arab rice to support the kid whose sad appearance led my mind wandering to the fountain of Bandusium, more shining than glass, while Alinur enjoyed herself, being gently chaffed by the Mansab, who likes her. It is pleasant to see her happy. She has a weary time of it just now, for the geology she would like to examine is buried under many layers that have filled in and levelled the wadi floor; so that she must feel like a surgeon who has to operate on someone monstrously fat, his vital parts all choked in superfluous matter. The age and alternation of these layers of silt are given by sheets of gravel, sandwiched between them, washed down in successive periods of flood—but these are only visible where some sort of erosion has occurred to give them in section. Later torrents will cut through them—but no current has eaten its way deep enough to reach the bottom of the great trough, whose history, with that of the world it belonged to, is buried like forgotten empires out of sight.

January 6.   "*The word and nought else in time endures.*"
(HUMBERT WOLFE.)

Alinur and I eat alone; our conversation is about easy things like English gardens, and we sit over our food much longer than we did. Science, I begin to feel, is a dreary affair in conversation and incompatible with meals. An omelette is undoubtedly a composite of eggs and butter, but to say so is usually devastating at table. My vagrant fancies are often being pulled home and confined to tangible objects such as potsherds, beyond which it appears to be unsafe to draw conclusions. But when, ye gods, should one draw unsafe conclusions if not at dinner? when the mind roams released, adventurous and playful, "scegliendo," like Matilda "fior da fiore," and leaving statistics, like the omelette's egg-shells, decently out of sight?

*   *   *

91

There is a difference, no doubt, between science and art, but I think it is not near so great as many men imagine. In all human adventure two types of mind exist—one formal and the other seeking for reality through and beyond the obvious bounds of form; and the formal mind as such is held to be scientific because it is in effect able to collect data for other men to use. In art, on the other hand, each artist must gather material for himself.

But the ultimate aim of *all* human wisdom is but the liberation of the spirit; and on the degree of this freedom the excellence of *all* intellectual endeavour must depend. The assembling of facts is a means only; the collector is no more master of his universe than the paving stone is master of the road: he makes it indeed for freer feet to tread. It would be ungrateful to despise his devout and necessary labour; but it is also singularly unfair to limit the majesty of science to so pedestrian a track, and to take from it those ecstasies of the imagination which alone transmute the dead array of facts.

In this more vivid rank I do not believe that art and science intrinsically differ. The data of the one is certainly no less accurate and no less indispensable than the other, though less tangible. Too elusive for the instrument of language, it *must be gathered by every maker for himself*, and the labourer and the creator, often separate in science, in art must ever be combined. A sentence in Jane Austen is the fruit of observation as conscientious, minute and catholic as ever was produced by a biologist. On its truth and honesty her excellence, as his, depend.

Apart from the fact that art alone is a creator, the difference between them is one of method rather than of accuracy.

Science and Art

The facts that the scientist simply *states*, the artist *evokes*. Instead of relying on words alone, he lets the reader's mind fill in the meaning, and, in the measure of his magnanimity, will trust to what his reader can supply. It is collaboration, as between player and instrument.

> "Avenge oh Lord thy slaughtered saints whose bones
> Lie scattered on the Alpine mountains *cold*."

In the language of science, the adjective merely applies to the rocks of the hillside; but the poet knows that in the mind of his readers it awakens the vision of the cold and stiffened bodies of dead men.

Almost any fine piece of literature exhibits this delicate suggestiveness.

Take the Iliad:

> "As far as a man's view ranges, as he sits in the haze on a point of outlook and gazes over the wine-dark sea, so far at a spring leap the loud-neighing horses of the gods."

Everything helps to the infinity of that great spring: the "point of outlook" eliminates the finite sense of land around one: the width of sea horizon is indefinite and vaster in the haze that makes it at one with the sky above it: the reader sees the horses of the gods leaping into an unbounded space of light.

In Lycidas two different passages close together show this art supremely:

> "While thee, alas the winds and *warring* seas
> Wash *far away* where 'ere thy bones are *hurled*
> Whether beyond the *stormy* Hebrides
> Where thou perchance beneath the *whelming* tide
> Visit'st the bottom of the monstrous world. . . ."

The Diary, Hureidha

The words scattered here and there press through one chaos of movement to the remote limits of the world. The next lines with their change, show how consciously the whole effect is gained:

> "Or whether thou, to our moist vows denied,
> *Sleepst* by the fable of Bellerus *old*
> Where the great *vision* of the *guarded* mount
> *Looks toward Namancos* and Bayona's *hold.* . . ."

All is rest and immobility—though only once actually expressed in the word "sleep"; the other words all imply it, and there is nothing in the whole passage to express motion except in the last line where the eyes that "look toward" Namancos are made with infinite skill to increase the feeling of immobility, of imprisoned stillness evoked unconsciously in the reader's mind by the images of age, of guarded fortresses, of enclosing walls.

The artist does indeed play his instrument on the living hearts of men—even he who stumps his feet on a box in Hyde Park. He has the whole gamut of his audience's capacities to choose from for his practice, and the permanence of his labours depends on whether the things he chooses to evoke are permanent or ephemeral in the human heart.

The facts that science communicates are, on the other hand, permanent as long as the peculiar linguistic convention in which she clothes them is understood. But I have noticed that science is of no manner of use for talking to Arabs. It is not a matter of language: I have watched the scientists explaining things in Arabic which, though painful, could yet be understood, but it produces nothing but a blank from the mere fact that they are thinking of their subject and not of their listeners. The despised artistic method builds to the tribesman's eyes a picture he can see: his ancestors dispersed after the flood, their gradual descent to the lands of Yemen, the scattering of their records before the days of Qahtan: the natural desire of all men to know the beginnings of their race: the possibility of unknown kinship among the races of the world; the possibility, indeed, that English and Arab were cousins long ago: all these are familiar chords that wake an echo. Over and over again the Ja'da tribesmen come and, puzzled by the science of excavation out yonder, ask to have the matter explained in the intelligible language of art: like a house delicately built, I see the light of understanding rise in their eyes stage by stage: and the explanation, lamentably deficient in what the Archæologist calls "objective truth," has at least succeeded in convincing them that our aim is research and not treasure.

January 8.   *" The world stands out on either side*
                 No wider than the heart is wide."
                                    (E. St. Vincent Millay.)

Nothing could be more lovely in its sober tints than the view of our wadi in the morning. Its farther cliffs are washed with transparent blue, a thin veil of those whose innumerable numbers make the sky. The naked brown houses stand on their brown steep. A little ragged mist still catches the low distance of the palms. The landscape is as simple and severe as an early picture, bathed in this luminosity of morning.

My heart no longer flutters so badly, I can go earlier on to the terrace and look at the first beauty of the world, and copy my manuscript in the cool and pleasant hours, under a sun-shade which Qasim ties to three nails in a corner. No sooner does it appear than the small voices of children are heard from the slope below, calling my name with an implacable soft persistence for hours on end. It is agreeable to be loved, but no one enjoys hearing it said for hours together in a word of two syllables only.

Salim this morning brought a gift in his hand, an amber bead from the necklace round his neck.

"I want no money," he said hastily. "I want to give it as a present."

He tied it round my wrist with a piece of cotton and an expression of trembling joy and looked at his work with pleasure when it was done. "It will bring you luck when you wear it," he said. "Do not say that I gave it you; it is my amulet and I should be scolded." Among his few possessions, it was the only precious thing he had to give.

He asked me if we use arrows for divining. This ancient pagan custom still persists here, and people go to visit the witch or the diviner in a cave, and, having brought him meat or flour or whatever it is he requires, throw their arrows, which the diviner reads as they fall. The children tell me this, but it is denied by grown-up Moslems if one asks.

*　　*　　*

Another charming object has been brought for sale to-day— a tiny green axe like polished jade; the Archæologist says it is called a celt. No one knows where the beautiful stone comes from.

*　　*　　*

I have a copyist now—a thin-faced student in a long gown who writes out for me the manuscript of the Sultan of Qatn for which I have no time: it has six hundred pages and tells, under red and green headings, the history of the sixteenth century in Yemen. It is called the Sirat al Mutawakkiliya and was written in A.D. 1600, and in it are described scraps with the Ferangi (probably the Dutch) in the Red Sea, and a mission from Yemen to Abyssinia and news too of this land. Whether it is known or not in Europe, I have no means of telling, but it is good enough in itself to be worth the copying, and it is a pleasure to perpetuate learning by this slow and ancient means. It is very expensive, for every two sheets of paper cost a quarter of a dollar ($4\frac{1}{2}d$.), apart from the scribe's time; and it is difficult too to deal with, for none of the pages are numbered.

The first section of my own manuscript is copied out now and has given useful information, such as the date of the restoration and final ruin, in A.D. 1298, of al-'Urr by the Arabs.

In the afternoon, before the sunset prayer, the Qadhi comes to locate for me names of places and tribes which no one in Europe would know. He sits, turning over with his delicate fingers the pages written by his grandfather and treasured above all the books they have. The Egyptian who came here last year was never even allowed to *see* this book, for the man who wrote it is a saint in their eyes.

The Qadhi loves these hours. He has in him a pure passion for learning, a small flame with little enough to feed it, that burns for itself alone. He is happy to come and think of abstract things, and looks up from his page at intervals with quiet and gentle affection in his eyes, infinitely touching. In the middle of it all, a slave runner came in with a mail from Shibam. He got a small tip and, wishing to make all he could out of the occasion, asked in a truculent way: "When do we dine? I should like to eat."

I laughed and said he should eat when we did, and after us at that, and the Qadhi, shocked, looking up to me, said: "We in Hureidha all thank you for the kindness of your speech."

Before he left I showed him the Christmas cards that the mail had brought. There was one with a field of buttercups among them.

"That," I told him, "is our country in spring."

He looked for a long time at the deep grass and the flowers, scarce believing, and at last, turning to me, said in a voice of wonder: "And why do you come *here*?"

January 9. "When Eudoxus shore his first lovely fleece of hair, he gave its childish glory to Phœbus.

(Greek Anthology.)

To-day is Friday, a holiday, and all the boys have had their heads shaved like convicts and only the "gamzuz" left, a streak about two inches wide like a ridge from front to back. Sayyid 'Ali says it is left till they are fifteen, so that nobody will kill them by mistake. I remarked that in that case I would leave it on all my life, which appeared to him an uproarious joke. One cannot help having a tender spot for him. He likes jokes and adventures, two considerable merits: but something will have to be done, for he is giving just one quarter of the money paid for donkeys to their rightful owners.

The whole of this country must be full of his creditors. One of them walked in yesterday, a bedu of the Ja'da with a beard, grey and curly, like a waterfall down his chest. He had an expression of permanent and cheerful surprise which many of the Ja'da have, and looked like one of those lascivious Tritons one sees in pictures, clasping a nymph by the waist, half out of the sea. He was rather abashed because he had wandered upstairs and met the convalescent Archæologist in her dressing-gown, and the nymph and the Triton had not taken to one another. His beauty was indeed a little spoilt by a very greasy European vest over the top half of him. He settled himself on the coffee hearth near my bed and, after a preliminary discussion on archæology and treasure, came to the burning topic of politics and the Wadi 'Amd murder. Could he have, he asked, a letter of introduction to Mr. Ingrams to tell him that the Qu'aiti government in the Wadi 'Amd was about to go up in smoke?

"That is interesting," I remarked, "but why not go and tell the Mansab?"

"Oh, we tribesmen think nothing of the sayyids. If it were not for you English we would have been fighting long ago. Why do your aeroplanes never come to look at us?"

"They are busy preparing to bomb the Se'ar, as you know. But no doubt if you do things to your governor in 'Amd they will come up to you soon enough."

The old man laughed. He went off with no official letter, but made me write a private one for him to a relative in Java, telling of the approaching downfall of government, and asked me in an off-hand way as he went to be sure and stamp it for him. In the afternoon he was back: the echo of my voice, he said, had remained sweet in his ears; but now the actual business came out in the shape of fifty dollars owed him by Sayyid 'Ali. Sayyid 'Ali walked in just as the matter was being laid before me, and took him, with many flourishes of oratory, safely out of earshot.

"It would be better," he said to me later, "if you would

not let people come in as they do. I could see them all for you first."

"You do see the donkey people first," said I. "And every one of them has been in after to tell me that he is not properly paid. Now I shall pay them myself, and that will be less trouble for both of us. Why do you take such a heavy tax? If you had taken only a little no one would have spoken."

"Do you think it much?" said 'Ali with perfect good humour. "You know that anyone would do it in my place."

He sat, with his mug of tea in one hand and his melon seeds in the other, spitting husks over my unhappy carpet at random, and told me how Husain "is stirring up plots." There is a feud between 'Ali and the House of the Children of Muhsin, and it is crystallizing over the problem of our landlord. Strange as it may seem to persons unacquainted with this country, it is quite impossible to find out *who* our landlord is. There is no doubt that the owner of our house is the old sayyid who lives in Du'an; but it appears that *he* is living in the house of his cousin, who, being our neighbour here, claims the proceeds of this house in exchange. The whole coil goes to prove what a mistake it is not to follow the customs of the land: if I had not suggested the innovation of paying rent, covetousness would never have entered the cousins' hearts, and a present at the end would have contented everyone. As it is, the most absurd contretemps has happened. Husain came to me this morning as usual and told me that the Du'an landlord is staying with him on a short visit, and would come for his rent. I was only too delighted at the thought of getting rid of it, and when a venerable, wall-eyed old man arrived this afternoon, and showed his holiness by wrapping

his hand in a striped green-and-yellow shawl before con-
taminating it by the contact of mine, and told me that he was
going back to Du'an and had come for money—I hastened
to ask Qasim for the fifteen dollars and pressed them into the
green shawl. They were accepted with equanimity, and the
old man's brusque departure immediately afterwards might
have been due either to excessive holiness or to surprise. No
sooner had he gone, however, than the assembled bystanders,
who had not breathed a word during the proceedings, informed me that he is not the landlord at all, but a wandering
religious man who had come merely on the chance of being
helped in his travels. No one had liked to spoil sport while
it was actually going on, but they all volunteered to scatter
over the town and find my fifteen dollars again. The old
man, meanwhile, had vanished from the house of Muhsin:
he was no doubt celebrating the mercies of Allah in a sober
way with some religious friend. Late in the evening he was
discovered and came, with the same equanimity, the fifteen
dollars tied in a little bundle in the shawl. It went to my
heart to take them back, but we cannot afford to be known
as squanderers of dollars. The old wanderer himself saw
them go with the same placid serenity with which he had
seen them come. Having handed them all back, he waited
in a dignified way while I selected two to give him. I had
to drop them into his hand from a foot or so above, so as to
avoid any chance of pollution, and we parted with another
handshake made safe by the wrappings of the shawl. As for
the rent, I have decided to hand it over to the Mansab, who
alone can deal with the complexity of the problem.

*   *   *

We are in a rather destitute condition here just now, for

Ba Obaid has not sent us our money from Shibam. Sayyid 'Ali found a man so old and toothless to go for it with a camel, that Ba Obaid evidently thought it unsafe and wrote to say he himself would send it by a messenger of his own. It comes sewn up in sacks of Maria Theresa dollars,[1] with some small change of the local currency minted by the Al Kafs of Tarim; and one man can hardly carry two of these little sacks, for each dollar (worth 1s. 6d.) is about the size and weight of a 5s. piece. It shows how safe the country now is, that this can travel unguarded—a thing impossible three years ago.

January 10.   *"No spring nor summer beauty hath such grace*
            As I have seen in one autumnal face."

                                        (DONNE.)

The Archæologist has a pleasant taste in beautiful things. Some time ago she suggested that we should buy a collection of jewelery and clothes worn by the women here. I am doing

[1] The history of the Maria Theresa dollar in Arabia and Abyssinia is of some interest. How it first came to be adopted there is not known. It was minted in a variety of places, including Belgium, until Austria came to have a practical monopoly. In 1933 Italy (already preparing for the Abyssinian war) bought the right to mint for L.6,000. In 1936 the British Government denied the existence of a monopoly and the minting of Maria Theresa dollars was undertaken privately by an English banker who had spent many years in Abyssinia; he bought the silver, the Bank of England minted it, and the production continued until a number of competitors came on to the market and the price of these dollars in Aden sank to a level so low as to make the trade in them no longer profitable. This enterprising banker then thought to reintroduce the old half and quarter dollar which had fallen into desuetude during the last hundred years: this currency had not, however, been sold by the Vienna mint, and the Bank of England refused to infringe a monopoly which, though not established by law, had long custom behind it. The introduction of a smaller coinage would be a very great convenience to the traveller in Arabia.

this, and the word has gone round, and rows of women come rustling whenever Qasim opens the door, with small round covered baskets in their hand, and their trinkets to sell inside them. They sit with anxious eyes behind their silver-bound eyelet holes while first I and then Qasim weigh the objects in our hand, and it is impossible to drive a bargain merely business-like for these vanities round which the female heart is curled.

"All the things we women love—scents and ornaments and wars—are taken from me," one said to me a day or two ago, whose husband has left her without money.

So many of them come that Qasim weeds them by a process of selection I suspect not to be strictly impartial: one can see the power of the Doorkeeper, and the growth of Favouritism in the East, born of the mere physical inelasticity of Time. It is to mitigate this danger that every Arab ruler sits at stated times in open places, accessible to all.

Yesterday one small boy, called Muhammad, used his power of access to bring his mother, and in her hand a necklace set with silver suns. Muhammad is a plain little boy with so enormous a smile that it seems to have a separate existence of its own like that of the Cheshire Cat. But his mother has the most beautiful mouth of any that I have ever seen, and kohl-rimmed eyes like black water. Such beauty in an old tired face comes from some loveliness behind it: in her dark shawl, her forehead bound in black, she might have been Motherhood itself as she looked down at her son and saw in his common-place features only the infinite extent of her love. Her husband has travelled to Java and has not written for three years. I asked if the boy would go too: and it was then that she looked at him with that unfathomable tenderness, and said: "No. Not till he has a child that I can keep, and then he will go to get money." Not out of books, but out of the very sorrows of womanhood, these have to learn their strange serenity.

It must be admitted that when they come to describe their illnesses, they take about three times as long over it as any average man. When the Mansab calls, Qasim shoos them away in a hen-like chaos, and they melt through the door with flutterings of face-veils and shawls.

The Mansab has been twice to-day, for to-morrow he travels to Seiyun to ask for a soldier or two, and to tell Harold of the turmoil of our wadi, where the government, as our old Triton prophesied, has now gone up in smoke. Or rather it would have done so, but the Slave-Governor of 'Amd, seeing himself in the rôle of the victim, and having neither salary nor soldiers to help him, thought it better to escape in time and has fled for refuge down our wadi to Qatn—much to our relief, for he alone is the object of the beduin's dislike. They, meanwhile, are busy pouring paraffin over the roots of each other's palm trees in an effort to imitate civilized war—and all because of one man murdered in his sleep and a little stirring by Italians from outside. It is monstrous how money is spent to stir distant troubles in unknown lands, to bring, for some petty and dubious advantage, chaos and death into the lives of men.

As for the Mansab himself, he is no longer against us after many long talks over politics and the future of Islam. And meanwhile he is taking with him his manuscript, of which I have only copied the first section.

He sat for a time, talking of various troubles that surround him, his long locks and the cap on his high forehead making him look like a Raphael portrait, with that rather girlish, delicate expression of Renaissance youth. Husain came, too, bringing finally our elusive landlord with him—an ancient Sufi nearly blind, with a tuft of beard like a soft white cloudlet under his chin, and a white turban wrapped round a skull-cap of sequins and tinsel of almost startling levity in one so old. He was very friendly, considering that, without consulting him, we have ousted him from his house. "If you had been others I would have thrown you out," he remarked with unexpected vigour, tossing frail ghost-like hands. But he has got his rent, for the Mansab's verdict went in his favour. He told me there is a quick way to Du'an over the jōl that takes off from this southern bay on which we look and comes out either at Ghaidun or Khureiba. There are indeed infinite interlacings of routes across the plateau, apart from the main tracks that follow the course of the greater wadis down below.

*   *   *

When they had all gone, and the evening was over, I stepped on to my terrace before sleeping and looked at the southern sky and its stars, thick as foam-flakes on the rising darkness of a wave. They are brilliant but soft, unlike the diamond glitter of Alpine skies. Orion is early now, and the Pleiades late, and an unknown star shines through many hours of the night at my window. In caves on the hillside opposite, where they keep their millet stalks cool and shut up their goats, live the Se'ar tribesmen who provide our milk. The young man is marrying to-night, and they are dancing round a fire in the cave; only a blur is visible as the figures pass before it, but the sound goes on for hours—three beats and a pause, and a rifle-shot now and again. The Se'ar

are free people, and can court their brides face to face a year
before they marry.

Above the cave and the dancing figures are the cliffs where
the valley divides, one mild already in the hidden radiance
of the moon. Illuminated precipices hang about it; its summit is whiter than the night. The other stands black, hiding
the climbing horns, and throws across the wadi floor a giant
cone of shadow; in its darkness, as in a harbour, the hillside
and caves and we and the sleeping houses of the town are
hid.

As one watches the shadow creep across the valley, waxing
and waning monthly with the moon, the mind wanders
back through the eternal recurrent monotony of seasons,
till the Se'ar beduin, leaping at the mouth of their cave, turn
to the men of the Stone Age, who dance wild nuptials under
the same dark and ragged skyline of the jōl.

January 12.   *"For verily the excellence of man*
               Is in two smallest parts, the heart and tongue."
                                        (Arab saying.)

Qasim likes holy men, but he has just been telling me that
he thinks little of the sayyids here. "We in Yemen," he says,
"know a good one at once from a sham, because the real one
cures you by a mere touch, or even a look at the place of the
disease: and even when they are dead—there is one I know
of who has an 'ilb tree over his grave, and your sheep die if
you take a branch for fun or to make a walking-stick, or else
you wound yourself as you try to cut it: but if you take the
leaves to use as medicine, they will cure you."

"As a matter of fact," I said to Qasim, "the really holy
people are nearly always stronger dead than alive. Look

Food for the dig

at the Prophets. Even here they tell me that the Saint who
is buried in the tomb below has pye-dogs who slink in to
him at night and keep him informed of all that goes on in the
wadi. I wish one could persuade the dog who barks below
our window to go and join them."

* * *

We are having a quiet time, for the Mansab is away and
Sayyid 'Ali has been sent reluctant to Shibam, ostensibly to
escort our money back, but really to enable me to hand over
the workmen's food to the household slave who draws our
water, a clumsy, ugly, huge and good-natured creature, so
remarkably strong that I have seen him with my own eyes
lift a petrol tin full of water with his teeth. He is happy with
no obvious reason for being so except that he has a nice hard-
working wife: she draws the water-skins from the sixty-foot
well when he is away. He has now spent our money honestly
on rice and dates, 4s. 6d. for eighteen men and boys, and there
has been general repletion and a holding of 'Ali's name to
scorn, but that is as far as it will go, for not one of these men,
who are peasants and not beduin, will stand up to him when
he returns.

January 13.　　"Qu'est-ce qu'une femme auprès
　　　　　　d'un papyrus Alexandrin?"
　　　　　　　　　　　　(La Reine Pédocque.)

I have been out for the first time, and have climbed to what
three years ago was the old mosque, with one of the few
square-based minarets left in this land. It is now all restored
and renewed, the interior filled with columns like a forest—
thirty-six pillars in six rows and a small square of light in the
middle—the minaret rebuilt with round holes like railway-

107

station architecture, and the two pre-Islamic slabs buried under the modern pavement. All this is the misguided beneficence of the old man who sold us the incense burner. The town climbs up to the mosque, on spurs of the cliff-side, and was lost to-day in pale unusual weather shimmery as a sea mist but not damp—since there is nothing to be damp with. With it a N.E. wind blows, sudden and cool. The people say that the mist comes "with this star," a pretty way of mentioning a month. It gave a strange look to the cliffs of the wadi, like headlands out at sea. Through it I walked to call on the Mansab's sisters, who live in various houses scattered in the town and welcomed me on my first venture abroad. They all live in pleasantly empty rooms lifted on carved pillars, and strewn with carpets, where, through low windows, the sunlight can make patterns on the floor. Even poor houses with ceilings of sticks laid on rafters, contrive to lay them in diagonal patterns, to give the effect of decoration.

All the sisters are pretty, especially when the veil frames the oval of their faces, for their heads are flattish at the back and the plaits do little to hide the shape. In the house of the Mansab's grandfather, who was the saint, his mother still lives, ill these three years with a gangrened foot which, for some small ailment, she cut about with a penknife. It should have killed her with blood-poisoning long ago, and is a swollen mass of sores. I took permanganate and explained the making of fomentations—without much hope: the mother must have been a lovely creature, and still has pretty ways, with little gracious petulant movements of her hands. She breaks off the talk of her three dutiful sons to say: "He loves me, you know," as if it were a wonderful and constant surprise.

The Sultan of Qatn

Two women from Ajlania were sitting there and sang their native songs, in which we all took parts like strophe and antistrophe in a Greek chorus, while little hands with hennaed nails beat time on an empty tea-box, used as a drum. Every town has its own dances and songs, and Ajlania is one of the most celebrated. The Greek chorus, with the household servants in groups discussing the affairs of their masters, and the masters asking for and listening to advice, is indeed a picture of ordinary Arabic life, very similar, I imagine, in all small towns that lived or live on robbery and flocks.

As we sat there, the Qadhi appeared, kissed his mother's forehead, and walked back with me to finish the notes for the manuscript, now complete. He stayed for a long time—indeed he always stays till I explain that I must go to bed—and told me of the troubles of the valley. The Ja'da have gathered about nine hours away on the jōl—a sort of tribal pow-wow such as von Wrede witnessed nearly a century ago. They have sent a deputation to Sultan 'Ali of Qatn, who is playing an uncertain game, misled partly by propaganda, partly by his ancient Kathiri hate into hoping that he can, by stirring trouble, remove Harold and the Seiyun influence altogether. "He thinks," I was told, "that if there is enough disturbance in the country, Mr. Ingrams will be recalled by the people in London who do not like to hear of agitation." How shrewd this estimate is, the reader may determine; the idea of playing off public opinion at home against the man on the spot has at all events entered the Arab mind. I have a liking for the Sultan of Qatn, and both the Mansab and Sayyid 'Ali are going to try to warn him of the ruin of his ways, of which the Mansab is now fully persuaded. Two R.A.F. machines, merely flying over this wadi, would keep the district quiet: it is distance and absence that allows foreign weeds to grow: and as soon as Harold appears, all will melt away before him. Meanwhile our presence does something to keep the place quiet; every day I get people from the wadi who ask advice, which I give, unofficially and reluctantly, for their own peace.

Their governor has fled; and the tribe have seized the daughter of the murdered man. It seems that she opened the door to his enemies or—according to the latest version—herself shot him in his sleep. He was bad and violent, all the tribesmen say, and had taken her jewels and shut her in his fort, suspecting her to be unlawfully pregnant: if a child was born, she would die. So she killed him in his sleep, and someone's blood is wanted to avenge him. But as there has apparently never been a murderess in this country before, the Ja'da do not know what to do about it, and have sent to ask Harold to set the precedent.

Having discussed this matter at great length, the Qadhi passed on to another subject and asked me if it would be possible to get a book with the whole of English Law inside it. He looked at me in silent wonder when I told him that it would take six houses the size of his own to accommodate it.

January 14.   "*Nec pietas moram*
rugis et instantae senectae
adferet indomitaeque morti."
(HORACE.)

We have been to lunch, Alinur and I, with the oldest man in Hureidha. I found him sitting in the dust of our kitchen floor, left there by Qasim, who is in love just now and quite unreliable, and he asked us to lunch with him to-day. His shoulders stoop under a greasy coat of silk striped red and yellow; his cheeks are sucked in with age; his eyes, still embellished with kohl, are flecked green and blue like the sea on a windy day, and his beard is dyed with henna. There is nothing left of him but a sort of ghost-like shell of antique gaiety, the flicker of a candle almost dead. He has been a traveller in his day, and knows South Africa and India and Malaya, and is rich and respected, and has had, it is said, fifty-five wives. He is a friend of all the British who come his way. On the doorstep of his great square house he was waiting to receive us, and deposited us with his wife, a middle-aged woman and plain, who quickly poured her troubles in my ears.

"I hate him, and I have pains all over."

"That comes from sitting in draughts," I said, separating the propositions which she seemed to consider as one.

She brushed this aside. "Who would not feel ill with a husband of ninety-five?" said she.

"You have a beautiful house," I tried to distract her.

"Pah, and he keeps all the keys and never lets them out of his grasp"; and just at that moment the old man returned, with a plate of ginger in one ancient hand and in the other, a ruby ring on its little finger, the bunch of keys.

The wife retired, we sat on the floor round an excellent meal, and friends and servants who had come to help with the ceremony entertained us with stories of our host. His age is the pride of the town. But he himself sat silent, his light eyes in some dream long past, and presently began to talk quietly of Nairobi and Cape Town and the far-away travels of his youth.

We had been rather surprised to hear that he was building a house at the other end of Hureidha. I asked him about it.

"It is my tomb," said he. "It will soon be finished." His old eyes closed in the middle of our conversation and he was asleep.

"He is old," said the guests for the twentieth time: "the oldest man in Hureidha."

With his servants about him, and the wife who hates him, with his keys and his silk coat and the dreams of his journeys, he seemed like some old Balzac figure perpetuating the vanities of mankind, till death

> "When he has wandered all his ways
> Shuts up the story of his days,"

in the tomb whose building he watches with tired eyes, among the tombs of his fathers.

January 15. "*Glory be to that God who slays our children, and takes away our wealth, and whom withal we love.*"

(*'*ATTAR: *Tadhkirātu 'l-Awliyā.*)

Mansur the postman walked in this morning, the same to whom I gave a lift on the way out here, and told me that Harold is in Seiyun with six R.A.F. machines, ready to bomb the Se'ar unless the forty-two stolen camels are restored. Sayyid 'Ali, who has returned, staggering under two sacks of new dollars, also confirms the news.

Mansur sat, with his profile, straight as a Greek head, framed against the background of the wadi, twirling his silver cane in his hands: it is only the ghost of a cane, for all except the metal core and the silver handle have melted off it, but such as it is it is an object of elegance and I have never seen him without it.

"The Government is merciful," said Mansur. "Ingrams is going to meet the Se'ar once more—and then if nothing comes of it they will bomb them. Those flyers bring a great peace into this land.

"Shortly before you first came to Hureidha," he went on, "my brother was shot dead from the house opposite ours in the palm grove, and we had the blood feud to carry on, and it was inconvenient because the door of each house could be shot at from the windows of the other. Then two years ago Sayyid Abu Bekr, may Allah widen his breast (with happiness), made a truce of four years between us and, from his own purse, gave me a hundred dollars bakhshish for my brother's death. And now the English peace has come, and the blood feud has ceased with no disgrace to me, and it is pleasant, for I and my next-door neighbour can walk together side by side and neither need shoot the other. Thanks be to God."

In the afternoon came the Qadhi with a new manuscript, and presently, talking of this and that, told me that he thought of opening a small shop in Hureidha, "for the passing of time."

"What will you sell in it?" I asked.

"I have not yet thought of that," said he, drawing a small sheet of paper from his breast. "But I have begun by writing a poem to hang by the door on the day that it is opened. I will read it to you. It is the shop, you must understand, that is represented as offering a welcome to its customers."

The Qadhi promised to send me a copy of this poem, but he has not done so. "It would be a delightful thing," I said to him, "if more people began their business ventures in this way. In our country we have yearly meetings of shareholders, when an account of all that has happened is read out: and why should it not be done in verse?"

"I should enjoy that," said the Qadhi. "When the Sultan came here I had prepared nothing, and my brother the Mansab asked me to speak, and I stood there and made up four verses straight away. And I made verses too for my schoolboys when our school was open."

He looked at me earnestly with his gentle eyes, a little tilted towards the temples: a light comes into them as soon as he talks of books.

"I did not like to weary my children by saying just: 'do this, do that': so I used to make them *wish* to do things by writing a poem about it."

"They must have been very happy with you," I said, wondering what the effect would be in an English classroom.

"Yes. It is a pity we have no money for the school. The valley is so poor. When I have a little that I can spare I buy a book or a manuscript, for there are numbers lying about in people's houses, and eaten by moths, and when I see that, I cannot bear it, but buy them, whatever they may be."

When he had gone the place's poverty came home to me even more than usual, for his sister, the pretty gay one who lives next door, came in, bringing, secretly, a lot of little trinkets of silver to sell. It is hard for them all, for the Mansab is like the vicar of a parish, and he has to be generous always, though quite poor. As she stood up to leave, shoving herself into the white dust-sheet for the street and trying to find the little square hole for her face, she apologized for coming. "We all have our needs," she said.

Love and magic

And the next need was indeed a more difficult one to meet, brought by a young peasant woman, who, throwing her veil back and showing the prettiest triangle of a face imaginable, asked for a charm to bring her husband back. He loved her and they had two children, and she had left him and his house in a fit of temper, and now could not go back until he sent for her and he showed no sign of doing so.

"And can't you go back and ask to be forgiven?"

"We could not do that," she said.

"Would it do if I wrote you a letter to send him?"

"We do not do that," she said.

Nothing but magic could help, and she went sadly away.

These women all come in with apparently the same identical soft brown eyes—and then, when their veils are raised, all sorts of different faces appear.

The only other news to-day is that our poor little Salim's cough gets worse and worse and he complains of a "long worm inside that bites his liver." I tried to nourish him with a sandwich of Marmite, of which he took one bite and leaped up and was sick.

I have also been told that Qasim receives ladies at night, and how one can deal with that I do not know; but I think I shall keep his pay from him till we leave this place, for he seems to spend it at a very great rate.

January 16. "*Partout, dans la vallée bien ouverte, la jeunesse timide et charmante de l'année frissonnait sur la terre antique.*"
(Le Mannequin d'Osier.)

It is strange how even in a land where scarce a thing is growing, a sudden benediction comes, and lo, the spring is there.

The Diary, Hureidha

So it was yesterday morning, or at least it was so to me, for I went for the first time these three weeks out from among the brown houses of the town to see the Moongod's temple, now fully excavated and already abandoned. I had meant to try the hour's ride, but Abdulillah stepped providentially out of space from his green-tasselled car and offered to take me. Sayyid 'Ali came: Qasim seized his white coat with the gilt buttons and leaped in: the Mansab's son boarded us in the High Street, and I snatched up little Husain, who was the only infant about, for a joy-ride: he was far too overcome to say a word of thanks, but in silence turned his face towards us at intervals from the seat in front, with an expression of such ineffable ecstasy that that alone seemed like the spring-time of the world.

But the spring was everywhere. Intangible yet, it lurked like a promise in the sharpness of the air, in the milky transparency of the sky, in the buzzing of an early bee and the faint pink pea-flowers that sprang from their small bushes in the sand. It washed with a secret beauty the brown town on its brown hillside, and threw its fugitive illusion even on the ancient ramparts of the wadi, making their implacable outline tremulous in the soft arms of air. Life, that mysterious loveliness, was moving; and even the sandy wastes flutter and stir as she passes. The little wizened spy from Yemen, who has been for some days in Hureidha and does not like our presence there, blinked his eyes in the sun as we passed him on our way. The Archæologist was digging out a small mud house a stone's throw from the temple : I watched the baskets of earth handed from boy to boy in line against the sky like an Assyrian frieze, and then climbed towards the abandoned temple on its mound, small but conspicuous, a human landmark in the flatness of the wadi.

It is really three temples, for it has been built and rebuilt three times, and even the earliest is far too late to throw any light, as we had hoped, on the origins of the South Arabian civilizations; its first good walls of dressed stone were followed by more and more careless building, and the old inscriptions, used as mere slabs, were thrust by later workmen into the walls and pavements, as they came; the stone itself out of which they are cut is soft and bad, and crumbling already under the feet of the beduin of the Ja'da who come to visit and wonder. But it is the first temple to have been excavated in the Hadhramaut and the second in South Arabia, since the plans brought by Halévy and Glaser were taken from ruins above ground. The first temple, dug by M. M. Rathjens and von Wissmann in 1928 at Hugga in Yemen showed the use of columns and of windows; what this one will show is of course not yet apparent, nor do I mean, in this slight note-book of mine, to enter on scientific preserves. But its excavation is an impressive piece of work; two stairways run up to it south and west, and below it is the scoop of the artificial basin, the pond or Karif, a pre-Islamic name still used in the Hadhramaut for this sort of water-hole.

I stayed a short time by the ruins wishing that Alinur were not away mapping, for she would have told me the details of the three weeks' labour with her usual kindness. Some travelling Ja'da climbed up and held their camels on the edge, and asked whether these people were before or after the Children of Qahtan; they have an aptitude for history, if one takes the trouble to explain it, because of their interest in their own past.

When we came home I pressed a few plants I had collected and asked Husain, still ecstatic from his ride, to put a heavy box on to the books with which I covered them.

"That is impossible," said he.

I thought he meant it was too heavy, and said: "Nonsense."

"But," said Husain, "one should not put anything on top of a book. The word of God may be inside."

January 17.   *"But O, this dust that I shall drive away*
                           Is flowers and kings,
                           Is Solomon's Temple, poets, Nineveh."

(V. MEYNALL.)

Mubarak, the Nahdi, who is paid three and a half dollars weekly to guard the excavations and all that belongs to them, lives in the hillside on the northern wadi slope, in a cave that was once a tomb. In its dim walls are the horizontal niches scooped for the bodies of the dead, useful now to hold Mubarak's goods. Our dig is on his land and we were recommended to him by a ten-year-old friend, an imp called Ja'far, who happens to be his feudal suzerain. "He will give you no trouble," said this small laird with his minute hands in the pockets of what was once someone's European coat. "He belongs to me and I have told him to treat you well."

Mubarak is the most good-natured creature anyway, and, living on sufferance, surrounded by Ja'da, is not in a position to make anything difficult to anyone; it is only because of the English peace that he can count on the safe and quiet possession of his own waterless strip of 'ilb trees and plough. His two naked boys were working on it this morning, manœuvring the plank-like machine with which sand is shovelled for the dykes that guide the waters to the ploughland. This plank has a shallow wooden border on three sides, and scrapes along, guided by one bare foot and drawn by a camel, and gathers the sand with it as it goes. When the flood comes tearing down the scree from the cliff above, over the necropolis in which Mubarak has his home, the strip of sand below, where his ploughing now looks like the scratching of a hen on a dustheap, will blossom into crops of melons, sown in the mud and ripening as it dries, till summer again burns the same blinding and waterless sand.

To the cave itself you descend by rough steps of boulders, through a door that lets in the tempered light. A few strips of goat-wool matting and a sand-strewn floor, a slanting pole to hang water-skins, guarded from rats by a bunch of thorns at the lower end; a few vessels, three naked children with lovely eyes and lashes, and a cat as small, wild and graceful as themselves, which they deposit at intervals, struggling, in my lap; and the wife whom I knew already, who sat holding my hand and fed me with melon seeds—such was Mubarak's home.

"And I hope you and the two harim will come to dine here soon, and if our cooking is not good enough, Qasim can cook the dinner for you."

The slope is full of caves, one above the other, under the cap of the limestone where two strata join. One of them is to be excavated, and the tent will be moved to-morrow to this wadi-side. In the plain below, the ancient people had their gardens; the main channel that fed them can still be seen, a broad avenue of sand outlined with boulders. Ploughing there, Mubarak finds palm roots buried. He was uneasy, because of the map Alinur is making; and only reassured when

The Diary, Hureidha

I reminded him how the sand is covering already the temple of the Moongod: "In three years' time, there will be no sign of it left: but the Harim's map will remain, and travellers who wish to find the ruins will read it and will know the place.   And that is why we make the maps."

I had ridden over late in the morning, when the workmen had gone.   No one was available to lead the donkey, till the small Muhammad, who has the beautiful mother, saw me and leaped at the chance of missing school.   He led the donkey by a chain, which he would throw without warning on its neck whenever he had a thorn to pull out of his foot: I had no stirrups, so the donkey and I both struggled for equilibrium when this happened, till Muhammad took the chain again and trotted on, saying at intervals: "I am not tired, I am strong."

Sick men came running as we went: peasants came up to shake hands and greet my reappearance: an old man spurring along sold me a bronze spear from Mekka.   It was pleasant to be alive again at last in the friendly open world.   As we came in I met again the spy from Yemen, who puckered up his sour little face swathed in a white turban much too big for him.   The Qadhi says: "He is not much of a spy, for he tells us what he thinks of our land, instead of finding out what we think of his."   When I reached our door my heart was giving some trouble, and I have had to rest it and see people from my bed again.

January 19.   "*Il n'a pas l'intelligence assez large pour concevoir que l'intérêt n'est pas seul à mener le monde.*"

(M. Barrès.)

I spent yesterday tracing Alinur's plan of the dig, a lovely work, full of delicate and careful detail, that has taken days and days of labour to collect. While I was at it Harold and two R.A.F. aeroplanes descended, but the landing-ground is an hour's ride away; I did not even hear them, and they had no time to stay. It is a disappointment. The donkey boys who rushed to their assistance have been fined; they did so without permission, but in lonely places in South Arabia descending aeroplanes may need help and certainly need transport. It is this miserable precedent of Egypt, where people possibly respond to fines; here, as a matter of fact, they have very little influence. The beduin, whose off-hand independent speech is taken for impertinance, never last more than a week or two at our dig; we could not think of excavating in purely tribal country to the west. But the peasants are philosophical: one man had to have his wage reduced because of bad work: "a blessing upon you," was all he said. Another, sent off because the present site is small and requires less labour, merely remarked, "so much the better." Half a dollar a day is to them the difference between poverty and riches, yet they treat it in this airy way. The Archæologist says that all they do is done for money, but this, I am privately convinced, is untrue, not only of them but of almost every human being in this world.

* * *

'Ali, in the evening, brought back the Seiyun news, where it appears that the last attempt at conciliation has collapsed. The heart of the Se'ar chief, who came down to Shibam for a conference, failed him at the last moment, and he fled from the house he was lodged in, back to his valleys, through the W.C. window, on the eve of Harold's arrival. As they will not restore the stolen camels, their villages, alas! are to be bombed to-morrow.

In our own valley the trouble is settling down. The Ja'da, who have decided to keep the peace, congratulate themselves on their virtue with a smug regretful air. But the wretched woman who has caused it all has been tortured with hot irons in her sides and nose to make her confess, and is being taken to Seiyun. The tribe feels the whole matter a disgrace and did not let her come through the town; she is kept in private by her own relations.

* * *

This afternoon I received a scribbled paper from Sayyid 'Ali to say that all sorts of objects have been found in the new cave, whose digging has begun. He is a scamp, but it was nice of him to think of writing; and in the evening all the boys came rushing excited to my terrace with baskets full of pots. They are rough and ugly, but they have pre-Islamic letters scratched on them, which will presumably help to date them: one has the word "māt" (he died), incised upon its edge. And two sheep are to celebrate the occasion.

January 20.   *"Death is now the phoenix' nest."*
                        (SHAKESPEARE: *The Phoenix and the Turtle.*)

A few drops of rain have fallen, and thin and melting clouds drift like browsing herds over the jōl northward toward the Se'ar country out of sight.

I set out to walk to the palm groves in search of flowers to press. Six children playing on the slope ran to join me, Husain and Salim among them.

It was a pleasant morning. We called the shepherdesses in their witchlike hats to come and help with the names of the flowers. It is not a simple matter, for the names vary from district to district and what is the Courage of the Wolf in one wadi, is probably the Mother of Grasses in the next. The shepherdesses know them, and know their uses, and which are liked by camels and which by goats; rumran (*Heliotropium undulatum Vahl*), whose leaves are chopped to put on wounds; dumma' (*Jatropha sp. aff. spinosa Vahl*), wild gooseberry, good for snakebites; deni (*Euphorbia aff. dendroides L. Spurge*), used for sticking the soles of sandals; and 'ishr or 'alas (*Capparis spinosa L. var. montana*), with whose milk or leaf respectively the inside hairs of water-skins are scraped away. The feathery ra' seed (*Aerua javanica Juss*) is used for stuffing pillows and that of the 'ishriq (*Cassia holosericea Fres.*, a Senna), eaten by human beings; senna (*Cassia acutifolia Del.*) and saqrab (*Corchorus antichoras Raensch*—a "Jew's Mallow") are purgatives, and hawir (*Indigofera argentea*—wild indigo) is used for dyeing. You wash your hair with soap of the sakhbar grass (*Cymbopogon schoenanthus L. Spreng*) and your hands with the powdered leaves of the khoteka. Sesame seed is boiled till thick and drunk for colds. The root of the harmal is good for the stomach, and its leaves, when mixed with kohl, make a medicine for the eyes. The ban tree (*Moringa aptera Forsk, gaertn.*) leaf cures snakebite; its seeds, soaked in water, reduce swellings; and the lithab leaf (*Ficus salicifolia*) poisonous to camels, is used in sesame oil as a flavour. As for the 'ilb (*Zizyphus Spina Christi*) tree, its uses are innumerable, and the Jinn live in it, and comb out and beautify the hair of those who fall asleep in its shadow. All these things the shepherdesses know, and some of them we found out this morning.

There were no flowers at all under the palms, but many among stones in the open, thorny scrubs mostly with blossoms bright and fragile, that fall as one picks them; and because the thorns are so thick and the flowers so delicate, the pressing is an almost impossible business.

Samr (*Acacia vera*), misht (*Anogeissus Bentii Baker*), habadh (*Zizyphus Hamur Engl.*) and hawarwar (*Indigofera Argentea L.*) —small trees in their own thin shadows, stood on the flat ground in the open, and goats browsed among them. On the sand-bank that surrounded the palm groves the shepherdesses sat, their eyes alone showing through their face-veils, for they are village girls. From Hureidha came the youngest of the Children of Muhsin, riding his donkey bareback. We sat and watched his approach. "Donkeys," said Salim, "are bad animals. The camel, when its master falls, is sorry: but the donkey laughs in its heart." The braying of the ass is always called laughing here.

The Child of Muhsin had seen me from his high tower as I passed and followed with his maligned animal in case I should be tired. He joined our botanical party, and we sat with the shepherdesses on the bank, looking down into the lattice shadow of the palms, green and pale as water, and out over the open, with Hureidha small in the distance like a landslide at the bottom of its cliff. A wide peace filled the wadi, and that etherial feeling that comes before the spring is there. The clouds had vanished in the north, a few birds hopped about. In its pale windless sunshine, in its almost colourless repose, the world seemed good. A dull sound, a distant explosion deadened by the waves of air, reached us; the children and I looked at each other:

"They are bombing the Se'ar," said Husain.

One after another, at a few seconds' interval, the dull explosions came: the children listened with delighted shining eyes. The notes, drifting sullenly in that clear sky, over the empty jŏl in the sunlight, seemed to be tearing a rent in the peace of the spring: their softness, like something falling on ploughed earth, was particularly deadly. But the children did not think so.

"Those madmen (the Se'ar) will now know how strong is the heart of Ingrams," said they.

We turned home and named the birds as we went, but as I know so very few English birds by sight, the Arabic names were little use except in the case of the wagtail which is called triz.

"You must wait for the seil, and then you will see the Green Bird," said Husain, "the bird which lives in Paradise and feeds on bees and is the friend of the Prophet, peace be upon him."

"Oh, Green Bird," they sang together,
"Who sees you rejoices,
    Even the children of the soldiers,
    Your father killed you,
    Your aunt put you in the cooking pot,
    But your sister Bough of Frankincense, laid
        you in the box of spices,
    And you came again to life."

It was the story of the Phoenix, sung by the children in the land of frankincense, cousin of many a similar story in other lands (in the first part of Faust, for instance); but I have never elsewhere met the "box of spices" in which the resurrection occurs.

"Oh, Green Bird," the children sang again:
"Where is your lodging to-night?"
"I shall lodge with my people:
    And you shall lodge in the seil."

"Oh," cried Salim: "there is a fox, and he is looking towards us. That is good. If you see his tail it is bad luck; you can say nothing worse to your enemy than to wish him 'the tail of the fox in his face.'"

January 21.   "*The first wife is marble,*
                    The second wife is sugar,
                    The third, send her straight to the graveyard."
                                        (*Bagdad Saying.*)

I had a quiet lunch yesterday with the Mansab's sister next door, whose husband requires some soothing over the matter of the rent of this house. He is a negative soul, and his voice is always heard through one or other of the little windows next door, querulous and disagreeable; he has a long theologic sort of face, and bad teeth, and I am sorry for the pretty gay wife and eighteen-year-old daughter just divorced. Divorces do not really matter to a woman. If her husband says so three times before witnesses, the thing is done, and in Hureidha it is more or less an everyday affair. The pretty daughter seems happy enough to be at home again. She has two plaits immensely long, and as we lunched together on the floor I told her the story of Rapunzel, who drew her lover in by her long hair.

They, for their part, told me that Husain had been invisible all these days because he is busy marrying his third wife. He marries only one at a time and then divorces. I have sent a sequin bag as a wedding present, but I gather that the whole thing is not very popular in the family.

*   *   *

I have had a relapse, and lie again in bed, filled with despair— for it seems impossible to get rid of this Arabian microbe. It would not matter if it did not affect the heart, and so make one helpless. And I have had to see endless beduin, who gathered like vultures at the news of the spoils of the cave. They have asked for bakhshish, and been refused, for our peace will be ended if money shows itself. The reason why we have had an easy time so far is that there have been no sensational finds, and I have now been impressing on the tribesmen that the whole of our possessions together would not fetch more than two dollars in the suqs of Aden. They look in a sad and puzzled way at the singularly ugly collection of our pots, and are forced to agree: they are reasonable people, till an idea lodges in their heads, when—like most of us—they have no room for any other—so it is vital to see that the suitable idea gets in first. I take it that this is the Art of Government. Meanwhile I have told 'Ali to counteract my refusal of bakhshish by the unofficial promise of a present to the tribes at the end of our stay.

Alinur is kindness itself and comes in the evening after her day's work with poultices in her hand. May her breast ever be filled with feelings as warm and happily comforting, but not as sticky, as the Antiphlogistine, which is really doing some good.

January 22.   "*The business of the kitchen's great*
For it is fit that men should eat."

(SIR J. SUCKLING.)

There is a mender of watches in Hureidha. He is an old man called Abdulla, and I first saw him digging out a canal beyond the town; he looked up from his labour, showing a singularly beautiful old face, and said:

"Ya Faraya, may God be with you. Take my photograph."

Which I did. Now he has been sitting over Qasim's watch, opening out its machinery.

I asked him where he had learnt, and he answered: "In Mekka."

"I learnt," he said, "from a sayyid who was able to mend anything in the world, and this not by study, but by the Generosity of God."

I could not help congratulating myself that it was Qasim's watch and not mine that he had in his hands.

His was a pleasant, restful interlude, for I have been dealing with more beduin than I have the strength for, all coming for medicines and news of the Se'ar bombing. They come sometimes from places three or four days' ride away, and the bombing has filled them with the pleasant certainty that they were right to remain quiet and good in this wadi. They have handed over their murderess to Sultan 'Ali who is not, apparently, forwarding her to Harold and the Hand of the Law.

Sayyid 'Ali added to my exhaustion by bringing in a relative of his from somewhere in 'Amd—a pseudo-Gothic creature like an invention of the Romantic Age, very black, with elf-locks on one side of his face and the fringe of a red-and-yellow turban on the other: I thought him the wildest sort of tribesman, but he turned out to be a sayyid, and the important business which made 'Ali refuse my prayers for rest was merely that of looking at me to see what I was like. This is done with dramatic effect, for I lie in bed under a mosquito net, which I gradually and reluctantly draw; it is my last barrier against the world, constantly with me. I sometimes feel that my bedroom is more like a railway station than anything else in Asia.

Husain, Ahmed and Salim

The children, who come in for their daily rummage in the waste-paper basket, have learnt to do so on tiptoe. Only three are allowed in: Husain, with his dirty little skull-cap, hair horizontally out beneath it, his funny snub nose and the smile that begins in his eyes: Ahmed, with tiny regular features, and violent loves and hates, that shake his small person like a wind—he will come rushing in to say that he wishes to shoot all the dogs of Hureidha (a wish we share), or that So-and-so steals the rice, or that unbelievers are pigs (with a kind exception in my own case)—and the anger will so possess him that he scarce sees where he is going. And Salim will come, regretting that I allow anyone else near me, refusing my peppermints when the others accept them, because he is so proud that it hurts him to receive. One sees more of a nation through its children than in any other way. To-day, a parcel reached me with new shoes, and I let the three open it for me, and watched rather sadly while they stroked the soft suède against their cheeks in love and admiration. How will they not fall to all the objects of Western desire, to which we have long ago succumbed?

*   *   *

There has been a great to-do about the feast of the two sheep presented to the workmen. It took place yesterday, and a deputation arrived before breakfast to ask about rice.

"And wood for a fire?"

"And *where* are the sheep to be eaten? Would we wish to see it done under our own eyes in the yard?"

After an interval the sheep themselves arrived to be approved of, and after another interval, the fore-quarter of one of them, already skinned, was brought to my bedside to have its plumpness admired. By this time I was beginning to get tired of the thought of mutton altogether. It now turned out that the wrong man had bought the sheep, and the one to whom I had actually given the cash arrived on the scene with, so he said, a better pair.

Of this matter I washed my hands, while Qasim dealt with the chaos that went on below. The ways of the Benefactor are hard. But the latest report is that the actual eating was carried out in gratitude and harmony and the man who lives some way off and only heard of the whole thing this morning, found his portion honestly saved up for him in a piece of somebody's shawl, and has gone off happy too.

January 23.   *"Noi sem pellegrin come voi sete."*
                                        (PURGATORIO.)

In that youth of our race when the souls of men were free, in the Athens of Pericles, Socrates was able to assume that "to live the good life" was the average aim of thoughtful men.

Here on my bed, wondering why I come to these disastrous lands when I have a comfortable home of my own, I can find no better answer than that old one. I reached the East with the mere wish to know more about the world we live in. But I suppose that now many other reasons have added themselves: partly that it is easier to think in this simpler atmosphere, partly that one would like to add some small arch to the bridge of understanding between East and West; but ever there is that Platonic hope, never perhaps to be attained, difficult in our chaotic Europe, to "lead the good life" and carry a small lamp of understanding across the shadowy world. This solicitude suggests perhaps an exaggerated value to set upon one's own infinitesimal powers of illumination; but there is this to be said for it—that if one thinks highly of one's own, how should one not be tender of the lamps of other men? Not willingly would one push, jostle or touch them roughly so that in surprise or trepidation their uncertain wicks snuff out: indeed, if it so happened that, knocking at the farther door, one could cry in the darkness: "Lord, though my own is out, yet never have I dimmed the light of others"—I have a hope that the gate of Mercy might yet open because of the harm one has not done.

It is in this heart of our philosophy that we amateurs disagree with your unmitigated expert, whose object is so supremely important that he cannot count, or at any rate notice, the jostling and hurting of others. Beside the pure acetyline of science, the souls of men are apt to look like glow-worms. To be too drowned in business to smile upon a child; or take the long way round because the shorter might corrupt some native mind or heart; or end the tired day with half an hour's pleasantness for others tired as oneself—wrapped in one's own affairs—to move solitary among earth's pilgrim-crowd of strangers—it seems to me that no finding of stones or oil or treasure will compensate this fundamental emptiness.

"The heart's division divideth us."

However important the appointment, one does not run over human bodies to catch one's trains.

If this were merely individual it would not matter, but it appears as the very core of difficulty in present dealings with the East, now flooded with experts, of commerce, of science, of oil: and though theoretically they are ready often enough to agree with our Platonic standard, yet when it comes to the point, and the amenities of life clash or appear to clash with the efficiency of their job, the amenities of life must go.

There is no doubt that to preserve them means a slight retarding of the wheels of work; it also means the laborious acquisition of humility and knowledge. Rather than undergo this loss and this labour the competitive business man or scientist prefers to sow the whirlwind in Asia. It is left to a handful of officials, who take their holidays hunting or fishing with the tribesmen and love them for themselves, to redress in some small measure the dangerously tilted balance of East and West.

Whatever happens, we may think of this with comfort—that in Hureidha no whirlwind will rise after our going, because of us. No vanity has been hurt, no comparison made evident, no alien mode of living has touched in its essentials the dignified economy of this little town: we have given money, but money has never been recognized as the mainspring of our dealings, degrading the minds of men. Nor have we lost in efficiency, so far as I can see. The time spent in pleasantness has harvested the love of all the countryside; even in immediate utility the expenditure seems worth while, and the sight of Alinur walking down the village street to her labours with a small imp hanging on each hand shows that the ordinary graces of life need not be divorced from the otherwise rather sterile paths of science.

January 28.   "*About both of them there was then and always a sweet wisdom that never went beyond what was due and meet for the land they lived in or the people with whom they dwelt, so that all round them the folk grew better and not the worser.*"
                                                    (W. MORRIS: *The Sundering Flood.*)

Like a silver fish slipping above the palm trees an aeroplane landed a few days ago, and out of it stepped Harold. He arrived here on a donkey in the course of time, with all the resident notables behind him, for Alinur had written to tell him I was ill. My sickness took a sudden turn for the worse, and I have spent four days inert, seeing neither sick nor beduin, nor children, nor anyone except the Ba Surra, old friends, who came all the way from Du'an.

Harold wears the Arab dress, which not only makes him popular, but also has the excellent effect of causing the people to esteem their own sensible and beautiful clothing. He walked in, looking very handsome and full of concern, while murmurs of applause from the Chorus of Elders welcomed the affectionate warmth of our greeting, and it was so nice to be affectionately greeted after so much female austerity, that I very nearly wept. He had only half an hour to stay, but it was enough to hear the news, to settle that a doctor, both for the Mansab's mother, for me, and indeed for all of us, would fly out one day if possible, now that the R.A.F. are going continually to and fro to Seiyun; and to feel that the normal world with breakfasts, teas and dinners was still in existence, beyond our cloister walls.

*   *   *

To-day another aeroplane has grazed the tops of our cliffs and landed. We thought it must be the doctor—but it was Prof. Pike, the oil man, who had been asked to make a detour on his way to Aden from Qishn in the East, to pick me up if necessary. Refusing to wait for the puny assistance of donkeys, he came striding from the landing-ground across seil beds and ravines, filling the inhabitants with awe, and with an admiration equally divided between his powers of locomotion and his beard. The Qadhi rushed to meet him and was apparently greeted by the question: "Do you love Freya?" I cannot think this is what Prof. Pike meant to ask,

133

but his Arabic is not very good, and the Qadhi replied in the affirmative. When the professor reached me he had only ten minutes to spare; the afternoon was waning, and Aden 400 miles away. I let him go, feeling that a donkey ride and air journey would be far more dangerous than convalescence in Hureidha. A feeling of doom went with him: another collapse simply must not occur.

Our position here is so smooth now that I am not needed, a comforting thought. Only one urgent affair arose during these bad days, and the Qadhi in his kindness went out late in the evening to deal with it himself and kept it hidden, so that I should not be troubled. It was a meeting of the local Ja'da, to debate whether they should blackmail us for digging on their land. They may have been encouraged in this by a new intrigue from Meshed, which has appeared in the shape of a document signed by five notables and sent to our Mansab, to say that our presence there is not desired. The Mansab there, my old friend, who had nothing to do with it, this morning sent another document, with the names of him and his son, stamped with enormous rubber stamps in its middle, denouncing the opposing party and begging me to pay no attention to threats. But as we do not think of excavating Meshed anyway, the plot and counter-plot scarcely affect us, and the local tangle may be left to tie or untie itself in its own knots.

The excavation here goes on. Pots and skulls continue to pour out of the hillside cave and something important may, one hopes, lurk in its depth.

Alinur is happy and busy tracing the ancient system of irrigation in what is now the desert wadi floor. It looks as if it had been identical with the modern system, an infinite

The workmen's food

labyrinth of small cuts that led the water to every separate palm tree. She is mapping it out, travelling from point to point on a diminutive donkey with our slave—now happily restored to us by the Mansab from Seiyun; and in the evenings she comes for a while and tells me the progress of the day.

I enjoy this peaceful interval of sickness and read the works of Jane Austen, released from a fear of death which, ever present in this land of unknown diseases, seemed for a day or two to be creeping near. But the peace, with returning strength, is coming to an end. The business of 'Ali and the workmen's luncheons has become acute. He gets three or four dollars a day according to the number of men, and he spends less than two of them on food. It would be easy enough to hand the charge over to anybody else, but there is not a single one of the workmen who will stand up to 'Ali; the very suggestion frightens them, and our slave has told me that he will buy the food only if I *order* him to do so, and explain to 'Ali that it is not because "we no longer love him." This I have done in a painful interview which reduced 'Ali to thoughtfulness, the prelude, I feel sure, to some circumvention. It will surprise me if the food is not back in his hands within a week.

January 30.   "*plaisirs d'une race pauvre, économe, eternellement jeune . . . trouvant son bien en elle-même et dans les dons que les Dieux lui ont faits. . . .*"

(E. RENAN.)

Fatima, the Mansab's sister, has called to-day, and sat on the floor turning over the leaves of *Vogue*. It had just come, and I had not had the time to tear out two naked ladies advertising bath salts: I hastened to say that it is a paper exclusively circulated in harims.

135

"Are they real?" said she.

"Oh no," I said with relative truth: they had the improbable silhouette invented by advertisers. "They are just Jinn."

"Do they *see* them," she asked, much intrigued.

"No, but they *think* that is what they look like."

Fatima was overcome by the female beauty of Europe. The specimens of it provided by ourselves in Hureidha had evidently not made a particular impression. She kissed her forefinger and pressed it on the prettiest of the mannequins and said: "May Allah shower good upon them."

* * *

Husain too has looked in for a little, and asked if I would like to buy a bee-hive. "Then," said he, "the honey could be sent to you in Europe every year."

A father bee-hive costs sixty or seventy dollars, a son twenty-five: they are kept in a village among the palm gardens, and the guardian, who looks after about a hundred of them, takes a quarter of the honey, but the owner keeps the increase of the bees.

Abdulla the watchmaker came too, with a pocketful of stones like agates, which they thread here on necklaces and think efficacious against various ills; he was disappointed because I could tell him of no medicine in them. He sat turning them over, his head swathed in a purple turban with a yellow shawl above. "Is it true," he asked, "that you are going to Beihan?"

Beihan lies in the north-west, and will eventually be found to have been an important place in pre-Islamic times.[1] We had planned to examine it at the end of the season, but it is

---

[1] Important inscriptions have since been found there by Mr. Stewart Perowne.

useless to think of our archæology among beduin, and now that the only civil aeroplane is out of action it will be impossible to go even for a flying visit. "But why do you ask?" I said to the old man.

"I would have liked to go with you."

"Have you friends there that you wish to see?"

"No," said he, "I have no reason to go, except that I have never been, and knowledge is better than ignorance." What better reason could there be for travelling?

January 31.   "*In squandering wealth was his peculiar art:*
                Nothing went unrewarded but desert."
                                (DRYDEN.)

This is my birthday. I woke up in the dawn, and looked out from my terrace with a feeling of gratitude for a universe one might so easily not be alive in to enjoy. It was another of those strange misty days, nothing but white softness visible, and in it the shaving of a moon, white also, tilted like a boat in waves of foam. Behind that curtain the sun came up unseen, the cliffs were lost and reappeared, intangible and blurred: it is the influence of the star Neth'a, they say.

Out of this dim world a hooting car produced Sayyid 'Aluwi, my friend from Woking with the beduin bride, who now attends to electricity in Mukalla. He appeared, placid as ever and a little thinner, and remarked that he had been shot at on the road, the same road we followed over the jōl, a little south of the place we camped in. Three ambushes lay in wait for them, they raced by the first two but had to stop for the third, which got them in an enfilading fire, and fifteen Humumi tribesmen came up and relieved them of 1,300 dollars. The camel trade of the Humumi is being damaged by the existence of a motor road—what can be more reasonable than to make the motor road unpleasant? It is merely done, said Sayyid 'Aluwi, so as to draw the government's attention to their troubles. The affairs of Palestine have impressed on the Arab world that arson and murder alone can open London ears to a good cause, and the Humumi have adopted the same tactics, forgetful of the laws of relativity. They have not as good a cause as the Palestine Arab, either, for no one can deny the right of a motor road to the inland cities of the wadi. Harold has long been doing what he can by taxing the motor traffic: but the camelmen are doomed eventually, as those elder Titans who strove against younger gods. For who are they, in their poor nakedness, to stand alone against the mechanical world?

Meanwhile the Mansab has returned. He walked in, handsome as ever, in a brown check greatcoat of the time of Lord Byron. A cashmere shawl, yellow and red, was thrown over one shoulder under a white turban, and his red-tasselled amber beads were in his hand. And he came to my bed and kissed me on the forehead, a greeting reserved to Sherifas, which caused another murmuring approval from the attending crowd.

His mother, he says, is better and everyone full of regret that she did not begin to use the fomentations when first I sent them, but allowed herself to be dissuaded by an old cousin who told her that Christian remedies are poisons.

"But now," said the Mansab, "if God wills, she will be cured and you need fear no one who may speak against you"; and he told me of an old woman who had come to ask if it would be allowable for her to pray for us, since—

138

owing to the fact that her son is working—she had been able to eat meat for the first time in a year.

The news from the great world, which as far as we are concerned is the Wadi Hadhramaut and Mukalla, is none too good. Doreen is ill, with the same epidemic that we suffer here: and the Humumi have raided another lorry on the Tarim road and stolen 2,000 dollars intended for Ba Obaid and therefore probably for us. It will be most inconvenient if we are stranded without money.

Having told me all this the Mansab asked to see the findings of the tomb, and sat with a skull in his hand, now varnished by the Archæologist with shalaq. I told him about Alinur's mapping of the ancient irrigation, a labour which makes her popular since everyone thinks it is meant to restore the original water supply. And we then discussed the affairs of the Mansab of Meshed, to whose letter I have written a friendly reply: the matter of the attempted blackmail has been raising a question never hitherto asked, as to *who* actually owns the waste areas of this country—the tribes or government?

No sooner had the Mansab gone than Sayyid 'Ali appeared. He has easily cajoled our slave into handing the workmen's luncheons back to his keeping, and now came to ask that, as he had provided a particularly good meal, he might be given a little more money.

There are limits to all things. "You wicked sinner," I said. "You want to be paid because for once your immoral profits are reduced?"

'Ali went into fits of laughter, and walked on to the terrace to laugh himself out—delighted to be discovered! If ever there is a Parliament in this country, he will be the first M.P.; he has all the demagogic arts. In spite of all, however, the luncheons will have to be taken from him, and I shall follow the Qadhi's advice and arrange with the owner of the Hureidha shop direct. Sayyid 'Ali heard of the resolution with equanimity; he merely remarked that we pay half a dollar for a donkey which he gets for a quarter; he omitted to mention where the other quarter went to.

"The people here," he said, "have light blood: they *talk* too much."

"Indeed they do," I said, reflecting that it is something to dislike one's own defects, even if one sees them only in other people.

February 2.   "*Where thieves break through and steal.*"
(Matthew vi, 19.)

Of all problems of travel in countries without a post office, that of money is one of the worst. Large notes, even if they exist, are little use, since only fair-sized towns will change them, and the small currencies are nearly always unmanageable. One cannot carry their weight on one's person, a strong box arouses more interest than is safe, and ordinary luggage is easily accessible to any Arab with time on his hands; the best way is to deal with the matter as the Arabs deal with it themselves, and to hand one's money-bag and all responsibility to one's servant, who has a free mind to attend to it. I have now done this many times, nor ever had to regret it, for nine people out of ten respond to a trust that is placed in them, and the tenth . . . one should have judgement to avoid. So Qasim has our cash, and keeps it locked in a tin box, and writes the sums on the wall as he hands them to me, a proceeding which the Archæologist, far from considering my financial method as the fruit of experience, looks upon with disapproval as the product of a flibbertigibbety mind. Since our arrival in Hureidha, however, where we possess large sums of several thousand dollars at a time, I have handed over the reserve to be kept in her bedroom, merely so as to avoid sleeping with it alone downstairs, for Qasim lodges in another house and anyone can walk into me through the non-existent terrace door. Her bedroom is locked with—she declares with innocent and surprisingly unscientific confidence—a European key. Now anyone might know that European keys and locks are bought all over the East by the dozen at a time, and one that opens one door will open another with equal ease; the only safe way of locking anything up here is to use one of the clumsy Arab contraptions made of wood. Our pretty little Ne'ma has long since looked into every secret corner of the Bluebeard room, one may be sure. I might have thought of this myself, but my own methods of guarding against theft are different, and, as I always lose keys, I would have given this one to Ne'ma to look after, and been sure then that no one except herself would rummage among my things. As it is, the danger never entered my mind, and fifty-five of our dollars have gone. I can remember hearing female steps and a chink of silver down our stairs, and noticing vaguely that the sound seemed different from the usual click of anklets, but who did it, or when, or how, we shall never know for certain. I hope it was Ne'ma; she can then buy herself another girdle to go with the dress we have given her for the coming feast. As for our bags of silver, they have been brought down again and handed to Qasim, who has locked them in our neighbour's carved cupboard, and now goes about with a large and very non-European key securely tied in his girdle.

*   *   *

He too has had to have a new *futah* for the feast and a white turban with yellow flowers. For days it seemed as if Hureidha could not provide these things, but at last our slave appeared with them unexpectedly—conjured to all appearances from nowhere—and Qasim has been smoothing them out on the dining-table, saying "Praise be to God" at intervals. His wages, however, I do not give him, and I have been talking to him like a mother on the subject of female wiles: he looked self-conscious and blushed, and will probably pay as much attention to my words as young men usually do when talked to by their mothers.

Meanwhile, unless we can get something soon from Shibam, we shall have no money to pay our workmen when this last bag has gone.

February 3.   *"He wished him to be a model of constancy, and fancied the best means of affecting it would be by not trying him too long."*
(*Mansfield Park.*)

The air is hot already, seventy to eighty in the shade, with sudden changes in it, and I have been sitting on the terrace for the first time wrapped in a quilt. Salih, the youngest of the Children of Muhsin, came and helped me to diagnose a woman who complained of a Sikin in her head. The Sikin is invisible except to a few exceptional people like Salih's father; it has a human form, though much taller, and can live in any substance—a stone, a wall, a door-post—and if you laugh at it, it creeps into you and hurts; if, on the other hand, it—or rather she—likes you, she will come and shake your clothes when you are ill, and bring one or other of the Prophets to cure you. Some Sikins pray and some do not. If she dislikes you, she spits as you pass (spitting is terribly popular) and you come out in a rash. It is very difficult to know her, because she goes about veiled like any other woman, even when she is visible. I thought Epsom salts might discourage her as much as anything; if they did not, I told the woman, Allah would do the rest, and Salih and I continued to discuss the matter after she left. He did not think it was a Sikin, but rather a Barkin, who—or which—is altogether milder and enters like a little cool wind by the great toe of the right foot; it then settles in the chest, swelling in lumps either in front or on one side, and it eats your food, so that you eat and eat and are always hungry. The Wali in the tomb down below can drive it away, out by the big toe as it came.

"Is it true, Salih, that the Wali has four 'Afrits in the shape of dogs who go to his tomb every night and keep him informed of everything we do?"

"Yes," said Salih. "Anyone can see them going in and out. No one can enter when they are there."

"The 'Afrits," he went on, "are men, and they creep into women by the ear" (how very true); "and the Jinn are women, and visit men. But the worst of all," said Salih, "is the Makhfi (the Hidden One): when He creeps in, you swell and swell and go black and die, may Allah preserve us."

"Amen," said I, for indeed our European morale is slightly shaken with all these diseases about us, and the Archæologist is now drifting towards sickness in her turn. Alinur says that this country "gives her the willies"; I must tell her it is only the Barkin.

* * *

Sayyid 'Aluwi, Salih's cousin, strolled in upon this conversation and turned it towards matrimonial complications, equally incalculable but far easier to cure. He tells me that his whole family are bringing pressure to bear on his brother Husain, whose divorce and remarriage are strongly disapproved of. "It may be," said 'Aluwi hopefully, "that in a week or two he will divorce again, and then he can remarry his former wife."

"That will make two divorces and two weddings in a month. Do you have a big feast for *every* wedding?"

"Not when it is the same wife for the second time," said 'Aluwi.

"But surely," I said, "he can't marry the same wife again till someone else has married and divorced her?"

Sayyid 'Aluwi looked troubled. "We do not follow that rule here," he said. "The fact is that the sayyids have made special arrangements among themselves so that they can marry cheaply and often—for there is very little else to do here. So they have a rule by which no one can pay more than fourteen dollars (21s.) for a wife, and a virgin at that; one can spend sixty dollars or so on a wedding feast, but that is all. This makes it possible for them to marry as often as they like. But the tribes are very much more expensive, and here in Wadi 'Amd one is supposed to woo one's bride for six months or a year, and one can see her as one does in Europe." A look of gentleness came over Sayyid 'Aluwi's kind and open face: "You went to visit my little beduin wife," said he. "She cost me three hundred dollars; and when I had been accepted, I had to give a present to her mother, who uncovered her face before me for the first time when she received it. It is called a 'coffee present,' and she gives half of it back as a wedding gift. And then I had to give presents to all the slaves. But the money for the bride is not actually handed over—not until there is a divorce."

The Feast of the Pilgrimage

"That will not be necessary in your case," I said. "She is a darling."

Sayyid 'Aluwi beamed. "We married for love," he said. "It is the best way."

February 6. "For so above thine altars will Philippus offer vapour of frankincense."

(*Greek Anthology.*)

The great feast of the year, the feast of the pilgrimage, begins in three days' time when the Elders of the Cities of the East see the new moon of Dhu'l Hajja in their sky. Then everywhere, from Samarkand to Morocco, is rejoicing and the slaying and eating of goats and sheep and lambs and the steam of sacrifice goes up in unison from the pilgrim fires of Mekka and from the pilgrims' homes. These are the greatest days of all the year, and already a fervour of preparation runs through our little town, and I am more harrowed than usual by the constant stream of women who come with the last of their treasures to sell. They never end their poor unhappy stories except by saying, "Allah will feed us," nor do they withhold their blessings and polite gentle words if, as it happens, one cannot buy: so that one is ashamed for one's easy virtues, compared to these whose goodness lives in the constant companionship of hunger. The trouble is that we have no money left to buy with, and Ba Obaid is sending nothing—he too, no doubt, cut off by the Humumi war. Our slave, poor as a rat himself, has just brought in a woman with children to feed whose husband has vanished in Java: it is a story I hear every day, but the slave has been doing what he can for it with his huge and clumsy eloquence, forgetting himself and his own needs in the anxiety to befriend. He has a great many friends; a moment will come when I shall have to ask him to bring in no more; but I hate to do so!

Little Ahmed, too, came asking for things—tea and sugar for his mother. I thought he was making it up and paid no attention: he turned at the door and said in a pathetic voice: "You did not believe me when I spoke," and in the evening the Mansab's sister herself came to fetch the things away for sudden visitors and told me that Ahmed had gone home cut to the quick by my lack of confidence. He is only nine years old.

Their great-grandmother, she told me, was a Ferangi Christian, brought from Batavia to Hureidha, where she settled and became a Moslem: a strange history.

* * *

Our wadi meanwhile is filled with troubles and rumours: the Archæologist is in bed with a temperature, and her cave has been disappointing, as it turns out to have been looted already by the pre-Islamics themselves. Our mails, slow as they were before, are now cut off altogether by the Humumi; and as for money, we are nearly down to our last dollar—and the time of the feast is not a time to borrow!

A chauffeur has been shot dead on the Tarim road, and Sayyid 'Aluwi will have to circumvent the troubled zone and return to Mukalla across the jōl by Du'an. Our only vision of the outer world was the sight of three aeroplanes flying from the Se'ar in the north towards Mukalla. Swift and infinitely remote they flew, unattainable as the sunbeams and clouds through which they travel, and if one lay sick indeed, one would see them as the shipwrecked see the distant passing ships beyond their call.

* * *

The Good and the Bad

The son of the Mansab of Meshed has come again, with a
sack full of pre-Islamic rubbish to sell: I would not buy in
any case, for it is a fatal thing to encourage promiscuous
scratching up of ancient sites. But I took from him a little
handful of incense, found in an antique fragment of a jar, and
smelled it as it burned, still faintly fragrant.

*   *   *

My stream of daily tribesmen now flows again and Sayyid
'Aluwi brought his brother-in-law to-day, who is a minor
headman of the Ja'da. The Ja'da used to emigrate a great
deal to Hyderabad, and their type is very mixed. The
question of blackmail has been a good deal discussed in the
wadi and the headman and his two friends looked at me with
cold reserve till I happened to ask after the rather remote
village they came from. When they told me the name, I
said:

"Oh, you are the people who are always killing each
other?" for there has been another murder among cousins
there; whereupon they smiled delightedly as a man does
when accused of being bad and gay. It must be difficult for
moralists to explain why one is more pleased with one's vices
than one's virtues. The fact is that one loves the Good, but the
Virtuous are rather a bore. Another Ja'da came asking to be
released from a sickness imposed, he thought, by the witch-
craft of some woman in Java; and he too looked as pleased
as possible when I suggested that his own unkindness was
probably the beginning of the trouble.

"Will your wali not give you a counter-charm?" I asked.

"Ferangi medicines are better for that sort of thing," said he.

A more difficult problem has arisen over a bronze axe I
bought for the Archæologist a day or two ago. The seller

had, it seems, merely borrowed it from a friend to do a day's chopping, and brought it to me: the rightful owner appears now, incidentally with a scalded hand which he has smeared with honey. The axe is precious, being the only object of the kind we have seen, so I have refused to relinquish it, and told the owner to summon his enemy before the Mansab, to extract the price I paid. One will become as ready as Solomon with constant practice here.

February 7.   *"Each in his narrow cell for ever laid."*
                                                (GRAY's *Elegy*.)

The tombs of the Saints of Hureidha, with their sons and their grandsons around them, lie under egg-shaped domes in the cemetery outside the town. They lie in wooden arks, heavily carved, and their size, pressed together in the small square space, gives them a jostling air unsuitable to the "vasty halls of death."

The oldest is that of Habib 'Omar al 'Attas, who died in the year of the Hejra 1182 (1768 A.D.); that of Habib Ahmed, the most venerated, dates from A.H. 1335 (1916 A.D.); but their elaborate carving and dusty neglect might belong to a much earlier time. The little buildings are naked, decorated only with scroll-work round the windows, a niche or two for lamps, and an old cotton sheet, printed in colours, tied by the four corners to prevent the mud roof from falling in crumbs on the coffins of these venerated dead. Habib Ahmed, the author of my MS., was the grandfather of the present Mansab; it was he who instituted the rule called *Taraf* in this valley, which made it sinful to destroy women, cat'le, waterways or trees. It must be pleasant to know that, when your worldly labours are over, you will abide in the love of your city, visited on holidays with banners and still consulted in the daily problems of all: resting there with your ancestors around you, while your descendants carry on the works that your arms have relinquished in the weariness of time: no wonder that with this before him, the Mansab of Hureidha walks with so quiet a dignity among his people.

They, gathering round, watched with dubious looks while I took my shoes off in the sun-drenched porch and prepared to photograph the tombs. A bedu assured me that the saint would object.

"That may be so," said I. "But do you think that your wali cannot look after himself? If he dislikes being photographed, all he has to do is to spoil the picture."

"That is so. That is indeed so. That is what happened to Doreen." The crowd was reassured, for Doreen's effort in the dim light had been under-exposed. They opened the windows, and I was allowed to photograph in silence, with only a murmur from the bedu now and then, saying: "It will not come out."

It was my first day abroad. A small bodyguard of children kept the crowd back with sticks, a proceeding which began to be resented and required another oration to explain that not pride or the desire to avoid conversation inspired it, but the existence of worms bad for illness which their bare shuffling feet are apt to stir about them in the dust. But it is an exhausting thing to take a convalescent walk through Hureidha, though to-day the town is half empty; all who can have gone on pilgrimage to Meshed, to return across the jōl in time for their to-morrow's feast.

The Diary, Hureidha

February 9. "*When a bad Muslim dies the angels take him out of his tomb and put in one of the good from among the Christians in his place.*"

(LUCIE DUFF GORDON.)

A small feminine sensation has been caused in Hureidha by the fact that my hands have been painted with henna for the feast: the news has rushed round the town and enthusiastic women come to snatch and admire the works of art as I pass. The truth is that I have long wanted to see how this operation is performed.

So I arranged to go to the Mansab's sister and her daughter "Rapunzel" of the long plaits next door, and found there the best beauty specialist of the town, 'Ayesha, with pretty little pointed face and thin fingers, sitting cross-legged making green puree like spinach out of powdered henna leaves and water in a basin. She asked me to wash my hands with the powdered Khoteqa to get the grease off, rubbed my wet fingers in turmeric which I spread over hands and arms to make them yellow; and then, having arranged cushions to support me on every side, took my hands over, beginning with the right one "for a blessing."

With her forefinger she scoops up the paste, which hangs in a thin drip, and with this traces out rings and stars and trees and anything she fancies. It was a formidable performance. I went at 1 p.m. and emerged at five. The ladies pressed glasses of tea into my free hand, looked at the growing work of art with criticism and advice, and told the gossip of the town. Fatima, the elder sister, came in a festal dress of embroidered silk, her eyes heavily kohled, a pair of white-and-black check socks "for best" loose about her ankles. The event of the day was a woman who had cut her throat but is still alive: I had been sent for, but Qasim refused to give

150

the message, to my relief I must admit, and I shocked the
ladies by surmising that perhaps the Sikin had got into her;
they were pained to think I should have learned of this un-
orthodox spirit. A feeling of infinite leisure hung over our
harim. When the news was interesting, 'Ayesha stopped
work with her finger and the drip of henna suspended in air
and everything came to a standstill. She kept a little stick
in her mouth to wipe away irregularities in the pattern and
stray drops, which she apparently swallowed. It could not
be bad for her because henna is one of the trees of Paradise.
When my hands were done, I was arranged on cushions on
the floor and told to sleep while one of the ladies did my
feet: the others had coffee in a far corner. I lay with closed
eyes, feeling the little cold drops as they fell; henna is cooling,
they take baths of it in summer. I dozed, and woke to find
the work finished, on each instep a sun with shining rays,
taken, the lady said, "from a printed book." My hands had
three palm branches on the back and one upon the middle
finger, besides other small patterns and circles: the first joint
and the inside of the palm were solid henna. This elaboration
is only for brides; matrons or unmarried girls have a much
simpler affair: it was the height of impropriety for me to
walk about so highly decorated. But though I pleaded in a
modest way, the ladies could not bear to lose the opportunity:
they lavished every bridal ornament upon me. While I lay
drying, they gathered round, fed me with bread and coffee,
and brought half a petrol tin to beat on while they sang: the
day passed, pleasant, restful and timeless: but I had to keep the
stuff on, caked like mud, all night, and go again this morning
to have the pattern worked over to make it strong. It then
lasts with no further attention for three weeks.

This morning a real drum had been provided to amuse me, and a woman expert in singing and trilling her tongue, while the little girls came and tossed their hair about in the dance called Rishi, or, very rigid, two by two and hand in hand, stamped their feet in the Safina to jingle the bells of their anklets and the little bells that hang from rings on the great toe. "Rings on her fingers and bells on her toes" is an accurate description of dance dress in the Harim.

To-day all are in their best, and the girls' hair is rubbed stickily with dates to make it fluff out at the bottom of their plaits. The women visitors sit in their medieval dresses; the veil tight about the chin frames their face, the black mask thrown back makes as it were a crown; in the shafts of light from the lattices, with the carved dark columns behind them, they move like the pictures of some fourteenth-century psalter come to life. I lay dozing at intervals, listening to the talk with closed eyes as the hours went by. I had a merciful heart, they said, and it is not true that Christians throw their dead into the sea.

A young woman came in with a timid manner to see me as one might a lion in its den: she teaches the little girls to read. She laid her fears aside gradually and, when I seemed to sleep, told the assembled company the story of Maiuk the Christian.

Maiuk, she said, lived near a mosque, and one day a widow and her daughter, travellers, came to this mosque, and being quite destitute, asked alms of the mulla. But he sent them empty away, and they wept. And Maiuk heard them, and sent his servant to enquire and was told that it was a widow and her daughter, and that they were travellers, and he sent them one hundred dollars. And in time the mulla died, and came to the gates of Paradise, and saw the rivers and the trees and the huris: and the angels said to him: "This, oh Mulla, was the place prepared for you, but it has been given away to Maiuk the Christian."

February 10. *"How shall we sing the Lord's song in a strange land?"*

(Psalm 137.)

The first ceremony of the feast began yesterday on the slope of our wadi, under the cliffs of the western side, where it is shady in the afternoon.

Here the men and children of Hureidha assemble on this day for the evening meal, which they cook in the lee of boulders that have rolled and settled on that stony slope. Small parties were going already with carpets and cooking-pots when the youngest of the Children of Muhsin came for me with his donkey and spread my white sheepskin upon it. Alinur came too, but the Archæologist is in bed with fever. We threaded our way among the reddish sandstones till we came to where boulders were spattered with the blood of goats and kids, and circular hearths were built, the same that I had seen and wondered at three years ago on the jōl; they call them *maq'ad*, or sitting-places, and build them with a ring of big stones a yard or so across, and charcoal and a kindling of dry palm leaves in the centre, and a layer of thin flat stones above, on which the gobbets of meat are laid to cook. These sacrificial feasts take place all over the country in the high clefts where the water pools are found; they belong no doubt to some rite whose origin is lost, and the places are still called *ma'bad* or "homes of worship"; but the people of Hureidha removed their *ma'bad* a hundred years ago and brought it down to the hillside near the town; and there on the day when the army of tents has issued from Mekka and the animals are slaughtered in Wadi Mina, the people of Hureidha, too, celebrate the Pilgrimage. Most of the men are away, 1,300 of them are said to be in Java, and no women appear, so the crowd among the boulders big as houses was thinly scattered, and from the mounds of the *ma'bads* the smoke rose only here and there, straight as the sacrifice of Abel.

From groups far and near greetings and invitations were called, and we paused by this friend or that, till, under the leaning wall of a boulder with carpets spread, we climbed to where the Mansab and his party were arriving. There we settled in a circle and leaned on cushions, rising at intervals to greet some Elder as he joined us. The land fell away to the flat wadi whose sparse houses and palm groves shone in the sinking sun. At a little distance sat the cook cutting chunks of meat into small pieces, a basket before him and a knife in his hand; he was swathed in a yellow fringed *futah*, with a wooden key tucked in at his apex in front; his portly back, enclosed in a machine-knitted sweater, rested against the mountainside behind it, two solidities meeting back to back. His assistant, half naked, with grey beard and woollen tam-o'-shanter, fanned the fire of our *ma'bad* with a shallow basket, and fed it with lumps of fat, while a man in a red tarbush sprinkled salt.

In the course of time the fuel consumed to hot embers, the roof of heated stones sank down, the pieces of meat were laid to roast upon it.

In our circle of Elders rosaries clicked; the conversation, tranquil and deliberate, pursued its way, imbued with the peace of the evening; the mind went wandering in Time

" God is Great "

through the feasts of mankind. Now and then the Qadhi asked all to join in a Takbir, the declaration that God is Great.

Allahu akbar, Allahu akbar, Allahu akbar;
La Allah illa Allahi
Allahu akbar wa lillahi al-hamdu
Allahu akbar kabirihi wa al-hamdu lillahi kathirihi
wa subhana Allahu bukratan wa asilan.
La Allahu illa Allahi
La na'bud illa aiahu mukhlasina lahu ad-din
wa lau kariha al kafiruna
La Allahu illa Allahi wahduhu
sadaqa wa'duhu wa nasara 'abduhu wa 'azza junduhu wa
   hazama al-ahdzab wahduhu
La Allahu illa Allahi wa Allahu akbar wa lillahi al-hamdu.

God is Great, God is Great, God is Great:
There is no God but God.
God is Great and to God the Praise.
God in His immensity is Great and to God much praise.
Glorify Him in the dawn and at the fall of night.
There is no God but God.
Him alone we serve, purifying our worship to Him,
Though the unbelievers hate.
There is no God but God alone.
His word is truth, He gives victory to His servant;
He gives glory to His army and puts the sectaries to flight.
There is no God but God and God is Great
To God the praise.

The voices sounded noble and manly among the frail columns of smoke ascending in the desert place of stones.

After every Takbir our neighbours turned thoughtfully and said: "There is no difference between us. We all believe in God."

A pleasant smell of roasting meat floated about. And presently cooked rice was brought in baskets, a tablecloth was laid, dates, bread, and honey were spread upon it, and the goat came up in relays, sizzling from the fire. In a small circle of their own nearby, eight of the children sat eating too, their little tummies visibly distending. When it was over the Mansab gave them fireworks to play with, while we again reclined. We perfumed ourselves with incense in small burners; we listened to the poets among us; and went home while the last brightness faded from the cliffs, red as the bands of henna with which old Sindbad the Sailor has streaked his donkey in honour of the feast.

When the dark fell we too had fireworks. I had a few with me, and some crackers, and the children let them off to sparkle over the edge of my terrace for the neighbours to see. Nothing, I believe, could have pleased people more, for many have come to-day saying: "You too took a part in our feast." We are more or less adopted as citizens of Hureidha.

February 11. "And as rest from labour is kept inviolate by the just man, so let the works of pious mortals endure."
(Macedonius, *Greek Anthology*.)

We had hardly done with the excitement of our sacrificial meal, when the young American oil-man from Mukalla walked in. He was gaily dressed in a long green *futah*, an Iraq *sidara* like a forage cap on his head, and had walked all the seven days with seven camels for his luggage behind him. He was so young, healthy and cheerful, so pleased with a universe unlike his own, so gay when he laughed, and so grateful for friendliness which comes when "you sit about and talk," that no one indeed could be his enemy. The perpetual charm of Arabia is that the traveller finds his level there simply as a human being: the people's directness, deadly to the sentimental or pedantic, likes the less complicated virtues; and the pleasantness of being liked for oneself might, I think, be added to the five reasons for travel given me by Sayyid Abdulla, the watch-maker: "to leave one's troubles behind one; to earn a living; to acquire learning; to practise good manners; and to meet honourable men."

* * *

Yesterday was the chief day of the feast, called Zina, and we dressed to a beating of drums, and made our way about 7 a.m. through our uneven streets till we came upon a little group of four rehearsing by themselves with banners unfurled. In the open space in front of the Mansab's house, another group was beating. The trident brass of the banner poles shines against the blue of the sky; on crude satins the name of the wali is embroidered; the crowd, collecting slowly, had put on all brightness it could find in the way of tablecloths, loincloths or shawls. The Mansab comes out from his carved doorway in a green turban and cloak, green jacket gold-buttoned beneath it, the men of his family behind him; he is so holy, people do not kiss his hand, they bend over and sniff at it audibly, so as to breathe up a whiff of sanctity as if it were snuff. The procession formed itself, some hundreds of men, the Mansab and the banners at its head; Alinur and I followed, snatching photographs as the colours wound round the brown corners of the town, across the dry ravine, up the slope in the sun to the mosque where the cliff of the jōl hangs like a ship's prow above. There they prayed, and then poured in a varied stream to where the egg-shaped qubbas of the saints shine vivid among dusty graves, past the shed where biers are kept that hurry corpses to their shallow beds.

There round the walis' tombs they gathered, and then scattered, visiting their own familiar dead. It is a fine sense of drama that so brings them in holiday attire to mingle their small living handful with the unobtrusive headstones, unwalled and uncounted—a recognition of Life and Death, inextricably neighboured. In that wide mortal space about the domes, the smallness of our town became apparent, its inhabitants so largely scattered in the world. For a day or two they have thrown aside the remembrance of their poverty, hanging ever on the sheer edge of starvation: the sight of them, so bravely dressed, among their tombs was infinitely touching. Poverty, not lovely in itself, has a splendour about it when it puts on a gallant show, whether it be a clerk in decent black, or a sayyid immaculately gowned with scarce enough food to last him half a year: in their humble way, like her who broke the box of ointments, they uphold the meaning of life as they see it, above its mere necessities.

When the visit to the tombs was over, the banners led back to the Mansab's door, pausing at cross-roads here and there while the Mansab and Elders stood with open and extended palms and prayed. We then returned to our houses, and I spent the afternoon with the children, who came to be photographed and to dance on my terrace, to the young American's delight.

* * *

Alinur made a sauce for a plum-pudding in the evening,

and we feasted our visitor with our only bottle of champagne, which ruined our reputation for abstinence and sent the Archæologist's temperature up again with surprising rapidity.

The American is going in a day or two up the wadi to 'Amd to survey. His news is not good. His cars are imprisoned in Mukalla by the Humumi, who hold the road; they have now murdered a local governor, a respectable man, and there are signs that the trouble may spread. As for us, we are marooned, but the R.A.F. will no doubt have cleared the road by the time we are ready to go. The Archæologist's illness has put a stop to all excavation for the time.

February 13.   *"From where with flutes and dances
                Their ancient mansion rings."*
                        (MACAULAY: *Battle of Lake Regillus.*)

The day after Zina is devoted to visiting. The Mansab goes round to the various houses where his sisters are settled and sits there over glasses of tea. The servants and dependents visit the sayyids on this day, the sayyids themselves having done their visiting on the afternoon of Zina. On the last day of the feast, which was yesterday, the beduin come to town.

Alinur and I again got up to the sound of a stray paraffin tin used as a drum. In the old days, before the young men of Java had weaned the hearts of the beduin from the sayyids of Hureidha, a vast crowd used to pour in from the neighbouring wadis on this last day of the feast. But now it is only a poor little contingent from the few settlements of our valley to the south. From the palm-tree distance they advance, a small dark crowd, and stop at intervals to recite a poem and wave their guns in the air, till the Mansab's secretary appears from the town to meet them, on a white horse painted with bands and rings of henna, and beside him the rival Mansab, whom nobody ever talks about, on a pony as small and unobtrusive as himself. These two come caracoling rather timorously from the brown cluster of the town, meet the advancing beduin with mutual recitations, stand, while the guns with their old barrels wound in silver are discharged over our heads—and then shuffle all together, singing, towards the houses. There in the Mansab's majliss they sit, while their wives and daughters visit the Mansab's wife.

It was Alinur's first view of a room completely carpeted with black and silver-spangled female forms. As we advance towards the hostess, friendly hands put our feet into invisible spaces; people we know smile through the deafening clamour: conversation is impossible. The Mansab's wife, a kind plain woman, resplendent in striped brocade, has bells on her toes and anklets, and a mane of silver bells from her coral head-dress to her shoulders: in a gratified murmur which ripples through the loudness of the talking, she rises to dance to her guests. The Singer of Hureidha beats the drum called *hajir*, which has red patterns painted at each end; her eyes are done with kohl in a theatrical line that sweeps to the temple and gives her an idol look. Other women beat small drums about the size and shape of a man's collar-box: they hold them shoulder-high and look at each other with delighted faces in the appalling noise. Among the general black, the sayyid ladies stand gorgeous in colour. The Mansab's sister is near me, pinning false plaits with silver hooks over each ear to help out her own shorter hair in the dancing.

"Don't you get giddy?" I shout as she totters back after the performance.

"You should not ask," said she. "It is not thought well to feel giddy—but I do all the same."

Our Ne'ma is there in the dress we gave her, her chin beautified with a smear of green like a small beard; she too is swinging long tails with eyes shut and a look of agonized ecstasy. Every colour is splashed on the women's faces: one lip green and one red is the most arresting. The dance is Rishi, done with the top of the body and the hair: the Safina, done two by two and hand in hand, with almost imperceptible movement, stamping of feet and jingling of anklet bells, there is no room for here. Our hostess smiles in a resigned way as we leave her; she has to sit in the clamour for the better part of the day.

*　　*　　*

The feast is drawing to its close, and in the sunset we stroll down to see the dancing before the Mansab's home.

On either side of the carved door a wide whitewashed bench runs along the wall: the Mansab and his friends sit there and anyone else who can find room, and because I am still delicate, a carpet is brought to spread upon it. Round our feet the children squat in a semi-circle, showing gold-embroidered tops of skull-caps as they look away to the performers; and behind them are the mass of townsfolk and slaves, the visiting beduin and their rifles on the outer edge; in the distance, against walls of houses, black shrouded ladies well out of any possible danger of being able to see anything at all, and little girls in their flowered dresses on a small knoll, where the houses open to an outline of cliffs two miles away. The crowd merges with the dancers; three drums are there and the cook, who is master of ceremonies with a stick in his hand. They begin the Sharh al-'Abid, Dance of the Slaves.

Two hold hands, moving quickly back and forward side by side, or in a circle, one forward and one back: this goes on till a third comes out, places his hand on the others, and one of the two gives up his place. The music is played on the mizmar, the plaintive and melodious music of the African slaves.

The Qatni then begins. A poet stands out and sings a verse taken up by the audience: "I left my loved one in the Wadi al'Ain." They dance this in groups, visiting each other, rather like the lancers, to a quick exciting tune.

The Bara'a of the Yafe'i then comes with knives held up, as I had seen it already in Shibam, and then the Sharh Dhaheri, two parallel rows of men facing each other. Abdulla, the old watch-mender, is the poet, he stands between the rows and gives the verse:

> "I called upon the Merciful and the gates of God were opened."

The two rows repeat it, the poet retires, the one line advances to the other, raises hands over head as they meet, bows nearly to the ground and withdraws: they do this several times, till the other line takes it up in turn. At intervals the verse is changed:

> "May the flood come from Ghaibun and bring prosperity."

Or

> "May the Mansab grant us gifts, to buy us clothes."

The music is spacious and rather sad: the dance like "Nuts in May."

The Sharh of Sur in Oman comes next: these dances are all local and every region has its own. This is a war dance with sticks for swords. The two performers come across the stage singing a wailing wordless tune and stand before a line of ten men with sticks; they then fight, leaping at a distance from each other. They trip each other up by sweeping the stick (sword) from behind along the ground; the menaced one springs clear; they kneel opposite each other and fence; when they get too close, one of the bystanders with his stick leaps between and again does so when, at the end, the victor holds his dagger over his enemy's body on the ground.

The dances become pure comedy in the Sharh Saibani, and the cook's assistant, the man of the tam-o'-shanter, appears with a pink-and-red *futah* draped coyly over his head and hides behind a line of clapping hands. His suitor, hunting behind them, drags him out: he—or she—follows in a bashful fluttering manner: the little grey beard sticks out from the pink garment in a waggish way. When another dancer appears, the lady goes gaily from one to the other in a manner not exclusively Arabian.

The comic was a great success, and having added a striped *futah* petticoat to his trousseau, became a Somali wife with a Somali husband also draped in a *futah*, a crook-handled stick in his hand. They danced and quarrelled, but what they said was probably too Rabelaisian for the Mansab to translate.

His colleague from Meshed now appeared among us, beaming with smiles, his own feast over a day or two before. We settled again to watch a juggler from Yemen. This was a sad-looking creature dressed in rags, who amused the crowd by pushing a dagger into his eye, over the eyelid I suppose; it seemed to go in nearly an inch and when he pulled it out again he had to rest his eye for a moment or two, covering it with his hand while his ragged old grey companion beat on a crooked sheep-skin tambourine. The sun had sunk meanwhile, and the crowd was thinning; the time for prayer was at hand. The two Mansabs, cross-legged on the bench beside us, rose to go. The rough dark man with the mizmar, with blue serge coat buttoned to his neck and a purple turban, walked away, playing a sad little tune, while the children followed. The feast was over with the last ray of the sunlight, and the call of the muezzin from the mosque.

February 14.   *"How better far at home to have stayed*
                 Attended by the parlour maid."
                                          (R. L. STEVENSON.)

I spent a domestic morning trying to teach Qasim to iron out my companions' shirts, which are of the severe kind invented by tailors to proclaim the equality of woman, and, like most hieratic garments, look wrong when crumpled. When Qasim has done with them they look worse than before; he uses his iron like a battering-ram: the Scientists seem to have thought of laundries as a feature of the Arabian hinterland, and look plaintively at his dilapidated efforts: but they did not teach him when they had him in idleness in Seiyun all to themselves; and now, as well as being busy, he is in love, and has also developed a boil like bubonic plague under his arm and has cut it with a penknife.

*   *   *

Otherwise the day was peaceful, apart from a visit from the Mansab of Meshed at 8.30 a.m. He appeared in his shabby white chemise, his green-and-red velvet sash across one shoulder; he has pinned on to it the Nizam of Hyderabad's

star, with the Mansab's own name carved in the middle:
120 rupees monthly to go with it. The Mansab has travelled
in India and Egypt. In Cairo, sitting in the lounge of the
Continental Hotel, he was distressed one day to see an
American woman at the next table in short sleeves in the
(to the Mansab) cold winter weather: "How can you stand
it?" he said to her in his cheerful Arabic, pinching the naked
arm which was close beside him. The outraged husband
called for a dragoman; Sayyid 'Aluwi who was present, and
told me the story, confounded himself in apologies; the
Mansab himself patted the irate husband on the chest, roaring
with laughter.

He came in beaming as usual this morning, his curly grey
beard bright and clean as water over the dingy gown.

"I will send you a new velvet ribbon from London as a
present, Mansab," I said.

He looked at his ancient adornment with a pitying affection.
"It is no longer beautiful," he admitted, "but it belonged to
my grandfather." It has probably been worn for about a
hundred years.

* * *

All the performers of the feast have been to call, on the tacit
assumption that some small present would appear; it is like
the Christmas box in England. We too have accomplished
our holiday duties and visited all the harims of our acquaintance, our Mansab's mother among them, whose foot I dressed.
She refused to have it done again until I myself appeared, and
as she lives up at least eighty steps and my heart is not yet
quite well, there has been much delay. She lives in the
house that once belonged to the Saint of Hureidha. On the
very top, opening on to the roof, is the room he lived in and

the mihrab by which, peacefully praying, he died. A little niche screened with glass on his terrace enabled him to sit in the cool air on summer nights and read his Quran. An atmosphere of brightness, of cheerful sunlight, inhabits those empty rooms. On a floor below, the Qadhi keeps his books. Two cupboards hold them all, and we sat and looked them over on the ground, a jumble of all sorts with manuscripts among them, their ink gone brown with age. There is a local history written in the fifteenth century by a man of Shihr: I photographed it, but the Qadhi cannot let me have it to copy because, he said, it belongs to his orphan nephews, and there is a canon against the lending of the property of orphans.

In the late afternoon I took Alinur to see the Mansab's sister, Fatima, the elder one, who lives in an old house on the ridge above us, high over the town. From her roof one looks away to the R.A.F. landing-ground in the north; one can see how the palms grow, in patches surrounded by banks for irrigation; one can see the roofs of the mud houses with all their domestic details spread below so that a competent censorship can be kept over one's neighbours; and one can see our house too, with Qasim struggling as usual to keep children out at the door. As we stood watching the lengthening shadows in the wadi, a man and a boy climbed the stony knoll behind us that overlooks the town. They beat on a tin for silence, the man raised his arms and, in a high shrill voice, called to the listening houses: "Hear the voice, hear the voice," he called. "All men of Hureidha, there is mud in the Tajrub canal: go to clean it, for the coming of the seil (the flood)." He repeated each sentence twice, and then walked down. Fatima listened, hiding behind the parapet, as she had no veil

Bombs and the Se'ar

on. All general news is published in this way. When we climbed down, her sister was wrapping herself in a yellow gown for prayer, a saffron colour made by dipping cotton stuff in the dye of the Yemen plant called *wars*. Her head, too, she covered, and looked like a Greek figure in her draperies, and knelt and rose in a corner of the room, while we sat by the whitewashed coffee hearth, hung with plates of Victorian landscapes, and chatted over the events of the feast. Our little town has now returned to its quiet ways.

February 15. "*The hungry sheep look up and are not fed.*"
(*Lycidas.*)

Our milk is brought to us by the young Se'ar bride whose wedding in the hillside cave I watched the other night. They are nice people. It is their tribe that has just been bombed by the R.A.F. I went to see them some time ago to ask what they felt about it, and found that they had been listening to the explosions with the most philosophic detachment. The fact is that, by establishing a rigid code in this matter of bombing, we have turned it into a sort of warfare which the medieval courtesy of the Arab can understand; when the affair is over, the R.A.F. are usually invited to come to the punished area and collect their unexploded missiles, and the question is considered at an end.

Many of this tribe come down to our wadi; their pilgrimage is to Qabr Salih and to Meshed, and the Mansab there has influence among them. Our own old Se'ari lives with a small herd of black-and-white goats in the cave where they had the dancing. He spread a piece of sacking for me beside him in the warm dim twilight of his home. The young daughter-in-law came in with the goats from pasture. She

167

has a snub nose tattooed at the bridge, and a new *thaqila*, the heavy dangle of coral and silver which attaches the veil. She has not yet learnt to keep it from falling forward over her face.

"Come and dine with us," she said.

The fact that one lives with one's goats in a hillside makes no difference to hospitality.

But to-day a catastrophe has overtaken shepherds and shepherdesses. Our Mansab, needing money for public works, has impounded all animals—goats, sheep, donkeys and camels—found browsing in the neighbourhood, and releases them only on payment of a dollar per head. This ingenious arrangement has a double advantage, as it not only produces money, but also discourages the eating by goats of everyone's young plantations; the Qadhi's best palms have all been nibbled away, and this perhaps hastened the Nemesis. By the time of afternoon prayer, 120 dollars were collected, and about 125 animals for whom the owners cannot pay, are abandoned on a compromise: the proceeds to be spent on the levelling of the streets of Hureidha. But a wail of sorrow rises on all sides. The impounded creatures are not fed, so that their owners must find dollars quickly or they die. The bride asked, weeping, if I would liberate hers. I drank the milk, she said. Nine are impounded. I have given her four dollars, and have been besieged all day by unhappy shepherdesses bringing their last little trinkets to sell. It is a harrowing affair.

*   *   *

Sayyid 'Ali has returned to us from a holiday. He has two wives, one here and one, whom he loves better, in the wadi a two days' journey away, with whom he spent the feast, and

A geological discovery

has brought me back, as a present, a leather bag with tassels, of the sort they carry about here when they go visiting, filled with coffee berries.

February 16. *"First was the world as one great Cymbal made*
Where Jarring Windes to infant Nature plaid.
All Music was a solitary sound
To hollow Rocks and murm'ring Fountains bound."

(MARVELL.)

Alinur, wandering about to map the irrigation, has found fossil plants embedded in tufa in one of the side wadis—data precious for the ancient flora of this land; in the flat below she has found flint tools bedded in wadi gravel, and pebbles of tufa with them, washed from the upper site. By this means the gravel can be dated, and the tufa also, since it must belong to the same paleolithic age as the flints which lie beside it: it is an exciting discovery, and we are now going up all the likely side valleys, one after the other. I have been to one, but nothing came of it; the next, called by the inspiring name of "the Drip," had fossils enough, imprisoned in great boulders. It was a considerable drip in paleolithic times, now perpetuated in stone round a semi-circle of overhanging cliff where the scree slope of the valley begins. The sun visits this place in early morning only, and there is an antique privacy about it: three earthen jars, half buried, overgrown with moss and maidenhair and bright leaves and white flowers, hold the few drops that still trickle from above, squeezed out of the incumbent wall of jōl. An old tin mug is left there for all to drink from, and a few remains of fires. Among white boulders below grows the tree called *ban*

169

drooping with thread-like leaves and pale pink flowers. The overhanging cliff is rounded like cobbles by weathering; the devious course of water in its heart can be traced by bunches of clinging shrubs whose roots creep in crevices to drink. There must once have been an amphitheatre of dropping springs; the tufa is honeycombed with hollow petrified tubes made by the splashing drops; they cling like bee-cells to the rocky wall. There is a feeling of natural worship in this shade. It must have been too wet for human habitation, and the flint-men, Alinur thinks, lived further down or in caves along the neighbouring ledges.

As we rode back, the three children carolled with strident voices:

"We caught the red Ibex and broke his horns
And 'Ali the Servant of God within the year
will take from us the sight of our eyes."

There is still a flavour of magic about the ibex or wa'l; a red one is supposed to be particularly strong. These short songs, two verses with pauses in the middle, are called *'amal*, and sung with any labour, such as the drawing of water from the well.

Down the valley we rode in the crisp sun, a little wind blowing through it. Hureidha appeared far off in sight, its white mosque and minaret before it. It is a charming town, so clean, clear-cut and brown, and not a tree to break its straight and delicate lines. It is a dear city. I shall think of it always as something complete and independent, a little oasis that lives its life in its own way. And of how few places can one say that in the world?

Arab manuscripts

February 17. *"From the old deep-dusted annals*
The years erase their tale
And round them race the channels
That take no second sail."

(A. E. HOUSMAN.)

Things are very gloomy. The Archæologist continues with a small but irregular temperature, Alinur is in bed with a cold; our American has left us to walk up the wadi to 'Amd, after receiving a message to say the the "deep wadis are unadvisable"; wadis 'Ain, Masila and all S.W. of Henin are forbidden: the road is still cut; and there is a wavering ripple here among our tribes owing to the fact that the Humumi are not yet dealt with; the British reluctance to bomb is very difficult to explain to the Arab. I am wondering whether, even if I am strong enough to attempt it, I shall be able in a few weeks' time to travel by camel to the coast.

On the credit side of this depressing balance is the fact that I have bought the fifteenth-century MS. from the Qadhi. Our Mansab, hearing of the difficulty about the orphans, decided that as the benefit will go to them one can *sell*, though one cannot *lend* their property. So the Qadhi appeared this morning early with an air of mystery, and drew the precious object, wrapped in a case made of mattress ticking, out of the folds of his cashmere shawl. I told him that I had no idea of its value, but would risk 100 dollars: he said he had thought of eighty, but the extra twenty would be a help to the orphans. He is the straightest, most honest of men, and goes out of his way to tell me which of the manuscripts exist as printed books so that I need not buy them. I have now got three partially copied, and have taken details and copied specimen pages of six others.

* * *

I have ridden out in the wadi, photographing irrigation channels for Alinur. Our slave took me. He is as huge and black and clumsy as a Labrador, and he has the smallest of donkeys, which he adores. He calls it McLean.

"Why McLean?" I asked, very much astonished.

"It was a steamship," said he. "It used to visit along the coast, from place to place—and that is why I gave the name to this donkey. He is like a steamship on land."

Anything more unlike would be hard to imagine. McLean has a wooden pack-saddle with a shelf on either side; one can balance one's feet there in a precarious way.

The sun and day were beautiful; a little film of cloud made one hope for rain, and the fields are being hoed with pointed hoes and the canals cleaned out in expectation. Yellow scented balls of blossom, soft as kittens, are out on the samr trees along their banks of boulders. The slave was so happy, he stretched his huge arm and slapped me on the shoulder at intervals, out of pure affection, regardless of the disturbing effect, like an earthquake, on McLean.

Hasan the boy came too, in a green *futah*, and walked ahead, cajoling the donkey onward with his skull-cap which he took off and offered as if it were a dish of carrots. "Walk ahead," I heard the slave whisper. "McLean likes to see someone in front of him." McLean was not taken in, even when Hasan filled the skull-cap with pebbles.

Hasan, smoking wisps of paper filled with green tobacco, walked on reciting poems composed by his father about Harold and the R.A.F. and chucked his long brown fingers to explain the verses to us and to the donkey behind him.

Songs of Ingrams and the R.A.F.

"When the flyers met them with their hum,
The tribes fell a height of four stories.
In wadi 'Alwa Ingrams will overcome;
Who disobeyed his order, he will bomb.
He commanded abruptly and there was no discussion,"

"Oh, Hasan, how can you say that?" I interrupted.

"They will throw down their guns
And their hearts will settle.
He says: 'Woe to you if you cause trouble,
On camels we will seize the guilty, with blows.'
Now everyone crows on the day of the month,
(the last day, when a truce ends: all being peace now, there
is nothing to fear)
Now all who sin, ask pardon of Allah."

"Ingram is very great," said Hasan. "Since he has been
in the Hadhramaut, every year the seil-flood comes."

I can see Harold and Doreen rapidly turning into legendary,
tutelary deities.

We rode along the north side of the wadi, to a burial cave,
now used for storage of fodder, dug in the hillside; its niches
were filled with drying stalks of millet. Below it the dead
oasis stretched across the plain, sandy waves dotted with
stones like foam. A train of four camels ploughed slowly
across that dusty floor, on whose immense peace the imperceptible, immemorial movement of Time alone was visible.

The irrigation seems to have come down unaltered; a
series of stone-built wedges cut the main stream and divided
its waters: they are called *sadd*, a misleading word, as it makes
one expect a barrage where none exists. From these sadds
secondary canals, small streams called *saqiyas*, are taken off,

173

The Diary, Hureidha

irrigate fields enclosed in high mud banks, often topped with a breastwork of thorns, and flow over a walled outlet into parallel saqiyas that run on a lower level. Little holes in the banks, called *harra*, let the water into smaller patches or plantations. In the main canals, here and there, great blocks of stone called *ras* are built to deflect the course of floods, and the waters are sometimes run through a narrow piece, walled on either side, where they can be measured: one such ancient measuring-place is yet visible, emerging from the sand.

As we rode there, a bent old man, his shoulders clothed only in his beard, came up and told me he was the head of a sub-tribe of Ja'da and lives in a small fortress on a rock beside the way. Alinur has been, and there is a cave below the rock.

"My sons will let you see it," said the old man.

But when we got there only a handsome, sullen grandson was at home, afraid to bring the key. "You might carry things away," he said to the slave.

It is annoying to be treated like a pickpocket, though the suspicion was mentioned with no malice. Our little party left in state and dudgeon, relieved only by the sprightliness of McLean who stops of his own accord at every water-dome, in case his rider may be thirsty. The slave then contemplates him fondly, like a mother her precocious child, but Alinur tells me that she secretly uses a packing-needle, gently to prod these pauses.

When we reached home I found the Qadhi and a host of people waiting, a new poet with a Qasida, and the Mansab of Meshed—delighted to eat marmalade and biscuits—surrounded by a train of men and boys carrying a small grey monkey with sad wrinkled nose and red behind: it sat on the middle of my terrace playing with old reels of photographs and eating melon seeds. They say there are numbers of them in the hills about. They are unbelievers, the Mansab says, transformed by God. It seems strange to think of God as so much more unpleasant than one's fellow creatures. Who would change his worst enemy into a monkey, with that sad look in its eyes?

February 18.   *"There is a pool whose waters clear*
                 Reflect not what is standing near."
                                    (WALTER DE LA MARE.)

Our Mansab has issued an order that spangles, sequins, cowrie shells and all such ornaments are to be abolished from the wardrobes of Hureidha. Consternation fills every harim. The ladies with sighs are snipping from their new dresses, just finished for the feast, the stars they wear so gracefully in the middle of their backs, swaying as they walk. And the sadness is that *we* are responsible for the tragedy. It is the sight of *our* dowdy clothes that inspires dress reform in the heart of the Mansab. He himself is a dandy, always immaculate, scented with sandal-wood, his nails now pink with my varnish, which he asked for. It seems unfair that he should be able to condemn the whole womankind of his city to plainness. I have been to the *majliss* to see what I can do, but the unanimous male vote was inexorable. "Sequins," says the Qadhi, speaking for all, "cost a great deal of money and are no *use*." Social distinctions will be preserved by other means. Sherifas can wear long black wraps to the ankles and throw the fringed ends both over one shoulder: slaves and the lowly born have to throw each end over its own shoulder and wear them short; this rule is now to be

enforced with strictness, so that a lady may be known for a
lady as she trails her shapeless garments through the dust.
But the pretty spangles must go. "They cannot *wash* like
your clothes," says the Mansab. It almost makes one wish
to dress like the Archæologist in trousers, which no one would
copy.

* * *

We have had a mail from Seiyun—the Humumi still
fighting, the road still cut, trouble spreading; Harold must
wish us away, though we are having a steadying effect in this
corner. Mr. Philby's article has come, and when Ja'far
destroys my afternoon sleep by murmuring "Freya" for an
hour on end outside my door, I like to think that we are a
spearhead of oppression.

* * *

I am now the poulticer of Alinur, while the Archæologist,
having consented to take quinine, has dropped her temperature. The young American is back from 'Amd, cheerful
but exhausted with social life and realizing to the full the price
one has to pay for a friendly footing in Arabia. He tells me
that he calculates the wear and tear of life here to be exactly
double that of home.

We took him yesterday to hunt for tufa fossils. For an
hour we rode south along the Wadi Nissim gravel, amid
dams and sluices and watch-towers here and there, until we
turned to the cliffs and lost the path under steep limestone
boulders. Alinur rode McLean and I had a still smaller
engaging creature called Daqiq who knows his name, lifts his
head, and brays if you call him. Hasan came and the slave,
and a strange bedu appeared with long smooth hair over his
shoulders, and walked with the young American hand in

hand. When the sheer walls narrowed we came to a ledge like a grand circle in a theatre, over an empty stream below: and saw at its hillside end in shadow a naked pool, rock-ringed and lonely, about forty-five feet across and its depth unknown —my thirty-foot tape could not plumb it. It lies dark there, reflecting nothing, beside a little beach of rock, where the limestone silt turns to tufa for the benefit of geologists to come, and is visited only by the violence of waters in their season, which foam down a scooped channel in those scarce shelving walls. In the ravine another group of beduin and five shepherdesses, children, were playing with browsing goats, and came to look. The lads wound their head-cloths round their loins and leaped into the water; or climbed the overhang, and, clinging like goats, sprang fifteen feet or more into the middle of the pool. It is a mystery how, with only a pond of this size in the whole district, they all can swim; they learn, they say, during the floods of spring. It was charming to see their dark bodies with curls loose on their shoulders, the cliff and the shimmer of green water around them. There are fish in the pond; if you catch and eat them you can see in the dark, the beduin say. The little shepherdesses sit shyly at a distance and eat dates out of the crowns of their hats.

The young American gave us an excellent lunch. The beduin lads came shivering, wringing their loin-cloths out of the cold water to the sun. Red dragon-flies flitted, a frog put out its head. I slept with the splashing and laughter in my ears, and in a dim dream followed the voices as they must have echoed century before century round the water-hole, since the days when first the leaves were fossilized around it, exactly, to look at, as the leaves that grow there now.

The Diary, Hureidha

February 20. "*And the great argument for long living is that you win lands of dreams and find them real too.*"

(Letter from W. P. KER.)

The Mansab of Meshed, still here on a visit, said that he wished to see our ruins and lent me his brown pony to go there; he himself rode the grey with henna spots. We set off in the morning from a heap of bricks just outside the town, with a sort of John Gilpin ceremonial and a chorus of admiration when I started to trot. A woman on a horse has never even been imagined here. The little Javanese pony called Nasib (Fate) is a charming beast. They train them to a quick pace between trot and canter, perfectly smooth as if impelled horizontally, with no ups and downs, and most pleasant. He pricked his ears and looked about with the friendly liveliness that makes Arab ponies so attractive. Hasan, running at remarkable speed, followed with camera and sunshade.

The Mansab was not really dressed for riding. He had a long white gown over a purple loincloth, with no trousers, and bedroom slippers on his feet; his velvet sash and the Sultan of Hyderabad's decoration pinned on to it kept him more or less together. He came thundering along like a voluminous Charon, beard, gown, turban and slippers floating about him, and enjoyed it hugely till his star fell off amid the ruins of the pre-Islamic irrigation, and Hasan had to run back to find it; but the bit with the name in the middle had gone.

We climbed to the temple of the Moongod, dilapidated already but peaceful in the sun; and then, crossing the main waterway of the vanished gardens, marked faintly by a double line of stones, saw the Nahdi and his boy labouring in their

178

fields on the farther side. He had hired a plough and two oxen for one and a half dollars for the day, and his patches of turned-up earth looked very small. The little boy was going over them with a camel and his wooden board, drawing the earth washed down during the winter up again on to the slope of dykes that hem the cultivated patches. The water, when it comes, escapes by a gap built with stones at one corner, like the lip of a jug, and descends to irrigate another field below. But as yet it is still desert, for every drop has to be carried three miles across the wadi except in the season of floods.

The Nahdi ran to meet us and kissed the Mansab's garment, now decorously perpendicular as he stopped to dismount. Hand in hand they went over the scree to see the excavated cave, a large round place with niches and fragments of pottery and skulls; and thence to the dwelling cave, in whose twilight, on goat-hair strips of matting, the Mansab settled cross-legged with his sash wrapped round him to support his knees. He was hot, and took off his turban, and beamed. He was pleased at my regret over his star, but himself does not mind, he says, losing his possessions; and this is evidently true, for he thought no more about it. He had a bag of tiny coins in the folds of his gown for the children, delighted and shy beside him; and presently in the middle of a sentence his eyes shut; he stroked his beard, said he was an old man, lay down at full length with his plump toes sticking upward, and was asleep.

The family had rushed to slaughter a kid, so that we had time on our hands. The twilight was pleasant and cool, filled only with a small buzzing of domestic flies. After a while when coffee had come, I too felt sleepy and lay down, and was touched presently to see the old man creeping quietly towards me, to cover me, head and all, with his green shawl. By the time I woke, the kid was there, carried like the head of St. John in a basket, and a mound of yellow rice beside it.

The Mansab washed with only a few drops of water, remembering how far it has to come; he is one of those happy natures who think spontaneously and cheerfully of others. His host, squatting in a dark corner, looked on while we ate, more pleased to see his food consumed than if we had brought him a present: and when we left soon after, the Mansab took Hasan to ride pillion behind him, my camera in his hand.

On the way back we stopped at the small fort of the Ja'da to see the owner whose grandson had received us so badly. I had seen to it that a complaint reached him by 'Ali, and we were now welcomed in a cave below the castle, where, under double rows of ancient funeral niches, the family lives in winter for warmth. There was another unexcavated cave, they said, in the hillside above, with ancient writings cut in the rock beside it.

I thought I would toil up, though it is hot now in the afternoons: our mornings are eighty in the shade at 8 a.m. The Archæologist has lamented the absence of rock inscriptions in Hureidha, and wishes to find another cave to dig: and this one is close to the town and nearly all day in shade. It is there, apparently untouched, where the steep cliff meets the scree, with pre-Islamic words scratched on the rock around it, far better than the graffites of Shibam and Seiyun, and the only ones, as far as we know, round Hureidha.

Songs of praise

"For charitable prayers,
                            Shards, flints, and pebbles . . ."
                                            (*Hamlet, v.* sc. *i.*).

As we rode home yesterday we saw a hoopoe and a butterfly, peacock blue with yellow markings at its outer edge of wings. There is a pretty little bird called qara, with a black flattish head white splashed, white tail with black mark, white underbody and black wings; a wheatear perhaps? The ba-ramadi is a small grey bird with a black head. The triz is a wagtail with black bib and neck and white on the back and underbody. And there is a bigger bird called makhala, with black head and tail and yellow under its body. But the bee-eating phoenix has not yet appeared.

*   *   *

When I reached home I found a man with a *qasida* in praise of Harold in his hand. "He has broken the horns of the wicked," it says. I wonder if this has any relationship with the Bible phrase: "His horn shall be exalted"? It was the breaking of the horns of the wa'l that brought the punishment of 'Ali in the children's song.

Harold and I are the subject of song in Hureidha at present. Old Abdulla the watch-mender came some evenings ago to present me with an ode in my honour. He had it on a piece of grubby paper and his wife and daughter came too, to hear. I had gone to bed, but it would have hurt the old man's feelings to be turned back; so they all sat by my bedside; and it was charming to see him playing with his song, singing every verse over with modulations and variations, making us observe every delicacy of rhythm, while his daughter looked at him with all the admiration of her heart, and the wife, a plain elderly woman with a quiet, sweet expression sat listening, sure that he would be admired. One felt that it was a happy little household, all blossoming from the charming nature of Abdulla, who is one of the many really good old Moslems that I know. Qasim crouched out of sight in the passage, so that the women might remain unveiled, and presently Ne'ma joined us, and understood no word of the classic Arabic, but approved the sentiments when they were explained.

"Is your son a poet too?" I asked. He is an intelligent man very like his father, who has been telling me about a ruined fortress in the jōl above Hajarein.

"He writes half a verse now and then, but he does not know the difficult words." The father and daughter are the real companions in this craft, and presently they began to sing together, recalling one *qasida* after another. She knew all his poems, and reminded him of them; and at the close of each verse the two voices sank in unison into that low bell-like note on which the Arab music ends.

*   *   *

News has come through to-day that the Humumi have surrendered, handed in their robbers, agreed to pay the fine, and that the Tarim road is open; so we are once more in contact with the world. We have arranged to leave on the 5th of March, and I have sent for a lorry; I go overland, if I am strong enough, and meet the Archæologist on the coast to examine the probable site of Cana before sailing for Aden. Alinur hopes to come, but may have to hurry back to Palestine direct. It is getting hot; a south wind blows in the late afternoon, and it is irritating and dry; it is ninety in the shade at 5 p.m.

*   *   *

In search of flints

The Archæologist was feverless in the morning and packed our collected pots, and now alas! is in bed again with a temperature. The pots are so depressingly ugly that a prolonged contemplation of them would make anyone ill. Perhaps if one spent one's life in close communion with such hideous efforts of the past the sweetest nature might become embittered and grow to hate the human race merely because of the things it is now preparing for excavations of the future. No other animal, when one comes to think of it, has littered the face of the earth with fragments except the creature Man.

*　　*　　*

I have been out with Alinur, looking for flints in the gravel which lies like a thick slice along the wadi bed, sandwiched in loess-like ground beneath it and above. The flints look almost as white as the limestone pebbles. They are fastened there as in cement, and Alinur hammers them out, striding along with a clumsy walk that is pleasantly restful; it seems to have taken something from the steadiness of the rocks with which she deals.

We lunched under the shade of an 'ilb tree with huge roots twisted in the stream bed, the favourite shade of an elderly thin white goat with hennaed forehead, who retired after an irritated look, stared at us from another tree to see if we would take the hint and go, ate a piece of our orange peel with an interested air as if it were a scandal, and refused to have anything more to say to us. Our slave and his friend had both forgotten to bring their food; they lay and slept while the donkeys licked their toes; "qui dort, dîne"; and in the late heat of the afternoon we returned, keeping up a trot by the simple but fatiguing expedient of swinging alternate legs against the donkey's tummy.

★   ★   ★

I have been enjoying myself rather wickedly with the people of Meshed, the same who wrote to say that they did not wish us there to dig. Having been taken at their word they are sorry and have paid two visits, during which we fence politely. They ask what my plans are. "To stay here," I tell them. "The ruins are important and the people's kindness makes us feel at home." The delegation leaves with a disgruntled air, but still hopes with persistence to retrieve the ground lost by that unfortunate manœuvre.

February 22. "He that blesseth his friend with a loud voice, rising early in the morning, it shall be counted a curse to him."

(Proverbs).

I am one of those fortunate people who can sleep through almost any noise, but my companions, with nights already devastated by pye-dogs, are now awakened in the first glimmer of dawn by the voices of the Children of Muhsin practising the call to prayer from the minaret below. Our Mansab and Qadhi have started a sort of crusade to make the people of Hureidha more attentive to their prayers, and every mosque is now filled five times a day. A road too is being built for cars: it is to sweep from the R.A.F. landing-ground to Hureidha and then on to the temple of the Moongod; the road is made simply by hoeing up hummocks into their original sand and clearing away boulders. All these novelties bring a restless atmosphere of civilization into our little town. The committee of Elders—five sayyids, one from each big house and two to represent the poor and the peasants—are afraid to

184

lose their powers, and difficulties are piling up for our Mansab and his ardour of reform. Reform, here as elsewhere, is expensive; the proceeds from the seizure of the goats have vanished already in the making of the road, and a new tax has been invented for litigants, who are now expected to pay · a dollar each for the settlement of their disputes, which the Qadhi used to do for nothing.

I went down one day to the Diwan when the Council of Elders was sitting and watched the application of the Law. It is a patriarchal affair. Round the walls of a pillared room pierced by seven carved windows, the committee of five leaned on cushions, clicking rosaries. Our Mansab, in one corner, sat cross-legged with a pillow on his knees to write on, an ash-bowl and litter of papers before him, and a large pair of scissors to play with. He has beautiful hands with narrow fingers, slender and square at the tips, nails pink with my varnish, and a gold signet ring. Opposite him, against one of the pillars, sat the Qadhi, explaining the cases to his brother as they came. Three secretaries squatted writing. Between them and the Elders the wall-space is filled with anyone who likes to come, chiefly beduin, and as I entered a litigant was hurling invective at his opponent, an old peasant whose every wrinkle was wrinkled twice over, as he crouched at the foot of a pillar and spoke with both hands held out. When they were dismissed two beduin stepped into their place. One was a fine man, in a striped *futah* with belt and vest and turban, the other poor and naked, with only a dirty cloth to tie his old grey hair; when his opponent laid a new gun before the Mansab (each litigant deposes something of value while the case is tried) he could only take an inferior dagger, much handled, from its shabby sheath.

He had not come prepared for the new rule about the dollar, and when he was asked, and saw the other pulling out a fat leather bag, a look of such misery came upon his face that I was just about to go bail for him when the case was postponed and both told to return to-morrow.

It is not a bad system. The Mansab's decisions are final and personal, but the Qadhi is there to see that they accord with the Law. As everything is done in public there is a strong control of opinion, and the listening Elders do not hesitate to say what they think. The feeling was pleasant, democratic and friendly. The news of the district came in rolls and wisps of paper tied with very grey bits of calico: news that the young American in his journey had reached Sur and spent two days there: that a Qadhi has been nominated for 'Amd: that the Archæologist must call for a registered packet in Mukalla, arrived nearly a month ago. (She has been expecting it for weeks; it is rather hard now to be asked to fetch it in person 200 miles away.)

While we were in the middle of it all, a banging of drums and a chorus were heard in the street below and all the Elders bent their portly forms to the ground-level of the windows and looked out. It was the workmen coming home after finishing the new bit of the road. They were headed by the fat cook, who came up to report with a new green turban on, and the Comic, his assistant, beside him. The road was described, the Elders asked questions, the Mansab gave the workmen the blessing of Allah; with mutual congratulations the employers parted from their employees, and the drum and its chorus were heard receding. The morning's diwan was at an end.

A pilgrimage on horse-back

February 23.   "*To turne and winde a fierie Pegasus.*"
                                                    (*Henry IV.*)

Sayyid 'Aluwi and I have been on pilgrimage to the tomb of a saint in the hills; it is on the way to Rakhiya and is known as the Wali Rukheime. No one can tell his origin; they say he belongs to pre-Islamic times, the times of "the first ones," and that, when the saint died, "the earth opened and he buried himself with no one's help, his sword and his servant beside him."

The Mansab of Meshed lent his two horses for the expedition, and I set off thoughtlessly at a trot at 7.45 a.m. 'Aluwi following with cries. When he caught up he informed me that he had never ridden before, and I watched with some concern while he wrestled with the difficulties of his horse, his loincloth—an inadequate garment—and the flimsiness of a calico skull-cap on the hottest day we have had. If he were not the most amiable and placid of men, his temper must have given out. As it was, the irritation was confined to his horse, the grey with henna spots, who foamed and zigzagged at a gallop while 'Aluwi did things with the bridle one could hardly bear to look at. He was luckily hemmed in by the landscape, hills on one side and sand-dunes on the other, and went like a shuttle between them. The sand-dunes have a steep western pitch on whose brow 'Aluwi would hesitate, faintly and reluctantly reminiscent of Olympia, with the same unhappy but amiable expression of surprise repeated every time before he trotted hopefully up the easy eastern slope of the next. He is an optimist.

We came to a charming Arcadian sort of country, plantations of 'ilb trees in sunk fields, and then turned north into the wadi, with Ruweidat village on our left. A fort with

187

four round ruined towers stands at the gate of the valley
and beyond it one enters on a wide and stony amphitheatre
inlaid with gravels; ravines, like stairs descending, open to it
from the jōl. In this shadowless place, scattered with flints,
marked by a few pale samr trees meagre and grey, and camels
browsing between their vicious thorns, the tomb of the saint
lies beside a lime-washed building and rough siqaya, and shines
white in the solitary meeting-place of wadis. It is shaped like a
mummy-case with a lump for a head, and about fifteen feet
long. These gigantic tombs are scattered over the Hadhramaut and are said by the people, probably truly, to date from
times before. Islam. This one is on an ancient route that
crosses to Wadi Rakhiya and the main Hadhramaut track by
Shabwa to Yemen; traces of a built causeway are said still to
exist along it: it is a short cut which avoids the Kasr detour
for travellers making northward from 'Amd.

The one-roomed building that stands beside the tomb and
the siqaya has two doorways opening south and north. Its
rough stick ceiling is supported on tree-trunk pillars, and
small thick shuttered windows open near the ground. A
strip of black matting, a coffee hearth with coffee pot and cups
in a basket, an incense burner carved in stone: and on the
walls drawings of horned ibex very like those found by Sir
Aurel Stein on Chalcolithic pots: such is the furniture of
the shrine. It is a humble place, with an air of cheerful and
secure sanctity about it: for none would steal its poor
possessions, which are guarded by the saint himself: and the
beduin will deposit their treasures here when they go on a
journey and find them safe on their return. A friendly
bedu had brought us a goatskin of water from the village
and hung it on a peg for our use: he held our horses in

the sun while 'Aluwi and I ate eggs and raisins inside. It was his duty, he said, to keep the saint's siqaya filled for the use of travellers.

When we left the valley of stones, we made at a canter through the hot sandy air, across the flatness of our wadi for home; we had ridden for nearly five hours altogether, scarcely ever at a walk, and my little Java pony had not a fleck of lather on him; he can go, at his half-canter, the whole day long. When one dismounts and throws the bridle on his neck, there is no need to hold him: he turns his head in a friendly way at the sound of one's voice. I have now sent Qasim to buy two measures of millet in the village, to give the horses a feed; their usual meal is only millet stalks, and it is because of the difficulty of feeding them that so few are kept in this country. As for 'Aluwi's grey, it came home white with lather from exasperation rather than fatigue: and it was not nearly so tired as its rider.

* * *

The news that the road to the coast is open was premature. Three only of the four Humumi tribes have surrendered, and the runner whom the young American sent for letters spent three hours in a hole on the jōl on the Du'an track, trying to escape the fate of his predecessors, whose mail-bag the tribesmen burned. He is an old man, with a small white wedge of a beard and a knitted sports cap, and came last night with a lantern in his hand through the uneven streets, hoping for a tip. But he brought us no letters, owing to some mistake of the people in Mukalla, and as we have been waiting a week for him, we parted in mutual disappointment.

The Diary, Hureidha

February 25.   *"Illae continuo saltus silvasque peragrant*
                 Purpureosque metunt flores et flumina libant."
                                                    (Georgic IV.)

In a village among the palm groves lives the keeper of
bees, in a square mud house of many stories pitted with loop-
holes for defence (*mishwaf*, look-outs, they call them) by
which the bees fly in and out. By dark low stairs one climbs
to the roof where they have their tunnels built of mud, and
shallow water trays conveniently fitted with studs of iron
for their tiny quivering feet: they see their pasture lands,
the samr, palm and 'ilb trees, spread in the wadi below, and
flit over the parapet in the sunlight. The bee-keeper's
grandchildren run naked in and out among them: it is a
happy little aerial world.

I passed there on my way as I went to dig tufa fossils for
Alinur by the pool in the ravine. I took Sa'id to hammer
them out, a dark meskin or peasant, immensely strong, with
little cheerful eyes, and a crowbar and great hammer on his
shoulder. In the village below, our beduin greeted us as
friends and joined us; a woman there was beating henna
leaves to powder in a stone mortar beside the well in the shade.
The boy Hasan led Daqiq, the donkey that answers to its
name. As we climbed the scree he told me his family affairs
and how his father has now remarried his mother, long ago
divorced. Forty-four other wives, which is the traditional
number of a centipede's legs, have diversified the interval.
He is an old, old man to look at, and wears a yellow
gown, and is a poet with a reputation for holiness, and
I see him now and then walking with a meditative air
heightened, no doubt, by all the female complications he has
known.

Breaking tufa

"Your mother must be glad to come back to you?" I said to Hasan.

"Yes," said he casually. And then added with a note of real warmth: "She is *clean*: she has cleaned the house."

He then told me about the other forty-four: "But now," he concluded, "my father does not trouble about their looks. He only likes them if they can keep the house clean." There is a touch of the patient Griselda in this story.

In the shadow of the ravine, we spent the day smashing tufa boulders, trying to do as little damage as possible to the delicate leaves and stems that lie embedded in their heart. The beduin are quick—they understood in no time what was required; but it took longer to persuade Sa'id the peasant to go gently with his clumsy tool. He lifted his iron with both hands and, as he dropped it, growled to let the breath out of his body; the two sounds rang back from the high buttress cliffs around. Camels grazed in the ravine, stretching their long necks to the boughs of trees, their bodies the exact colour of the rock, both in sun and shade; they looked like primitive drawings against that ancient background. When our boulders were split, and a number of manageable pieces collected, I sent for one of these camels to carry them home, saw them packed in flat saddle-bags woven with palm leaves, and watched them down the steep scree slopes, borne with that look of aloofness which camels seem to acquire without any education at all.

As we ambled home through the evening, friendly wayfarers came up to say there were letters from Mukalla: "A letter from your Mother, if God wills." From the tops of the female palms, which men fertilize with spathes, greetings were called. A golden light was spread in the evening air.

A bedu overtook us with a bough from the incense tree, (*Boswellia Carteri or Bhuadajiana*) sent for from the jōl for my companions to see; its crinkled leaves, rather like ash with frilled edges, were drooping, its bark flaking off, but the milky frankincense dripped from its veins.

When I reached home, I found eight people to see me, among them an old man who came for medicine for himself, his wife and his son of ten (remarkable at his age). It took Qasim's and my united efforts to make him distinguish which was which, and he will probably wash himself with Epsom salts and feed his wife on permanganate.

And when we had done with him, Sayyid 'Aluwi was waiting to say farewell: he goes back to Mukalla by Du'an, the only open way across the jōl. His brother Husain, who married a fortnight ago, is now divorcing and going back to the wife he left, to the joy of all except the latest bride. It is his third wife and fourth wedding.

February 26.   "*At all events my name will remain.*"
               "*Inscribe it on a stone and it will remain just as well.*"
                                                    (EPICTETUS.)

My cave is not to be dug. The Archæologist went up to it and finds it too big and the inscriptions, not worth photographing.[1] She has now started another cave and we shall have had seven weeks of excavation if we leave, as we still hope to do, on the 5th of March. She has had to lose five weeks altogether through illness and even now is not well enough to face happily the insidious microbes of

---

[1] The inscriptions, however, turned out to be interesting because of their calligraphy and have been published by Professor Ryckmans in *Museion*, Vol. 52, parts 3 and 4 and in the Journal of the R. Asiatic Society for July, 1939.

Learning : luncheon : divorce

this dust, but there is a heroism about her, which carries her successfully where softer natures fail. Even Sayyid 'Ali, elastic under snubs, whose virtues, such as they are, have nothing of rigidity about them, recognizes this harder metal when he sees it.

"Her learning is great," he told me: "and learning must be honoured."

* * *

Alinur and I lunched with our Mansab to-day in a carpeted room which seemed luxurious after our draughty bareness. He was waiting at the bottom of his long whitewashed staircase to lead us by the hand, scented and immaculate as ever, but dressed in Italian colonial khaki with a blouse effect at the back. His colleague from Meshed in a clean white gown, various sayyids and a Nahdi bedu from Henin were sitting there, and we heard the news of the young American who, also laid low with fever, has had to return to the civilized comforts of Seiyun. When our lunch, cooked by Qasim, was over, I climbed the many stairs to the harim next door and saw my patient's foot, its sores now red and fairly healthy with freshly-flowing blood. For the first time in two years the old lady has been able to stand on it, and I came away happy, not only because of the misery eliminated by a little permanganate of potash, but also because the credit of Ferangi medicines stands or fails in Hureidha with the Mansab's mother's foot.

The only other excitement of the day is Ne'ma, who has, it appears, been divorced yesterday morning, and has taken it to heart in a surprising degree considering how she carries on with Qasim. I had in fact thought her divorced long ago, but it seems that that was only partial.

"Now," she says, "it is finished, and I grieved all yesterday; but to-day it is over."

"I hope it will be a good husband next time," said I.

"Inshallah," said Ne'ma.

*   *   *

Alinur has found four berries among her fossil leaves and hopes they may identify the tree. Great palm fronds petrified appear in the heart of her split boulders; she chips them delicately out with a chisel.

February 27.   *"For there was shed*
                 On spirits that had long been dead,
                 Spirits dried up and closely furled,
                 The freshness of the early world."
                          (MATTHEW ARNOLD.)

The beduin of Bahr, who turn out to be related to those Murshidi of Kor Saiban who call my friends the Ba Surra their "Father," said that there is an inscription and another pool in a valley to the south. I showed them some pre-Islamic letters from the temple and asked if the inscription were like that; they looked dubious, glanced about till their eyes fell on a packing-case marked *Shell*, and told me eagerly, that *that* was the writing on the rock. But it isn't. It is pre-Islamic, rough letters smeared with red ochre on the shelving overhang of a great boulder which has rolled to the valley bottom from the cliffs: opposite, a track leads up the 'aqaba through rocky gateways to the jōl, and that is a short way by Redet ed-Deyyin to Bir 'Ali. Many of these inscriptions appear to be at the branching off of tracks.

The valley runs a long way back, in a southerly direction, empty of villages beyond Shujjeira where the beduin live.

Rocks and pools

It is open and feathered pleasantly with trees, and camels graze there, and the deep seil-bed carries its gravels to meet the seil-bed of Wadi Nissim and flow towards Hureidha together. We turned up a side valley to the left, towards the pool Samu'a. Sa'd, the bedu, led us, walking with lovely freedom, his black rag like a cloak over his shoulders, a kid for lunch bleating confidingly on top, the thermos in his hand. He has a most engaging smile and light-green eyes, and all these beduin are plump, not fat but well covered: their muscles ripple as they move.

On flat ground a little beyond our inscription, we left Daqiq, the donkey, and began to climb under the huge overhang of cliff. The waters, when they flow, drop here from ledge to ledge into cathedral shadows; they have worn round pits in the limestone, where trees find coolness and grow among huge fossil shells one foot or two feet long that lie about clumsily convoluted, petrified remnants of the forgotten sea.

The ledges recede in tiers and the second holds in its recess a dark pool full of fish, cool in the shadow of the wind-hollowed cliff above. But the tufa rocks are beyond, on the highest step below the jōl; to reach them one must climb barefoot by smooth-lipped little hollows that scale the lime-stone wall. The four beduin gambolled here like goats, carrying my camera, carrying my shoes, seizing my hand in difficult places, until we reached the third ledge and saw there, enclosed and warm, a small mirror of water, peopled at its shallow end with rushes in the sun. Two trees with leaves like those of the fossil trees drooped over it, and at its far end, like a barrier, built in the slowness of time by the waters of spring, was a block of tufa, green with maidenhair. In this cloistered place, seen only by the beduin and the sun, wild palms, and twelve various sorts of shrubs and trees were growing; small limpets lived on the rocks, and the surface of the water was scattered with tiny things, cuirassed like polished steel, who pushed themselves about in a world so remote that man himself, one felt, was but a new intruder.

He looked at home however. Sa'd was already squatting, grinding the salt for our kid between two stones, while another bedu used the white smooth limestone floor to paste our flour for bread. Under the tree, in the shade, on a boulder, two beduin and a boy roasted a scaly-tailed lizard (*dhabb*) which the boy had caught below. They roasted it in its skin, and brought me the tiny liver and sweetbreads and a bit of tail, which tasted as good as chicken: the rest they divided and gave the boy who had caught it the head as his rightful spoil. "We are friends now," they said, as we finished this hors d'œuvre.

On the same boulder, with wood from a misht tree, they built a fire, set in a circle of stones. The kid, carried inside a poor little bundle made up of its own skin, was stitched into suitable pieces with shivers of palm. The wood burned, the blackening stones fell flat upon it and made a floor for the sizzling meat to rest on, while the bread cooked round the edge. When it was done, and the pieces evenly divided in heaps, the guests handed their daggers to Sa'd; he, with the bunch over his head and without seeing, laid them at random on the divided portions and each man took the meat that fell to his lot.

"On a feast day," said Sa'd, "we build these hearths on our house-tops so that the smoke goes up into the sky." And such, no doubt, were the hearths of Cain and Abel. We, in our easy lives, have forgotten how natural it is to combine religion with food. Here at any rate, in our meal, there was nothing that could not have been just as easily prepared with the flint knives of prehistoric men.

And when we had eaten, and climbed down the buttresses of the jōl to the middle pool below the upper ledge, the beduin fished in the afternoon sun. They held a shawl with crumbs outspread under the surface till the curious fish came floating above it and were slowly, very slowly, lifted out. The green, paint-like water rippled behind the men's shoulders; they glowed warm and brown through the indigo skin; they worked like the world's first inhabitants at their light-hearted toil.

When we left the pool they dropped me from the ledge by my wrists, with a bedu to secure my feet below, inspiring no great security considering their small foothold and the drop. On the lower ledge a circle had already gathered for medicine and talk; a bundle of grass and misht boughs, collected for their camels and Daqiq, were given me as a pillow. Shepherdesses of the black-and-white flocks came to join us with small axes in their hands and fish in their high hat-crowns, and sat to build their fire. One of them was prettier than the rest. "We brought her from the Samuh of Kor Saiban," the beduin said, as if she had been some sort of communal possession.

These beduin are socialists without knowing it; in their small communities, losses and gains affect them all. They were pleasant to talk to; their art of conversation has been elaborated through many summer afternoons spent in the shadows of rocks. It had the charm which comes to people who observe and do not merely copy; their similes spring vivid and racy from their lives. "The eye of a cock," they said of a small shiny stone; and the boy, when he held up his lizard in a languishing attitude in his hand, said: "See how it sits like a bride." The great ledge arched over us like the tier of a theatre; only a vertical strip of sky, narrow as a meander of spilt milk, was visible between the ravine's high walls: we discussed the place in a detached way as a refuge from bombs, and decided that we should be safe where we sat.

In the hot sun, at 2 p.m., we descended, found Daqiq on the lower level, and rested in the shadow of another boulder while he ate his grass: stopped in the village a moment to talk to Sa'd's mother, adorned with blue tattoo and saffron-coloured with turmeric from head to toe as far as one could see: and are home now with the Rip van Winkle feeling of one who has stepped from an earlier into a later Time.

March 1.   *"Stone walls do not a prison make,*
                  Nor iron bars a cage."
                                    (LOVELACE.)

The last of the Humumi rendered themselves up on Friday and the road is to be opened to-day. Our strange remote confinement is at an end. No difference is made in our visible lives, but the feeling of prison is gone, and with it also the feeling of safe separation, a pause and a stillness of time. I can imagine how one might throw a lingering glance of regretful affection as one leaves the quiet of a cell.

'Ali brought this excellent news last night, together with an immense bag of mail, the accumulation of weeks, and all the gossip of the valley, including that of the visit of Lord Dufferin and Sir Bernard Reilly to Seiyun. These excitements have come and gone and no ripple has reached Hureidha. We, on the other hand, have just escaped being involved in a new little war in our district, because Sultan 'Ali's governor in Haura, a few hours' ride away, was roughly spoken to by a Nahdi tribesman in court. He sent five of his men to follow and kill him, but they were luckily intercepted by the son of the Mansab of Meshed, who happened to be in the street. The Nahdi was able to escape, and the trouble of a blood feud is avoided.

The other news is that our lorry will come on the 5th to carry all away, and I shall start a day earlier, so as not to be late for the rendezvous at Cana, for there is little enough time as it is for an overland journey.

*   *   *

I took Alinur for another good day at Samu'a, to what she too thought the loveliest of hidden sanctuaries, climbing in her stockinged feet. She aroused respectful affection in the heart of the beduin, who had doubted her being able to reach the upper pool; but we did not sling her back down the ledge. The pool, she says, was once a lake whose lower fringe finally broke with the weight of water and let the torrents through. But how the fish got there not even she, with all the resources of geology at her disposal, can explain.

*   *   *

I have spent a meandering day taking last pictures in the town with the Qadhi, who read out the carved inscriptions of the tombs, and standing with upturned palms while he chanted his prayer for the dead, smiled in his gentle way as I said "Amen."

We examined the door of his house, which is the oldest in Hureidha, about 300 years old. It is two inches thick, made of 'ilb wood, eaten by the sun, and further strengthened by horizontal bars; a wooden bolt lets down into the floor, another one of iron drops from above, and beside the usual wooden lock there is a huge bolt held by a carved latch and a small, particular bolt to lock the hole made for the hand to pass through from outside. "My beloved put in his hand by the hole of the door," says the Song of Solomon.

We then inveigled the Mansab into his green coat, with yellow ribbon like an order over his shoulder, a blue turban and yellow shawl on his head, and so photographed him on the threshold of his house. There we lingered and discussed antiquities, and particularly the Cufic inscription said to have been found in the old mosque, dating it to the days of Husain Salama, the great Yemeni, in A.H. 315 (A.D. 927). This relic has unfortunately disappeared. The Mansab went on to tell me of the pre-Islamic words still used, especially by the women, in Hureidha: *shatata* for moon, *qaqa* for dates, *dada* for bread; whether they are Himyaritic or not, they sound peculiar. Having exhausted the wonders of the past, we reverted to our own modern coils, and discussed Sultan 'Ali of Qatn, whose agitations, the Mansab now admits, are all of Italian origin.

"I dislike the Italians," said he, "though they are always ready to do anything I ask. But one knows the reason for that." And we left them and their distasteful politics to discuss the more congenial topic of the ancient habitations of the Children of 'Ad.

"There is a place," said the Mansab, "called Wād, mentioned in the Quran in the chapter of Daybreak as the home of the Beni Thamud. It is somewhere in Hajr, I do not know where, and they say there are ruins beside it."

"I will look for it," I said, "when I go."

The Wadi Hajr is a legendary place altogether. Old Abdulla, the watch-mender, has ridden to Bir 'Ali by that way in ten days and tells me that the Wadi Hajr once belonged to a king called Be'be', who sent for one thousand virgins from Somaliland across the sea; they were all shipped in a sambuq, but when they reached the Arabian coast it was discovered that every one of them was pregnant. So they were sent up into Wadi Hajr, to do the best they could, and the population there, said old Abdulla, is still quite peculiar, neither African nor Arab, and their hair stands straight up.

March 4.   *"Welcome ever smiles*
                And farewell goes out sighing."
                            (Troilus and Cressida.)

To-morrow I start over-land west and down to the sea through what was once the old Incense Route. To-day the Archæologist has decided that she cannot meet me at Cana after all; so now there is no certainty of a boat at the far end of the journey. Had I known I would probably not have arranged to go, for the low-lying roadsteads of Arabia are unhealthy places to arrive at.

*   *   *

There has been one last little flutter over Sayyid 'Ali and the workmen's luncheons. The shopman appeared with an unpaid bill long overdue, but begged me not to make the matter public or else, said he: "Sayyid 'Ali will not pay me the other debts he owes."

This was a little difficult. "How can I get him to pay you, without telling him that I know that he owes you something?"

The shopkeeper pondered and admitted reason on my side. "We will leave it," he said: "and I will manage."

He was an ugly man with a squint, and I asked the Son of

Muhsin, who tells me about these things, whether the defect was ever taken to coincide with the evil eye.

"Oh no," said he. "And anyway there are plenty of remedies for the evil eye. You can either spit, or say Mashallah, or—if you can get hold of a piece of the dress or hair of him who has the eye—you can smoke it and pass it three times round in a circle, over an incense burner, for instance. It is quite easy to tackle."

Having dealt with this small matter and done some packing, I spent the rest of the day in farewell visits to the harims of the town, climbing first of all up the many steps that led to the Mansab's mother. Her foot improves day by day, and would have been well by now, but for the cousin who told her that Christian medicines break one's leg, and so caused a month's delay in the beginning.

From the pleasant quiet of her room, I went to the harims of the sisters, all sadly busy snipping the stars and spangles off their gowns. Dressmakers are not allowed to put new ones on, on pain of punishment, and, as we rode along some days ago, our men called out to a gay little bedu girl, walking in festal glitter, and warned her of prison if she went to town. What with the men who have to pray so assiduously, and the women who are allowed no spangles, and the shepherds whose straying flocks are seized, a resentful feeling is stewing in the town.

The melancholy of the harims was enhanced by the sadness of the occasion, the genuine sadness of good-bye after a whole winter spent together. A small snapshot of my mother came in the last mail and the women kissed it when I showed it and rejoiced because three letters at once had come from my home: they stop to congratulate me in the street as I pass

Last farewells

and say how sorry they are to see us go. And now Fatima, sitting and talking of our journey, bursts suddenly into tears; and what words can one find, when one says good-bye for ever? The kohl, as she wept, came streaming down her cheeks, and I too left the room with eyelids wet.

In the house of Muhsin they are too busy for regrets; for they are celebrating Husain's return to his second wife from his third. She looks about sixteen years old, and is dancing with a nervous air of endurance to an assembly of ladies, her pretty silly little face ornamented with orange eyebrows.

And now, when I reach home, the camels are here already on the hillside with the camelmen from Samu'a, and Sayyid 'Ali all prepared to come and protect with the holiness of his presence, and Qasim, lovelorn, with a boil under his arm, quite useless under these two disabilities. We hope to get away early to-morrow morning.

The lorry is to come by then, the packing-cases are all prepared, the tins of food left over—apart from small stores for ourselves—are already stacked in heaps for division among friends.

All this goes on in chaos.

My room, now furnished only with boxes of skulls and its carpet full of holes, looks derelict like a ruin; when everything but my bed is packed and I am resting, a child creeps in, one of the many who slip their hands into ours when we go out for walks. She pulls a saucer out of her blouse and asks for one last gift of Epsom salts for her mother, and when I have given them, suddenly buries her face in my arm and cries out: "Oh, we love you so much, we love you," and flits into the darkness. It is the night's last farewell in Hureidha.

THE JOURNEY

Chapter V

THE JOURNEY BEGINS[1]

"Society is all but rude
To this delicious solitude."
(MARVELL.)

WITH OUR STAY IN HUREIDHA THIS DIARY ENDS. THE OPEN
road begins again and the single-threaded story of travel.

Ever since the Moongod's temple had been disentangled
from the sands, I had grown more and more convinced that
Hureidha never was on the main trade-route of the ancients.
The littleness of the temple, the poverty of all objects we
ever saw or found, compared to other more westerly sites,
showed it to have been a small oasis, living on its gardens
much as it does to-day. The main road probably lay in the
west, through Beihan, and that we could not visit. At the
same time I felt sure that there must have been some sort of
ancient traffic through 'Amd to the coast, just as there is
to-day; and it was in the hope of verifying the vestiges left
there, and judging, as far as I could, of their relative importance, that I decided to travel by camel to Bir 'Ali. This was
not meant to be an exploration: Van der Meulen and
Von Wissmann had already travelled down Hajr, and not

[1] More geographic detail of this journey will be found in the Royal
Geographical Society's Journal, January 1939.

only they, but Doreen Ingrams a year ago, and the young American the other day, had visited 'Amd itself: it was only by accidents and happy chances that my steps were deflected to new country in the west.

At about ten in the morning, in the sunlight, Alinur and I walked down to meet the camels in the town. Everyone was about. The Mansab had called, scented with sandal-wood, pressing both hands in farewell, his eyes full of tears; the Mansab of Meshed had come, affectionate and cheerful; and the Qadhi sat through the last moments, cross-legged on the camp-stool, copying poems in my book. The children came, but little Salim, proud and sorrowful, kept away. Around the camels, struggling since 5 a.m. to get themselves packed, a little crowd had gathered.

Alinur was anxious because of my health, still precarious, and the new vagueness of my prospects on the coast. She would give up Palestine and come to me, she said, if I sent her a runner in Mukalla. Kindness and friendship could go no farther. The three camels drew up, with the Mansab's orange quilt spread as a saddle, and the paraffin lamps brightening the luggage as they swung; and now a new excitement appeared at the opposite end of the street—Abdulillah in the car, and a red lorry behind him all ready for the Scientists to-morrow.

A last delivery of letters, a last crowd of good-byes—I was in the car with Sayyid 'Ali and Qasim, and Hureidha small and brown in the distance behind us. A fat repulsive man, owner of the lorry, had climbed in too. They drove us for a stretch along the loess-like wadi flats, through the tangle of the old irrigation, past the scenes of the winter's labours, till in the silent noonday of the wadi they set us down, waited a little to let me deal with the lorry-driver's efforts at black-mail, and finally departed.

Qasim had forgotten lunch. He had been too busy pouring armfuls of dingy cooking vessels into the receptive arms of Ne'ma. He now sat with tears rolling slowly down his cheeks, his shirt bloodstained from his boil, a distasteful object which it would have been cruelty to scold. I wandered off and left him.

I was *alone*. The first time for months, so it seemed. An immense and silent peace lapped me round. By a little isolated samr tree, its thin lattice of shade a cobweb in the blaze of the wadi, with my head on its warm wrinkled roots, I slept.

Chapter VI

WADI 'AMD

"And it affords some ease
To see, at eve, the smoking villages."
(HERRICK.)

I OPENED MY EYES ON A YOUNG SE'ARI LAD SQUATTING BESIDE
me, a bracelet on his arm and his knife in his hand, the same
whose tribe the R.A.F. has been bombing. He had come, as
many of them do, by the Wadi Rukheime, whose opening
lay just opposite, dusty in the sun; and had been sitting watching my sleep, his curls loose on his shoulders. He looked like
a small, solitary brown animal with soft eyes, and asked me
if Harold belonged to my tribe. In the peaceful heat of the
wadi the samr tree above my head was thrusting out new
leaves between thorns that shone white like daggers in the
sky. There was no sound except faint, far-off puffs of wind
and the hum of a few small flies. A mud-coloured saqiya
stood in the foreground with goats around it; the world
scarce breathed in the noonday heat.

Our camels appeared presently, breasting in their ageless
stride the equally ancient dunes that cover the wadi floor
and its dead gardens. We mounted and rode reclining, the
orange quilt arranged like an armchair round me. The camel
is an ugly animal, seen from above. Its shoulders slope
formless like a sack, its silly little ears and fluff of bleached

curls behind them have a respectable, boarding-house look, like some faded neatness that dresses for propriety but never dressed for love. My camel was called Ibn Mafrush, and wore three spots of henna on its neck: the other two, Qibli and Sa'ada, followed, tied head to tail. You would think that in all these centuries they might have learned to walk of their own accord behind their beduin, but the wretched men still have to lead them by a rope, as they did, no doubt, when they departed down the dusty way that led from the Garden of Eden; and the rope must be held so high that it is tiring. They change at frequent intervals, one coming to take it from the hands of the other with that silent helpfulness of theirs. The wadi stretched around, sand-coloured and unbroken; to our swaying motion the landscape seemed endlessly the same, till, at two-thirty, we turned a sudden corner to the south; a big wadi called Tabra'a opened on the right; and Qarn, two feudal clusters on a hill, showed that we were entering the fortified village landscape of upper 'Amd.

It was still desolate enough, a land of rocks and sun, and we rested to eat in a little husn (fort) called Sinhaj, with not a blade of grass in its mud-walled court, nor any vegetation but a few stunted 'ilb trees in the land around it. The people who sit in this poverty, beating their friendly coffee berries on their hearth, are contented enough, and tell ominous tales of fertile Hajr, where the water is sweet as sugar but poisonous, and the people go about with short loincloths (which I do not mind) and large tummies (which I do, because it means malaria).

Qasim was still weeping over Ne'ma, so copiously that I began to wonder whether the human body contains more water in the tropics than elsewhere. It was time to talk to him for his good and I explained that separations are the will of Allah; and one woman very like another; and when he married a Yemeni girl in Aden he should have our paraffin lamp that he desired. "And now," I concluded, "say your prayers for which you are very late already, and in the name of the Merciful stop weeping into my cup." Whether it was this homily or the natural adaptability of youth I do not know: but he came from his prayers with Ne'ma apparently forgotten and became a gay and excellent servant for the rest of the journey.

In the waning afternoon we rode by beds of gravel in the sun. Great grey banks of them lie here, capped with loess, dividing wadis Hebde and Kebir. The cliffs run in a noble sweep above. And in the dusk we came to fields ploughed and brown, like corduroy velvet, and gardens dyked with walls; and saw Zahir, our little town, growing towards us, a ridge of houses against the sky. The cliffs in straight lines beyond it shone like a stair on whose last step the sunlight lingered. In the dust of the valley amethyst evening tufts of smoke were rising. Shepherdesses trailed home with the patter of their flocks behind them. This is perhaps the best joy of the journey, to come at evening to your unknown resting-place. However many the disillusions you have left behind you, no habit blunts the thrill of this unknown. The little village, swathed in its own life as in a veil, lies waiting there like a bride before you: and one cannot but feel that it is a passion for mystery chiefly which explains the optimism of human beings towards both polygamy and travel.

The whole male population of Zahir was out to receive us, for we had sent our Mansab's letter on ahead. They led us to a dark house on the hill and sat down, about forty of them, round the mud walls of their room, for conversation. This social exertion at the end of the day is, I think, the chief hardship of travel: I bore it for an hour, and then crept dead-tired to sleep, till a straw mat with rice and a kid appeared in my bedroom with 'Ali and Qasim and the headman to share it. Another hour of talk in the guest-room below, a visit to the harim, the luxury of a wash, the last effort to write one's diary, and then the boon of sleep.

*   *   *

It was eight-thirty before we started next morning, already exhausted by one and a half hours of medicines and talk. Even so, I was cross before the packing was done with, and to be cross in Arabia wastes more energy with less result than any other form of self-indulgence. But after this the day was pleasant, a leisurely progress through almost continuous stretches of gardens of 'ilb or palm.

The Ja'da tribe own the whole valley of 'Amd and live here in feudal unity; and attend in peace to their irrigation, which is infinitely more careful than that of Hureidha, though their water is sometimes 75 Qāmas down instead of 45. (The Qāma is the distance between a man's outstretched finger-tips.) At the upper end of their wadis, where the seil torrent rushes in spring, they build their dams, and lead the water off in canals cut for miles along the edge of the slopes. From there it is terraced gently in relays, four or five levels or less according to the width of the valley, till—having watered the gardens and ploughlands—it again reaches the bed of its own stream that runs through the middle of the wadi at its lowest point.

Long dry-walled dykes protect the terraces. In some of

the towns, such as Nafhiun and Nu'air, water runs into deep
rectangular cisterns with rounded corners, lined with mortar,
medieval or ancient as the case may be. Von Wissmann has
written about these cisterns in the Yemen, where they are
still in use from pre-Islamic times:[1] those of Wadi 'Amd,
from the quality of the mortar, are most probably medieval.
The biggest of them, at Nu'air, which is the best-watered
place of the wadi, was 30 metres by 16.6. Its water, like that
of several other places in the valley, was brought not by the
floods, but in conduits from a "gelt" or pool in the ravines:
"A pool," said 'Ali at Nu'air, "twice as big as the one at
Samu'a." The pre-Islamic people may have used conduits
far more than is done now, for there are bits of wooden
troughs, scooped out of tree trunks a foot or so across, still
stuck into inaccessible faces of the cliffs. The men of 'Amd
say they are bee-hives, and brought one to show me from a
high ravine: I think they are more probably conduits for water,
of which the more easily reached portions have naturally
vanished. But I have not seen them in their proper places,
and cannot therefore speak with assurance.

There was a feeling of seclusion about us as we rode. Not
in the landscape itself, for that was lively with men ploughing,
or shepherdesses under the 'ilb trees with their goats; but in
the pastoral quiet life of the valley, remote and self-sufficing,
where stray travellers alone bring news of the world outside.
Even murder here is dealt with in a family way; as we rode
we passed the house where the girl now lives who shot her
father, happily settled with a brother in a decent quiet like

[1] *Vorislamische Altertümer* (Hamburg University): Band 38. Reihe B.
Völkerkunde: Band 19 (Hamburg 1932). Carl Rathjens und H. von
Wissmann, pp. 145 ff.

half-mourning, and anxious only about the possible activities
of Harold and the methods of the West. The towns are
strong and poor, their walls all brown without whitewash,
their windows built small for defence; as we passed one of
them a voice called "Faraya" from its unseen darkness, for
many of the people of 'Amd have seen me in Hureidha; they
come running with welcome, very different from the watchful
looks of those who do not know us, for I am only the fourth
European here. Doreen took the eastern bank by 'Aneq,
but we kept to the west, through Rahm, ditched on its
northern side, by Qudha'a, a watch-tower on a hill, through
Nafhiun of the cisterns, to Sarawa and Rihib, whose pile of
houses is crowned by a castle with four towers. Here in the
open cultivated land we rested at noon for an hour, with a
pleasant temperature, eighty-seven in the shade. 'Ali, thinking to bully me into lunching in a village, brought nothing
for the company to eat; passive resistance on my part and the
remarks of the camel men made him go back to Sarawa in
the sun in search of dates and fodder. The passers-by stopped
on the road beside us, their curly heads tied with cloths like
garlands; they are Se'ari mostly, who come down here to get
food, and use the Persian form *kheir* to ask you how you
are. They are among the ugliest beduin I know, with huge
mouths and bony faces and eyes rather near together. One
of them brought his hookah and passed it round, and made
a pleasant bubbling noise of leisure in the shade.

In the afternoon the land grew more barren, the water and
the cultivated stretches lay mostly on the eastern side, where
the town of 'Aneq, the largest between 'Amd and Hureidha,
lies basking in the sun. As the level shafts slant towards us
from the west, I notice more clearly strange tumuli that line

the scree-slopes of this wadi, more numerous near 'Aneq than elsewhere. They are cairns built, either at the top or bottom of long lines of heaped stones, one cairn, hollow in the centre, at the end of every line. Sometimes there is only the line of stones, without the cairn. They are not necessarily parallel, but they always run down and never across the slope, five or six of them sometimes, radiating like spokes. Perhaps they are tombs? Beyond saying that they belong to the Ancients, and that they were probably meant for shooting from, the beduin have no theories about them. They give to this valley the same sort of feeling one has on Dartmoor, riding between forgotten Druid avenues of stones.

Chapter VII

SICKNESS IN 'AMD

"*Dolce color d'oriental zaffiro*
Che s'accogliea nel sereno aspetto
Dell'aer puro, infino al primo giro,
Agli occhi miei ricominciò diletto,
Tosto ch'io usci' fuor dell'aura morta
Che m'avea contristato gli occhi e'l petto."

(Dante's Purgatorio.)

SAYYID 'ALI IS GENEROUS; HIS ONLY TROUBLE IS A GUILELESS
indifference as to what he is generous with; and the virtues
that come out of someone else's pocket are apt to irritate our
Anglo-Saxon ethics based on property. I share this prejudice,
but with the uneasy feeling that perhaps, when final sums are
drawn, the man who hands his neighbour's pennies to 'the
poor may find an advocate: one cannot deny that civilization
has ever been based on the vicarious use of other people's
lives. Nevertheless it is irritating to be used in the mere capacity
of brick for the building of the edifice of our neighbour's
soul, and all the winter we have suffered. But now, riding
at six o'clock of the evening to the little town of Nu'air
where Sayyid 'Ali belongs, I—as a recipient—was to see his
other side. Already in the *majliss*[1] of Zahir he had come
into his own, holding the village entranced with comic
dialogues. He had omitted lunch both for our camel-men

[1] Guest reception-room.

217

and our camels: but he was obviously used to that, and it sat light as a feather upon him.   Now, as he saw the whole town gathered to meet us by the five great cisterns and the unknown giant's grave beside the little mosque, he gathered himself together with all the dignity of a small but public man.   I watched his cotton skirt and grey jacket and the drab ends of shawl fluttering before me surrounded by compatriots in the dusk.   The best house in the town was borrowed for my reception.   Tower-like and forbidding, the houses of Nu'air rise from the flat ground of the wadi; by fifty-seven steps, up stairs lighted dimly with shot-holes, I climbed to my room, where 'Ali's wife and his children were waiting in a row.

After supper the whole town sat cross-legged round three sides of a court under the stars, while Sayyid 'Ali, the lapels of his jacket gathered neatly under folded hands, addressed me in a speech of welcome whose adjectives, delicately chosen, brought credit not only to me but to those whom I visited.   "The Beloved of Government," said 'Ali, "is with us here to-night."   I thought of Harold, who must just now have heard of my unauthorized departure here into the west, and smiled.   But as a climax to the great evening, I failed.   My poor little speech of thanks wavered unadorned after those florid sentences, and, exhausted beyond the demands of politeness—I soon asked to retire.   The harim still had to be visited, a seething mass of ladies.   Coffee was there being pounded on a raised hearth like a dais by an old slave-woman who at intervals paused in her labours to intone a prayer.   There was then a moment of silence, like a pause between waves.   When I left I was so tired that I thought I could have lain down to die: I was running a fever, I took quinine and discovered that my heart was unable to stand it;

the prospect of a malarial journey into Hajr seemed madness to attempt. With infinite sorrow, when 'Ali came in the early morning, I told him I could not go; he must send the camels back and a runner to fetch a car as far as Zahir, the nearest point to which, it was said, a car could come. I lay quite still in misery, waiting for the beating of the heart to steady itself, thinking how once already I had been frustrated by illness in this land. 'Ali was good, he kept people away, and as the day went on the fever dropped, and I looked at the map. The track to Hajr runs almost due south, over a jōl that has Wadi Du'an on its eastern edge—only a day's ride from our route, so 'Ali said. This was incorrect, but it served its purpose. If I got on to the jōl out of the villages and their endless talk, I might, I thought, recover: and at the worst, I could make shift with a day's ride to Du'an and there find a litter to carry me to the new motor road now building from Mukalla: by this time it must have reached a point not more than two or three days' journey from Du'an. And if I turn back I shall never, I thought, feel mistress of my body again. To be twice defeated was too much. I called 'Ali and Qasim; they both thought it a reasonable plan: a second runner was sent to countermand the car. I spent a day of quiet in bed with only one visit from the headman of the Ja'da, and next morning crawled out to see the sights of the town. It has round wells enclosed in little walls with locked gates belonging to private owners. In seil-time the floods wash right up to the houses, the 'ilb trees have their roots in the air as they have on the banks of streams. The giant's grave is like that of Wadi Rukheime, a long rough heap of stones: but the pre-Islamic slabs around it which they told me of have all disappeared.

Sickness in 'Amd

In the afternoon, full of doubts, on a donkey and with three new camel-men behind me, I set out for 'Amd, only an hour's ride away.

But we were not to reach it that night. As we passed under the battlements of a fortress on a mound, called Hedbet Shamlan, the headman or Muqaddam of the Ja'da himself came out to meet us and, seizing my donkey's head, led me inside. My protests, addressed to him and 'Ali alternately, went merely unheeded. Prestige was in question. In pursuit of it my sufferings, like those of the nations of Europe, did not count.

The headman of the Ja'da was a fine old man. His bare torso tufted with white hairs had the marks of six bullet wounds, shot into it two years ago from the houses across the wadi. Sitting against the dark wall of his guest-room, a red and brown turban on his head, in the dim light of small shot-holes from above, his long face and the venerable tuft of his chin-beard made him look like some Rembrandt patriarch half lost in the shadows of his background. He alone is the real ruler of the Ja'da through all the length and breadth of 'Amd. Elders and chiefs of sub-tribes, as they dropped in, greeted him and settled along the walls beside us. They talked of the slave who is their governor from Mukalla, whom they hate.

"He does not know our customs," they repeated at intervals, "and he takes twice two dollars for every case he tries."

I believe that it is a mistake to send slaves to govern tribes-men.

"You know your own people," said an old man, turning to me. "You know what they like. Are we to send a deputation about this governor to Ingrām, or shall we murder him first?"

Out of general principles I advised a deputation.

"And how is it," they asked, "that in all this time Ingrām has not come to see us?"

"Merely," said I, "because you have no motor road. His time is important, and to come here and back means four days even from Hureidha. It is only we of the Harim, whose time as you know is of no value, who can give ourselves this pleasure. But if he had not liked the thought of seeing you, would he have sent his wife to you last year?"

A murmur of approval greeted this explanation, and the entrance of supper brought the conclave to an end. The Muqaddam's wife stayed. She, with tribal freedom, had been sitting alone among the men, veiling only if some stranger came in, who was not a kinsman, as most of the Ja'da are among themselves. But now, when our meal was finished, a horde came pushing from the narrow stair. All who were sick, or curious, crushed their way through, fierce and good-tempered, unused to denial, unsuitable visitors for a convalescent. After they had gone I lay sick through the night, feebly resentful of 'Ali, who had promised to spare me. When one collapses in Arabia, it is the moral strength that sinks under pressure of too many human beings. In the morning, having dressed with difficulty, I lay fainting at intervals on some sacks in a corner of the room while Qasim packed the bedding. 'Ali, shocked by the sight of me into a passing spasm of repentance, rushed out to find the donkey which the Headman had promised: forgot till he saw me descending, hopeful of departure; and was only roused from the last embraces of his creditors when, outraged beyond the power of words, I led him by the arm and placed him face to face with my donkey, which had at last appeared . . . without a saddle. The two, I felt, could best talk out the matter by themselves.

This was the culminating point of misery. From now onward the gods of travel, perhaps touched by the trust I had shown them, grew kinder. Every evening I noticed, at first with almost unbelieving wonder, that there was no fever to pay for the exertions of the day; until in a week's time, that short and painful nightmare was forgotten.

The donkey—eventually saddled—and my donkey-man and I, having left the camels to their packing, moved through the morning fields, with the high-built houses of 'Amd carefully on our left. We followed the white gravels of the seil-bed, till we came to places bare of gardens, where palms and tillage end beyond a right-hand village called Damhan. Here we soon turned south, passing beside the well-built stones of some pre-Islamic irrigation, possibly a sluice. Beyond it the valley forks, the western branch leads to Jardan, the southern by Wajr into Shi'be, which was to take us to the jōl. Somewhere near here there is the cave of Kanūk, the father of Nebi Salih, in a ravine called Bilghirban. The Van der Meulens had followed a slightly more easterly track, so that I was presumably the first traveller in Shi'be, a pleasant thought in its Arcadian peace.

It is a narrow valley, less than a mile across, but scattered with villages, threaded in their season by ribbons of water, where old canals are dug into the slope. The force of these waters in spring is shown by the great height of the dry-built dams of Shi'be, chief of the little towns. On top of them the causeway runs that leads below the houses. All around is tillage, or palm trees whose tops give a feathery luxuriance to the cliffs behind them. The 'adhab (*Poinciana Elata*) stands tall here, with white and yellow flowers; 'ilb and misht hang park-like over the canals or spill their shadows on the ribbed ploughed earth that waits for rain. Last year for the first time in memory no seil came to feed the fields in spring, and the folk of the wadi had to do with what little was left from before. So all are living now with hungry anxious hope, and if you say to them as you pass, "May your seil be good this year," they cry: "If it please God," with voices that come from their hearts. There is something infinitely touching in these fields, so carefully terraced for rain which may never come, on which their life depends. To believe in a God, who deals in miracles, and to watch him refuse the simple gift of rain, would, one would think, put a strain even on the endless forgiveness of mankind.

The population of Shi'be trailed across their wadi to watch me asleep after lunch in a field, and, when I awoke in a circle of over fifty strangers, introduced me to the son of their Mansab, a gnome-like man on little spindly legs. He had thick black hair fluffed out from a tight head-band, and his face was dyed blue with indigo, which made it pinched and hungry; he looked pathetic and bad from being so small and miserable in himself. He was too timid to invite us, but this was done by a friend, a man with hair parted smooth from the middle in long ringlets and a knot at the nape of the neck, an astonishing Victorian vision to see with one's opening eyes. He had travelled in India and Malay, and answered sharply when someone asked Sayyid 'Ali why he brought Christians to the land.

Nothing, I had felt, should make me enter those dark little

towns again till I was well. But the people of Shi'be possessed a library, and with this inducement led me triumphant up their narrow streets, over the seil-walls that are twelve feet high and under a fortress that hangs above the houses.

The houses are brown and strong; they have a good room with lattices and perhaps a little one for the harim above—all windows else are small for defence, and it is dramatic to see a head come out of one of these openings, just big enough to let it through. Many heads were out to-day, and the roofs, decorated with ibex horns, crowded with women: in the shadow below we moved in the dust of feet, suffocated and weary. And the library was not worth a visit after all; a whitewashed room, it had three little cupboards in the middle carved 140 years ago and very shabby: and they were locked, and the absent Mansab, the father of our small Misery, had the key.

So we left Shi'be, after coffee and a visit to the Harim, and went on to where the valley divides and becomes uninhabited, beyond the village of Radhhain, a four hours' ride from 'Amd. A westerly track there goes off towards Jardan, vanishing into an apparently perpendicular wall of cliff, while the main Wadi Sobale continues south-eastward to the jōl we should visit to-morrow.

In the dry bed of the canal, close to where it takes off from an ancient "damir" or dam, we pitched our camp. A lithab tree (*ficus salicifolia*) hung above with long and pointed leaves; from its boughs my mosquito-net and the guns of the beduin were suspended. The men of Radhhain came after supper—a sophisticated little crowd that talked of cinemas and had learned to read maps in Java. They sat some yards off round the fire while the camels browsed at my feet and the donkey

Under a lithab tree

at my head.   As I lay in bed I could hear Sayyid 'Ali enter-
taining, and the entranced laughter of the company: he was
imitating the sayyids of Meshed, and the voices murmured
on into my sleep; till a shock-headed man, creeping round
my bed for his gun, woke me—the last inhabitant of Radhhain
going home.   I lay then, enjoying the warm delicious night.
A sickle moon was shining; the pointed leaves of the lithab
hung black before it, in Chinese loveliness; a small wind
woke suddenly from nowhere, flapped the leaves against
each other and died as it had come.   The moon sank.   Voices
of foxes echoed in the cliffs—echoed and re-echoed, like some
lost chorus high above the world.   When I woke again it
was to the singing of birds.   The branches, so lovely against
the moon, were the everyday branches of the lithab.   Only
their enchanted memory remained.

Chapter VIII

ROBIN

"Balaam said unto the ass : because thou hast mocked me . . ."
(Numbers: 22.)

MY DONKEY HAD NO NAME, HIS MASTER AHMED TOLD ME, so I called him Robin. I had been charmed to see that Ahmed fed him on dates, sharing his own lunch in equal portions. Now, as I began to know the pair more intimately, Ahmed's attachment to this soulless animal began to show itself for what it was—an obstacle to the whole progress of our caravan.

Everyone knows that a donkey should go faster than a camel; the seven days from Mukalla to Du'an are five days only to an active ass. But this unspeakable Robin knew that he had but to droop his ears and look pathetic, to pause knock-kneed before a boulder perfectly easy to circumvent— his master's heart went out to him, thoughts even of gain were forgotten—if the hillside happened to be moderately steep, I would be asked to walk.

This happened at the very beginning of the 'aqaba of Khurje, by which we climbed from Radhhain in the morning. I had already fallen off once beside the ancient dam, and been held by Ahmed in his agitation firmly pinned among the donkey's hoofs. I had been roused in the earliest dawn by braying when the millet stalks which Robin looked upon as

226

breakfast were accidently rustled by a passing foot. And his lethargy was mere pretence: the sight of a female donkey, even on the far horizon, would set him off with cries, Ahmed hanging to the halter for his life, nearly pulling me off under the obviously inaccurate impression that a donkey and its rider are inseparable.

So I refused to dismount, and we crawled slower and more slowly up the hill with a feeling of coldness between us. Ahmed was a tall angular peasant with high cheek-bones and narrow eyes, and a mild expression due largely to the fact that he had none of those small wrinkles produced by thought. He walked with his head down, asleep to the landscape about him, considering small financial problems in his soul. The peasant and the beduin are two different species. But when I had spent a day wearying of his dullness, I would see him go with his ungainly walk to say his prayers apart, or watch him spreading the millet stalks with an air of tenderness before the indolent Robin, and would feel ashamed when I considered how these endless small sums of his were devoted to the support of three orphan relatives besides his wife and daughters and two sisters—burdens accepted without murmur or repining. I would feel ashamed but I would also observe how the accumulated efforts of Christianity have failed to make us enjoy the sight of mere virtue unadorned, for the fact is that Ahmed was quite unattractive.

Far different was Awwad of the Deyyin who was leading us to his castle on the jōl. Black-bearded with a large, lascivious mouth and always cheerful, he had come as far as 'Amd partly to meet us, partly to arrange for a third wife, since the second one says the work is too hard and wants to leave him. Apart from the difficulty of providing funds for this

227

transition, which was still rather problematical, Awwad's head was not troubled by finance: freer than a millionaire from its problems, he was able to concentrate on pleasant things when they came—the cooking of a sheep for dinner, or the brewing of tea in the shade. Now, at 6.40 a.m., with the sun pouring in to the Wadi Sobale as if it were a cup, he led the way up a zigzag track where smooth milky stones laid neatly still show an antique causeway to the pass.

They have remained intact in a protected place, sheltered from winds and landslides by the cliff: and where the cliff breaks away in a perpendicular tower, the causeway creeps behind it, through a tunnel in whose semi-darkness lies a smooth block of limestone, with pre-Islamic letters scratched upon it, sign of an ancient roadway to the sea. It was the first *certain* pre-Islamic object since Hureidha. The cleft was made, said 'Ali, by the sword of a saint of Islam.

"Do you imagine he wrote the Himyaritic letters?" I asked.

'Ali looked at me nonplussed for a moment. Then he laughed with his usual generosity, admitting defeat. "Nothing escapes the English," said he.

Our camels lumbered by, their quarters gigantic in the shadows: a few hundred yards on, an hour from the bottom, we broke by a chasm into the white sunlight of the jōl.

Into the thin and clean reviving air. Over the edge, far down, Wadi Sobale pursued uninhabited windings between gnarled cliffs. But over the plain a silver mistiness made every distance gentle in the sun: our journey lay flat and far and visible before us, flanked, like an avenue, by brown truncated mounds. Flints of palæolithic man lay strewn here, glistening on the ground; and I thought of the Archæologist with a gleam of warmth; grateful for the

Reception by the Deyyin beduin

pleasure of now recognizing these small and intimate vestiges of time.

Awwad the bedu rejoiced at being out of the lowlands and encouraged us with fallacious distances. Three hours, he said, would bring us home. We therefore rode gently through the morning, leaving on our left hand the track to Du'an. I had decided to push on for the south.

The jōl was dry as a bone: the water-holes we passed were waterless; two years had gone by without rain. At eleven-twenty-five we dipped into a valley, the head of Wadi Zerub.

The charm of all the western jōl lies in these shallow valley heads where, just below the upper rocky rim, rain-water collects and trees are sheltered from the wind. A few solitary towers, or small fortified villages stand there, surrounded by thinly scratched fields. In the distance, on our left, we could see several of them as we rode—Berawere and Berire, fair-sized clusters, belonging to sayyids. Through them ran the Van der Meulen's track to Dhula'a, a tiny market town. That was the main way for caravans to Hajr; but we, led by Awwad, kept to the west among the Deyyin beduin, and rested till three-thirty at Zarub, under the shadow of their 'ilb trees. Three little forts stood up and down the pastoral low valley, and the few inhabitants, friendly and wild and shy, stood in a fringe around. The men talked and accepted us as guests of the Deyyin—but a young woman, advancing carelessly and seeing me of a sudden, stood petrified with fear. The whole party, hers and our own, urged her on, saying that I would not bite, or words to that effect, and she finally came gingerly, touched my hand with frightened fingers, and fled to safety. She had five wild little children about her, and a brass-bound girdle at her waist. It is strange to feel that one is a monster. The children looked at me with solemn interest, then turned their heads, weeping, to their mother. Only the smallest accepted me, not having reached the age of understanding; it lay in a leather cradle, with leather fringes and a leather top to cover it, head and all: its mother carries it, slung like a basket on her arm; and when she has to labour in the fields, erects a tripod of three sticks from which it swings. These women are unveiled, small and sturdy like their men; they look as if their families went back to the beginnings of time. Their tiny, solitary villages must be very old, with careful pebble-lined half-empty ponds.

At three-thirty, rested and happy, I noticed that Awwad's perpetual optimism seemed ruffled: he was chafing to be off.

"But," said I, "we must be quite near. You said three hours this morning and here we have been riding for three and a half already on the jōl."

"Ah, well," said Awwad, "it is not very far."

"Shall we get there by sunset?" I asked. When it is impossible to get exactitude even for the present, it is simply waste of time to wrangle for it in the past.

"If we hurry, we may," said Awwad doubtfully.

We still had, I found, two valley ravines to dip into—Mlah, and Sobale, our wadi of the morning. They were delightful places, with the charm of things which live for their own pleasure, serving no utilitarian end of man, like the loveliness of childhood, free of conscious purpose. These cradles of valleys had the same innocent happiness about them. The waters had scooped them with a rush and left visible traces as one scrambled from ledge to ledge, undercut by the violence of the past. Little tufts of wild palm grow there and a great variety of shrubby trees, that keep their branches low, not to emerge into the wild currents that sweep the jōl above. You go steeply down and steeply up the other side, and the slow-footed camels take their time; and, in a blank space of the map, the existence of these ravines makes it impossible to guess even roughly how long a journey will take across the jōl. I was finding it just double what I had been told.

Awwad was anxious now, and tried to urge Robin and the unresponsive Ahmed with unavailing words: lengthening blue shadows began to lie to the east of every mound. In the emptiness a curly-headed lad from 'Azzan had appeared, flapping in sandals made of a ragbag of leathers stitched any-how. I have read somewhere that the people of 'Azzan wear these to brush away scorpions from their path. How-ever this may be, the young lad adopted us and took matters in hand. He trotted singing behind Robin, with a sharp stick in his hand: Robin understood. Awwad and a black cousin of his, with guns upon their shoulders, joined the chorus. Robin trotted, while his master sloped behind us begging the company in vain "to have a heart." I laughed; even Robin enjoyed it; the jōl now was flat as a landing-ground with limestone snouts pushed here and there along it. The sun dipped and blackish clouds sailed from the east with spots of rain. At this moment we came to an edge and saw Romance in the varied light of evening—a little castle, walled and towered, in an island of 'ilb trees gilded by slanting shafts of sun. The long barrow of Awwad's Himyaritic ruins was there beside it; two more towers among trees on the left; and on the southern horizon, improbable as some medieval background, a cluster of five towers, the fortress of Hajlein.

As we climbed down the blocks of limestone Awwad's baby son toddled in the path to meet us: his father picked him up on to the shoulder that had no gun. The little family of the castle were at the gate. The place looked poor and bare when we drew near, but strong, built of small jōl stones laid flat and stuck with mud, the central keep with battlements crowned with brush wood, and brushwood also round the outer wall: inside it were pens built with low roofs for cattle.

The only two women of the place, the precarious bride and a sister, took me by the hand up shallow slabs of steps to the guest room in the keep—a good room, old and black and low. Its door was carved, its small windows one foot by eight inches shuttered with thick blocks, the ceiling sustained by a tree-trunk column. The men hung their guns and cartridge belts on pegs about the walls. Two palm mats and two black strips of goatwool were all the furnishing, except a hearth for coffee dug in the earthen floor. Here a bedu soon sat down with husks in a mortar, and beat with an alabaster pestle picked from the ruins nearby. His hair, with a fillet bound around his brow, flared out above his shoulders, his big nose and thin mouth made him look like some medieval page. The smoke from the fire curled through a hole in the ceiling. The restless wind, pushing against the tower, as the darkness fell showed the wisdom of small windows. When the camels were tethered and my bed made in one corner, our party gathered here—'Ali and Qasim, three camel-men, Ahmed and the lad from 'Azzan with the men and women of the fort in a circle. They talked, and spat at intervals on to the middle of the floor. On the outer edge Awwad's small son rolled about playing with a toy—a tin bucket with Charlie Chaplin stamped in gaudy colours. Awwad did not know where it came from. "Is it a man or a woman?" he asked, "or *what* is it?" Apart from my bed, it was the only touch of Europe in our sight.

Chapter IX

THE HIGH JŌL

"The myriad hues that lies between
Darkness and darkness."

(RUPERT BROOKE.)

LIGHT, LOVELY AND GAY, SHONE ON THE WORLD WHEN I OPENED my shutters next morning. The south wind, so hot in the wadis, blew with a freshness of spaces about it, and a nip. The goats were out—all black, the white kind seem not to inhabit the jōl. The small tilled fields, and the limestone threshing floor, lay flat and shining in the sun.

The two sisters-in-law came to see me as I finished dressing, and brought Awwad's first wife. She had walked over from Zarub, a sad-faced but pleasant woman who might have been his mother, with a ring with silver beads threaded through one of her orange nostrils. Their made-up eyebrows give these beduin a curiously sophisticated look. They wear dark clothes woven at Hauta in Hajr or at Gheil Ba Wazir on the coast. They had never seen a European, and sat enraptured, looking at all my things, until I gave the younger wife my mirror, which she hovered over, torn between her longing and the reluctance to take something from a guest. She accepted at last, and came at intervals through the day with offerings, first her poor little silver nose-ring and then with an egg in her hand.

233

It was pleasant to feel that the day and its leisure were ours to play about with, for we had not far to go, and the whole morning could be devoted to the ruins. The long mound, flat as a table, lies opposite the fort.

On top of it stands what was once, I believe, a pre-Islamic mausoleum[1]: it is a small square building of stone slabs, neatly cut, and roofed also with flat slabs of stone. The lowness of the ceiling, and the small size, show that it was no human dwelling place; it is divided into three by two partitions, and the whole thing is less than nineteen feet square. Three cairns of rough stones are piled at the far end of the mound, about five feet high and hollow like those of 'Amd, but with no stones leading towards them; and, in the western slope below, two graves had been washed bare by rains and ruined by the beduin. They were different from the graves near Hureidha, and indeed from any found in the Hadhramaut hitherto, for they were single chambers built square with roughly dressed stones into the hill, and closed by slabs that ran in grooves of stone. Trinkets—two bronze rings, cornelian beads and a potsherd or two, had been found inside them and the mutilated remains of an inscribed slab lay buried in debris close by. The slab is written in the Hadhrami dialect and commemorates the renovation of the tomb for someone who was to be buried inside it; this, of course, I did not know at the time, but I thought that the place was probably a general burial ground and that more might be discovered if one dug. The beduin had done so

[1] For this and all other antiquities visited on this journey see my article in Royal Asiatic Society's Journal, July 1939. Professor G. Ryckmans, of Louvain, gives texts and notes on the inscriptions in the December (1939) number of *Museion*, Vol. 52 parts 3 and 4.

much damage already that I was careful to let out no word of these surmises, but confined myself to expatiating on the advantages they might have got out of their site if only they had left it untouched. It was a gloomy theme and after scrabbling over half the hillside in search of more inscriptions we turned mournfully back to our tower. When we had lunched there, Awwad took me up to the battlements where, under the brushwood, I saw a poor orphan girl whom he keeps in charity. "She is subject to fits on Fridays," he said, and asked if I could send some medicine; "even if it costs money," he added touchingly—and who can say more than that?

Near four of the afternoon we left the tower of Suwaidat, and rode for an easy hour to that of Madhun, which stands on the same lowland basin draining to Sobale north-west. Awwad came too; he would bring us, he said, to Yeb'eth, beyond the Deyyin boundary. With his gun on his shoulder he trotted beside me. Hajlein on our right hand shone in the light; its five battlemented towers had turrets on their tops.

"One tenth of the biggest tower is mine," said Awwad; and went on to tell the story of his grandfather's sister, who was being carried off from it against her will when the ravisher was overtaken and killed.

"Did you make sure that it was against her will?" I asked.

"It didn't matter," said Awwad.

Around us as we rode, pre-historic flints glittered like small mirrors—only those worked by man shine when they are caught by the sun.

The chief lord of the fortress, with a few relatives beside him, was squatting on his hams where our track crossed that to Dhula'a from Hajlein.

The High Jōl

"Come and spend a night with us," he said.

But Awwad pushed on to where Madhun stood in sight in a bay of the jōl, two towers and a cluster of huts, with goats and peasants drawing towards them in the evening. Here, in a windowless room, I slept well under the cold and wind-swept stars.

Qasim is now an excellent servant. I got up in the dark and found him busy with breakfast, and rode off on Robin at 6.40 A.M., before the surprised camel-men had finished with their dates. It gave us a morning of unhurried peace on the highest upland of the jōl, the watershed of Hajr. As we reached and topped it, a new lowland basin rolled out below us, filled with sea-clouds and steam, even to where Wadi Minter ends in shallows at our feet. This is inhabited country: Lingaf was in sight on our right, and there were four castles in Minter; the middle one, under whose triangular shot-holes we passed, belongs to a solitary marooned tribesman of the Ja'da. And when we had crossed this oasis, rich with the singing of birds and the vague sweetness of grass underfoot, we came, after an expanse of jōl and stones, to the tower of Ba Taraiq, and the valley-head of Luqna, and Ra'un with its mound before us on the left; and in our sight, whenever we stood on rising ground, faint as clouds, volcanic pointed hills of 'Azzan.

Thither would we travel, I decided, and avoid the cloud-steaming lowlands of Hajr, where, the camel-men said with one accord, all who go when the dates are in flower, fall ill of a fever and die. We would but dip down and out again at Yeb'eth and new camel-men would take us across the unvisited jōl. We had the new men already; for as we had skirted Hajlein, a young bedu of surprising beauty ran out and took our 'Azzani by the hand, and the bargain had been made then and there.

Our Ja'da camel-men were not heroic stuff. Friendship rather than efficiency ever guided Sayyid 'Ali in his choice, and he had picked these cronies of his from peaceful fields to travel through what they considered a hard and bitter world. They were not real beduin at all. They had the "Arab" type with long regular faces, very different from the square-set little aborigines of Deyyin or Saiban. I myself would never have looked at them twice, but I had been far too ill to bother about such things when they were chosen. And now whenever we reached some denuded spot to rest in, they sat despondent, lamenting the fact that they had forgotten both food for their camels and water for themselves.

Abdulla their leader had evidently been told by 'Ali that his presence rather than his work was required. He was, said 'Ali, who has a passion for grandeur, a gentleman of the Ja'da. He had a cross and twisted face like that of the dwarf in the Nibelungen, and suffered from indigestion. Whenever we dismounted, he would gather all he could in the way of rugs and sacking, pile them into a heap to recline on, and prepare to watch Qasim and the beduin do his work.

"Do you never do anything yourself?" I asked at last.

"No," said he. "The women cook."

"And when you are alone, I suppose you die of hunger."

"No, then I work."

"Praise be to God."

Qasim, gathering firewood, looked amused.

But now, on the bare jōl, the camels have had nothing but samr leaves to eat for the last three days, and as for the men's lunch, 'Ali admits that it has vanished. Abdulla reclines and wails—no food, no feed, no warmth—as if most of these troubles were not of his own making; the donkey and I are the only well-fed members of the party. But no one is very bad-tempered about it; they cook a thin disgusting gruel and laugh at the suggestion that it be treated as a day in Ramadhan. They rest in the clear hungry air among the thorns and boulders, with the basin of Hajr breaking to shallow far cliffs below, and play with their guns to distract their minds and chew a mixture of tobacco and ashes, which, they say, improve it with a salty taste. What happened to the food 'Ali alone will ever know. He, universally blamed, sits contented, smoking a pipe with a stem made of an old cartridge-case. Cartridge-cases are used for all sorts of things. The beduin who come for medicines empty them out to use as bottles, make holes to stand them in the roots of trees, and give them a berry of the 'ilb tree for a stopper.

At this place called the 'Aqaba of Mothab the rest of our day's route lay all in light before us, winding towards Ye'beth in Hajr between the ravines of Mothab and Injit.

Their devious twists, eating into the jōl below, looked irresponsible like the paths of worms in wood. We rode there delicately through the afternoon between the heads of wadis that drop as if a trap-door had fallen, till sunset made the gravel silver, like wavelets on a stream; then we camped on the Van der Meulen track, 1,255 metres above the sea, at a dry waterhole called Nuqba of the 'Ilb Tree.

The sun went, its gold ribands trailed and died quick as snuffed candles; from the Injit ravine at our feet shadows rose with the climbing night. Through the ocean green of the sky an icy wind came blowing; the food problem grew acute.

Shortage of food

The camel-men shivered and gathered by a fire: "We will be patient," was all they said. There is a disarming, and also invincible quality, in patience and stupidity combined. But Awwad, gay as ever, trotted about almost naked with his operatic smile, while Qasim, in tennis shoes, dealt with the tea. There were said to be beduin of the Mushajir somewhere in the darkness below; Sayyid 'Ali must get meat from them; he was the villain; it was he who had economized our supper. He sat talking, unconquerably cheerful, while snubs, reprimands and accusations hung about him—and having looked in vain round an unresponsive circle for some victim to send in his stead, girt up his petticoats and went. After a long interval a woman appeared on the shore of the shadows with a bleating kid in her arms. The kid was for me, but there was nothing for the men.

There was an outcry. Gladly would I give my little scapegoat, but it was a mouthful among so many; it trotted downhill again, happy and despised. I now handed the woman two dollars for a bigger dinner, and again we sat and waited, saying things about 'Ali, warm and well-fed, we supposed, with the beduin harim. Next time, I decided, I myself would take over the financial management of the camel-men, who would not have, like these, the privilege of being Sayyid 'Ali's particular friends.

I now went to bed to the chant of Ahmed's prayer, his gaunt peasant neck and shoulder statuesque against a sky that held a yellow planet; and when I woke again the moon was high, though not yet high above us, tangled in a samr tree, flooding it in light, shining in a cluster of stars; and there was business going on round the fire. A sheep was cooking. 'Ali thought it pregnant and said it might be bad for me. I decided to risk this, and Qasim soon came along to reassure me and to say that it was merely fat, and reappeared in due time with the liver on a plate, an exquisite meal. I handed out such coats as I could spare in the thin cold air, and fell asleep again not far from the crackling fire, wondering with a pleasant gratitude at the general courage and gaiety of men in a hard and beautiful world. In the dawn we woke under a red sky to find everything wet with dew as if it had been raining: I usually sleep on all my clothes to keep them dry, but had forgotten about these heavy dews; my sheep-skin and my quilt were sodden; and even at eight-thirty, when already we had been riding for two hours, the fat little scrubby plants in the shade of boulders were still heavy and luminous with dew.

The company had not slept; they had sat all night heaping logs on the embers. Ahmed and Robin and I left them and went on with the young 'Azzani lad, dressed in somebody's discarded Norfolk jacket with the collar turned up and his curly head above. 'Ali came behind, riding slowly, because his camel was so hungry. And as we made south, a three hours to the 'Aqaba, by dry water-holes and cairns—sites possibly of pre-Islamic burial—we met a runner from 'Azzan, walking lightly with the morning shadows behind him to Du'an. Harold, he told us, had landed on his Sultan's new landing-ground and he was rushing across country with the news. I might still find him there, said the young man, leaning like Tobit on his staff. It would be amusing to coincide un-expectedly with Harold in a place unvisited by Europeans for the last twenty years.

When the news had been given and taken, we parted and continued, till we came to the untidy spur of 'Aqaba that falls to Yeb'eth, and saw the oasis below us, spread out in groups of forts and houses by their seil bed, with 'ilb trees and small dusty gardens of palms. The place lies like an island embraced by high moraines of loess, carried down by Sufra and Injit.

From our height we could see small dark towers where the unmapped caravan routes wind north and west to the table-land upon whose farther edge stood yesterday's blue hills. Perhaps it is some echo of the days when we too, unburdened with possessions, wandered lightly on the surface of the world, that gives the unexpressible delight to the sight of a road that vanishes, a road that winds into a distance, the landscape of to-morrow melting into the landscape of to-day. Some books, like the *Pilgrim's Progress*, give this feeling and, recognizing it, we know that the charm of the horizon is the charm of pilgrimage, the eternal invitation to the spirit of man. To travel from fortress to fortress, over the high jōl where men still walk with guns upon their shoulders, and at the end of days to see before you land that is yet unknown—what enchantment in this world, I should like to know, is comparable to this?

Chapter X

THE DRAWINGS OF RAHBE

" Which yet survive, stamped on these lifeless things,
The hand that mocked them and the heart that fed."

(SHELLEY.)

As WE CAME OFF THE 'AQABA, THE YOUTH WHO HAD PROMISED camels at Hajlein was squatting there before us. His name was Salih, of the Badiyan, who are a portion of the Beni Nu'man, who live in those volcanic hills to which our face was set. He was graceful as a panther, with features perfectly regular and eyes brilliant under long lashes, and his blue torso was naked to the waist; he had wound a dark turban round his head and his *futah* was gathered full like a ballet-skirt about him in the manner of his province. Hand in hand with the 'Azzani under the 'ilb trees of Yeb'eth, his indigo wildness and the other's Norfolk jacket green with age walked together under my sunshade.

We had been travelling four hours and it was still morning when we reached Shuruj, the village where the caravan route from 'Azzan comes down. The news had already spread and a roomful of visitors was waiting, for—apart from the Dutchmen six years ago who hurried through—no European has been seen here. The head of the Mushajir was there, to whom Yeb'eth belongs—old and deaf and friendly with white hair over his naked shoulders—and a sayyid, old too and holy, who looked more dubious. The holy are ever more chary of their welcome, and politics here, untouched by Harold's truces, moved in suspicious grooves.

"What of the Government?" the beduin would ask as they met us. "Does it mean to let us live or will it kill us?" They asked it without irony, convinced that governments can do without question what they please. But the villagers of the oasis were anxious for help with their orchards, their roads and canals. "Why does Ingram not visit us?" they asked, ignoring the cameldays that cut them off. Any government would do, they said, provided it were strong, for the prosperity of these inland places depends upon safe access to the sea. According to the distance and the danger, the price of commodities varies, so that a load of rice costs three and a half dollars less at Yeb'eth than in 'Amd. The price of weapons too varies, according to the temporary security of the land, and rifles on the jōl have dwindled from five to three hundred or even to two hundred dollars.

The port of Yeb'eth is Bal Haf rather than Bir Ali, and they reach it by a newly opened three days' route across the hills; but before this they would go round to 'Azzan, they told me, rather than by Hajr, because of the safer road, while their traffic eastward was less with 'Amd than with Du'an. Their wells are easy at a depth of fifteen to thirty qāma; and the oasis and the land around belong almost entirely to the Mushajir, with a few 'Amudi Shaikhs scattered here and there.

Their villages are fine medieval groups of towers, barely furnished and poor. When I had sat there among them for an hour, I took refuge in the comparative seclusion of the harim, where the women welcomed and petted me, piling cushions and looking at all I had brought. The smallest boy of the house came and sat close in the circle; a tin lion, machine-made in Europe, hung about his neck, because Asad or Lion was his name. The wife was plain. She wore a necklace over the top of her head in a fashion I had not seen, and her mother sat beside her, a woman still beautiful, from Du'an.

"Do you see any good in me?" she asked. "An old woman, far from my people?"

"The old are nearest to Allah," I answered and pleased her. Nothing, to the Arab, appears to be so sad as the living among strangers. Her eyes were still lovely and dark.

The husband and master of the tower had been to Massawa, and told me how hard the Italians make it for Arabs who come with British passes. Some, however, they use for propaganda, and three brothers who had long served in the Eritrean army were busy now spreading rumours against us all over the lands of Yeb'eth, not, as far as I could see, with very much effect.

A mosquito was humming in this lowland and I meant to be off before the afternoon was out. But the chorus of Sayyid 'Ali's accusers had to be dealt with first. Everyone was annoyed with him and everyone said so. Even Awwad, the Deyyin, having bestowed my present in his cartridge-belt, complained that 'Ali owed him five dollars.

"Why do you lend him money?" I asked. "You knew, when you did so, that you were throwing it into a well? He has promised new dresses to all the camel-men because they are his friends? Can I do anything about it? You ought to know him? He is an Arab, not an Ingliz."

A hasty chorus assured me that no one would dream of confounding 'Ali with the English, and I then turned to deal with Ahmed, who had become a merchant in Yeb'eth where things are cheaper, had spent all he had, and now had nothing left to pay for Robin's fodder. In an evil moment, reluctant to see that unsympathetic animal starve, I paid five days' wages in advance.

Now all was ready, except for the buying of food. The new beduin had been strenuously told to provide their own, and dates and rice were soon got together; also two goat-skins of water which 'Ali had forgotten in 'Amd. In a final chaos, complicated by hosts of callers, by farewells to the Ja'da now completely friendly, and by the close-packed presence of half the oasis children, we got off. It was four o'clock in the afternoon. At the top of a gentle scree the jōl received us, its tawny landscape dotted with round *qaras* (hillocks), empty and silent, an arid but ineffable peace.

The evening too was peace in a small wadi recessed into the flatness of the jōl. It was called Shi'b al-Gin. The huge *qara* of Kalab is east of it; and in its pastoral heart wooded with 'ilb trees it had a pond and a fort, and a few families of beduin beside their goats, penned for the night with thorns. Here we too camped at six-thirty in a sandy hollow on moonlit ground strewn with berries of the 'ilb trees. 'Ali, after so much tossing, settled into the respectability and ease of holiness, and the beduin came running to kiss his hand. He takes it well, without undue elation, and is ever anxious to push me also into a creditable limelight; he is indeed a magnanimous little soul, in spite of all.

Two other sayyids joined us here, young boys home from school in Tarim. They were making for Nisab in the north-west, and asked if they could add themselves to our party as far as our roads go together. One feeds them, it goes without saying; it is the custom of the land. But the fact that no one can ever know how many there will be for dinner over a two or three days' foodless desert, does make housekeeping difficult. The elder of the two lads had devoted himself to grammar and religion for four years already.

"For how much longer will you study?" I asked him.

"I do not know. Perhaps always," he said. "Learning is like water to the earth. There is never enough."

Salih the Badiyan was unloading the camels, helped by a friend and a small brother. The goatskin of water and the gun, the two necessities of life, were deposited in safety beside us in shelter of a tree. These are good beduin, resourceful, cheerful and quiet: of me and of 'Ali they think little, but they care for their camels and know their road; and it is pleasant to watch their deft accustomed movements and to sit eating the yellow berries that lie strewn about in profusion and to smell the bitter smell of the evening fire.

* * *

Next morning at six-thirty we left the small dip of our valley by its western side and saw the grandeur of the unknown jōl about us, ruined and desolate. The waters and the wind have worked, and the flat surface is eaten into and threatened on every side. The great ravines roll themselves down to Hajr, over an immense fan of eroded tortured lands. Here is no water, except what lies in pools of the limestone below in shady places, or rushes in the channels of the rain. The little forts, invisible and single, are separated by days of rough journey; Ganamnam in Shi'b Jereb in the north, Ghiutek in the south, were all I could learn of in the wide broken landscape that lay in sight, naked in the morning; to right and left as we rode on a narrow shelf of gravel, the uninhabited valleys fell away.

The houseless beduin live here and know the water-holes. The ravines themselves hold in their sheltered hearts pleasant oases of high-growing trees. Long before the days of Islam, the forebears of these tribesmen must have known them, for their rough red ochre letters are painted with increasing frequency as one travels westward, on many a flat or over-hanging surface of stone.

Two such we stopped to visit in Wadi Rahbe, where the track zigzags down into a valley and the two great water-bitten desolations of Saiq and Rahbe meet. Not far from a pool like a well in the limestone, words and drawings are painted on the northern overhanging cliff. The words are strange, perhaps magic formulas, with the same letters often repeated, and a name here and there; but the pictures are plain enough and drawn with spirit—ibex and camels with rudimentary riders, men—a man with bound hair or a turban—and three oxen without humps unlike the modern cattle in this land. In the bas reliefs of Deir al Bahri, that show the bringers of frankincense in the fifteenth century B.C., the oxen too are smooth-backed like these, and the fact has been taken to strengthen the claim that Arabia, rather than Africa, was the frankincense land once known as the Land of Punt[1]. If this is so, the oxen of Rahbe strengthen the claim; and show also that there was probably tillage in this lonely valley at that time. The drawings are rough enough, but observant, the shambling camel-legs, done with wavy lines, are distinguished

[1] *Periplus of the Erythraean Sea*: ed. Schoff, 1912, p. 270 ff. The people of Punt in the Bahri sculpture have their hair tied in a top-knot exactly like the Beni Nu'man.

from the straight strength of the oxen. They are far better than anything of the kind we had come upon so far.

In the body of the valley, arching over the seil-bed, is a stretch of thick trees and wild palms. The trees are of the kind they called Tzaraf at Samu'a, brilliant as if a thin coat of varnish were spread over their leaves and with trunks two feet across; the palm trees behind them grow tall and push their spiky fans into the sky, and the beduin distil a drink from them (which is, I am sure, forbidden) and call them *nos*. Under their pleasant shadow 'Ali was thinking to rest through the heat of the day, and looked apprehensive when more drawings were mentioned down the valley.

"Only two hours to go and come," the beduin said.

"You do not know beduin," said 'Ali; "you do not know what they mean when they say two hours."

What I did know was that no one can inspire a caravan with antiquarian enthusiasm after lunch. We would set off before our rest—it was only ten in the morning—and come back when we could, and we took pity on Sayyid 'Ali and left him reluctant under the trees.

Down Rahbe with the heat increasing we rode through the morning, by park-like sweeps of tamarisk and flame-flowered shrubs and pools of water left from the winter-flowing of the stream; till we came after two hours to Ghiutek, a fort with huts around it, and were made welcome because our beduin were related to the beduin of the valley. There we drank from a goatskin of muddy water, took a handful of 'ilb berries that lay drying in heaps in the sun, and asked why no one tilled the earth in this lonely little paradise where trees would grow.

"We tried," said the men of Ghiutek, "to blow a canal with

dynamite out of the hillside. But it did not come and perhaps we will try again, and then we can cultivate and use irrigation, but otherwise we will live on these berries that you see."

"And when you go to a town, where do you go to?"

"To the tower of Joba, one day's journey down this wadi." ·

"And from Joba, where does one go?"

"Another day, to Hajr."

They live, shut up in their cliffs in a world of their own, unless they depart altogether for places like Singapore.

Twenty minutes beyond Ghiutek, down the valley, we came upon the other drawings on the under tilted face of a boulder the size of a house, close to the track. These also had rough letters, and two pictures of *husns* with towers—the same *husn* probably whose descendent stands at Ghiutek to-day.[1] We returned, riding briskly. In the furnace heat of the valley, Robin, encouraged by the beduin behind him, behaved like a proper animal, while his master, crumpled up with fatigue, trailed too slowly in the distance to protest.

We rested, and it was almost sunset when, after long żigzags up the terrific 'aqaba of Saiq, we reached again the windy spaces of the jōl, and made camp in the deepening dusk in a cup of the limestone, with the ruins of the world as it seemed at our feet. Among the rocks, still and warm in the moonlight, our camels scattered and settled, immovable and ancient in outline as the rocks themselves. No animal looks as permanent as the camel in its own landscape. And as we sat round our fire, a bedu appeared out of the darkness, with

[1] For details of all these see my article in the Royal Asiatic Journal for July, 1939, and Professor Ryckmans's *Museion*, December, 1939. Vol. 52, parts 3 and 4.

straight hair and a straight small nose, of the tribe of the Ba Qutmi of the Beni Nu'man.

"Are you one of the Ferangi," said he, "who are coming to make us free our slaves, and pay taxes, and to make our women do as they please?"

"I do not know," said I, "about the first two, but I know that your women do as they please already, because I am a woman myself."

He laughed and squatted down in the glow of the fire.

"All the jōl is talking," said he, "about your aeroplanes. The Sultan of 'Azzan told us they were coming, and none of us believed him; and they did come; and now *you* have come just after. What is it all about? Are you coming to spoil our country?"

"Indeed I hope not," said I.

"We have given up all our guns because of your English peace, and now the Sons of Himyar who live in the hills have stolen two of our camels a fortnight ago, and we Ba Qutmis have given up our guns." (A whole circle of German rifles was gleaming with smooth barrels round the fire.) "We have had enough of the peace, and soon we shall go into the lands of the Himyar and pour petrol over the roots of their palms. We do not like you." He smiled at me in a good-natured way as he spoke.

"We are going to have a kid for dinner," said I, "and you will like me better after that. In our country we think that a man never likes people till he is fed. But as for your country, we have no wish to take it from you." I looked over the vast lands tumbled in the moonlight and thought of English woods with blue-bells just coming. "We have a better land," said I. "And if we are here it is not to do you any harm, but because your sultans invite us, to keep out other people, whom you and we both dislike."

"If that is so," said the Ba Qutmi, "why all is well. But if you make a peace, you should keep it, and not let the Sons of Himyar steal our camels."

Chapter XI

ACROSS THE WATERSHED

"Their arms the rust hath eaten,
Their statutes none regard:
Arabia shall not sweeten
Their dust, with all her nard."

(A. E. HOUSMAN.)

THERE ARE, I SOMETIMES THINK, ONLY TWO SORTS OF PEOPLE
in this world—the settled and the nomad—and there is a
natural antipathy between them, whatever the land to which
they may belong. Perhaps it is because we are comparatively
recently barbarians, because the stone age lingered longer
among us than on the Mediterranean coasts that the English
have remained so frequently nomadic at heart. It is the more
imaginative attitude in a transitory world, where a man who
tries to feel settled must appear to the eyes of eternity very
like someone pretending to sit in comfort on an ant-hill.
And the nomads are without doubt the more amusing.
With a mind receptive to the unexpected they acquire a Social
Sense. The roughest bedu has it, and it is this that so happily
distinguishes him from a peasant like Ahmed or even from
a Banker, people who walk through landscapes with their
heads down, thinking out sums. The nomad, moving from
place to place in mind as well as body, is ready to take an
interest in any odd thing that meets him; this makes him
pleasant and I am inclined—especially after last winter—to

think it is better to be pleasant than to be virtuous, if the two *must* be looked upon as mutually exclusive.

'Ali however, with nothing much to show for it in the way of stability, is developing the attitude of a Settled Man, and has fallen out with the Sons of Nu'man. They, poor things, were happy in the thought that this journey to 'Azzan could be made to last days and days: already it has stretched out to three instead of the promised two, and it seems doubtful if even the fourth will see us there. Apart from the fact that the Aden Government has no notion of where I am and is probably getting restless, I am delighted to go slowly; the calm nights of the jōl pour strength into one day by day. But 'Ali has Reason on his side. He spoke roughly to make the camel-men go on; a moment of uncertainty followed, and I had to intervene with tactful words; Salih explained with black brows as we continued that—if 'Ali had been alone —they would have taken their camels and left him in the desert—a grim unpleasant thought.

"But," said I in a shocked voice, "isn't he a Sayyid? You couldn't do that."

"We are beduin," said Salih. "We like people, or we don't like them. We like you," he added with a disarming smile, and henceforward showed his affection by leading my camel round the branches of the samr trees that might happen to scratch my face, instead of through them as he did before.

We had been riding all the morning along a tongue of jōl between two ravines—Mudha'a with a track running towards us on our left, and on our right the hollow depth of Rahm in whose far sunlight we could see moving the tiny figure of Salih's friend looking for water to fill our skins. Presently a depressing small range of rubble limestone blocked our north-western view, though the jōl before us was still lovely in morning, flecked with pits of shadow. The road wound in decorative unnecessary loops made by the feet of camels in the past; the bedu behind me sang as he swayed on his saddle, in a high meaningless voice, shrill as the wind. And then, climbing the foot-hills of Jebel Aswad to the Dzera' Pass, we reached the ridge that had been our horizon on the jōl of Mothab, four days ago; and saw before us, red and black and fading in misty air like the Celestial City, bounded on its far side by crests of Jebel Himyar, the huge bowl of the hills of 'Azzan.

Dark indeed must the heart be that does not lift at the sight of the journey's goal set out before it; and I have often thought that, if one lived well, such perhaps may be the hour of death. Even the beduin to whom it was so familiar felt the strange joy that fills well-regulated minds when they step across a watershed, and paused in the morning breeze beside me, to point out the hills of their land.

We were now between two systems, white and black, where long ridges of limestone break and meet volcanic peaks of Aswad, home of the Beni Nu'man. Wa'l, the Peak of the Ibex, is the highest, standing about half-way along this range; but the most northerly and last peak is Merkham, under whose dark shaft our pathway led. On our other side and far higher above us were the crumbling buttresses of the last of the limestone ridges, whose long and even headlands break down and end here in three isolated, flat-topped derelicts called Qadas, Qishé and Himar. Beyond the former, where it joins the headland of Jebel Ali, is the Fughà Pass, fit for lightly-laden camels only, where the Gulgul track from Yeb'eth comes down, travelling through uninhabited lands. Another track, from Husn Ganamnam, comes in from the north and met us as we descended from the pass; a long string of camels, like some Egyptian carving, was threaded along it round the pyramid edge of Himar.

The two tracks join and together follow a dreary defile stifled in sand and yellow ironstone; and at the head of this in a naked dell we rested, finding such shade as we could, A delicate black-and-white wheatear hopped about here, which they called Rukheime of the Hills.

We had ridden for four and a half hours, and the afternoon sun was slanting steeply when we started again.

"He who has not many men, the Sun comes and eats him at night," Salih sang over and over as he saddled the camels. The beduin use of language is a perpetual delight; if they wish to tell me that something is for me to decide: "It is nearer your heart than ours," they say. They set off now, still sulky with 'Ali, led by Salih's friend, a figure so girlish in his barefoot grace, his curls tied away from his ears in a bunch at the nape of the neck, his face and hands so delicate and small that the tuft of beard on his chin seemed a monstrosity of nature.

He led out of the defile over the last swellings of Merkham through a land of barren hummocks black as slag-heaps from coal. All was volcanic here.

They were sulky with Ahmed too now, and so was I, for I had to ride a camel. Robin had given out altogether, his master having spent all the extra wages I had given him on stores sent back to his home. Poor Robin, with nothing but a few millet stalks inside him for the last two days, drooped along, his master brooding behind him, head sunk on breast, appalled at the cruelty of a desert you would think he might have known, or at least have enquired about, considering how he has lived all his life beside it. Down a long corridor we went, shady and dark, for two hours: volcanic cliffs shot up in perpendicular strata like flames on either hand, pitted with holes like honeycomb, where the deformed white stems find root of Adenum Obesum. Of that dead rock the outer skyline edges only catch a polish, like dark shoe-leather in the sun.

I went stumbling far below, reduced to walking by the fatigue of the camel and the debility of Robin.

"Your face is blackened, Ahmed," I said. But Ahmed is one of those people who think it is the Universe and not he who are wrong when they happen to differ, and disconcerted me by saying that God would judge between us. This is always a disquieting thought, and—though angry—I did remember that the bag of rice to which Ahmed had misapplied his wages, was intended to nourish those eight female relatives of one sort and another; when next I drank from the goatskin, I offered him a share; he promptly finished all.

"He can go home," I told Sayyid 'Ali. "But not alone, or he will die. Let him join the first caravan we meet."

"I have written already to the headman at Yeb'eth," said 'Ali, "to seize him as he goes by and take the six dollars away that you gave him in advance."

"You can tear that letter up," I said. "And we will look upon the dollars as alms given to the feeble-minded." But I almost regretted this decision next morning, when Ahmed came to ask for a second edition of his wages. He needed them, he said. He had an almost Teutonic incapacity for seeing other points of view.

Men of the Ba Qutmi

A late shaft of light struck us as we emerged at last from our long corridor into samr glades that lined a sheltered valley. It came down from the left to meet us, from Jebel Nahr on the ridge of Aswad, and was called al-Aisser, or the Left-hand valley. It joined our Lijlij track, and we turned west together, into a sunset country of varied and sudden hills. Violet shadows already lurked among them; and in the twilight we turned from our track and found a sandy place and traces of camp-fires, by the well of Lijlij that lies in its hollow alone; here the men of the Ba Qutmi come walking by with unechoing tread on the sand, leading their camels, and rest their guns against a tree to talk beside the travellers' fires.

"May one sit near her?" they ask when they see me. And then: "Where did you pick her up?" They turn to Salih. "And who brought her?" meaning from which tribe did they take me over.

And when these matters have been settled, while they sit cleaning out cartridge-cases to fill with lotion for their eyes, they ask for news in their beduin way, saying: "What is the war in your wadi?"

They live scattered about in huts or caverns of these hills, and tell of rock drawings everywhere in remote ravines too far to visit now. Their illnesses, collected through doctor-less years, are laid before me—a snake in the stomach, wind in the elbows—an expert would find it hard to diagnose. The well nearby, protected by a few dry walls and sheltered with faggots, is busy with the men of the place watering their goats for the night, who join us presently, when the full moon is out over flat-topped trees and pointed hills.

Two young married people come, with the straight hair

and beautiful small features of these very ancient tribes. The bride is unveiled, hung and braceleted with silver, one smooth plait showing under the shabby cloth they wear here in folds on the top of their heads. Her anklets are broad bands of brass, with bosses. Her face is beautiful as that of a Madonna. With a charming gesture of affectionate confidence she lays her hand on her husband's bare knee as he squats beside her, and in her other hand holds a bowl of milk to exchange for the medicine. Presently a small cousin joins them to find something for his grandfather's cough, hitherto "helped by Allah alone," and to ask for medicine against wolves which eat the goats they take to pasture. He is so full of affection and concern that I have to part with some of the most precious camphor oil that I use for myself. It is hard to keep anything in this land; at every turn one meets with people whose need is so disproportionately greater than one's own. The beauties and charities of their code, the hardness which a life among the perpetual poverty of others must engender, become clear as one travels among them.

In the dawn we too watered our camels and travelled in early sunlight into those little hills, making due west, over a low red pass called Naid, where many small cairns lie scattered, resting-places where the beduin dead are prayed over on their last journey, as they pass from their houseless wilderness to where, round habitations, they build a city of their graves.

Two hills flank the pass, and in the dip below lay the small oasis of Aroma with a fort and well and the mountain called Horhor behind it; and a long train of laden camels were zigzagging up the boulders towards us. The bearded beduin shook hands as they reached and passed us; they shake with a clasp, sidewards. One asked if I was a

sayyid, and looked surprised when 'Ali said "A sayyida."
There has been in this region a female Mansab of the Junaidi
sayyids; she inherited the position from her father, and was
much respected and did not, in fact was not allowed to,
marry; and my beduin were delighted when I told them
that I was to be thought of as a Mansab also, and forthwith
called me so. They told me that there had been three of
these ladies; the last one died a year or two ago, and the tribes
are now divided as to whether to have another woman or no,
so they put papers with the names of various candidates into
her tomb to see what she felt about it, and in the morning
found the masculine names torn to shreds.

It took us only an hour to reach Aroma. There before us
lay a great sandy basin, blown up by the sea-winds and lapping
to the edge of the hills. These sand-drifts are common
here and they call them "kaut," and I was anxious to cross
while the morning was still cool. But the master of the fort
of Aroma stood by the wayside to meet us and seized my
bridle and looked threatening when we asked to hurry on.

"What does she mean?" he said, turning to 'Ali. "Is
it to insult me?"

'Ali carries over his shoulder my leather-fringed bag filled
with coffee berries, which are produced in the houses one
rests at, according to the custom of this land: the host is put
to no expense, and his prestige suffers if one passes him by.
I could not help feeling rather relieved at the thought that we
were travelling in such uninhabited country; in a populous
region one would never get on at all. As it was, we sat
under his 'ilb trees for an hour, while the pretty wife who
ruled him and his fort beat out the coffee berries on a stone;
and, in the heat of the day, continued down the valley, barely

scratched for cultivation here and there. There were drawings on the hillside above Aroma, too high to be reached
without the sacrifice of another day; and there were some
under a rock on the wayside, almost effaced and rough;
as we crawled in to look, we saw a snake coiled there with
puffed cheeks, about eighteen inches long, coloured white
and buff and faint red like the ochres of the drawings—the
only animal seen on this journey, except for some conies
among the rocks of Rahbe. With no further incident we
turned north to skirt the edge of sand and reached the third
and last well on our road, where the small square forts of
Mesfala, the capital of the Ba Qutmi, stand on little hills.

Chapter XII

ARRIVAL IN 'AZZAN

"La soledad seguiendo,
Rendido a mi fortuna
Me voy por los caminos que se ofrecen."

(GARCILASSO DE LA VEGA.)

THE CHIEF OF THE BA QUTMI WAS ABSENT, AND HIS TWO
sons sat in their tower and did not come to see me, so that I
took this opportunity to uphold the prestige of my sex and
nation, refusing to visit their mother in the harim. All they
had to do, I said, if they wished for my company, was to come
and call on me first. The social deadlock was very welcome,
for it allowed us to rest in peace under the shade of a tamarisk
and enjoy the open spaces of Mesfala.

This is the beginning of the great Meifa'a basin where
four wadis flow into the open. A huge amphitheatre holds
them, intersected only by the Dhila' range which lay, half
blanketed in sand, across the Kaut before us. The long
snouts we had looked upon from Hajr now showed their
other side and formed our eastern barrier. They shone dia-
phanous behind us in the noonday light. In the foreground
the resting flocks, and men drawing water in the sun, looked
sharp and vivid as the Book of Genesis to a child.

This was the home of Salih and his friends, so that our
departure was even more dilatory than usual, and it was four

o'clock and cool before we started on the crossing of the sand. The Wadi Muhit comes down here from the Fughà pass, and, having circumvented the Dhila' range flows into Meifa'a below it; here also the Yeb'eth track from Gulgul comes into our track from the north; and the whole land- scape, framed in the steep strata of its range, its sands ribbed by south-east winds, slide gently south-eastward to low hills and the invisible sea. New plants appear here, different both from the limestone flora of the jōl and the volcanic fragile flowers we had left behind us: shersher (*Tribulus mollis Ehr. Caltrops*), ribla (*Heliotropium undulatum Vahl*), mārikh (*Leptadenia pyrotechnica (Forsk) Decne*) and grasses—sherh (*maerua crassifolia Forsk*) and thumam—that make hillocks beneath them as they clutch the wandering sand. The camels eat all these.

As we rode I watched the camel before me, admiring the perfection of its desert ways. Its ugliness is the ugliness of the east, that has some strange attraction; its colour is the colour of desert dust, with the same innumerable, impercept- ible variations; its tail, which looks like a dead palm frond, is merely ridiculous. But its feet are so strong that I have seen a camel, fully laden, raise itself up on a foot *that was twisted beneath it*, apparently without noticing, and so delicately made, with concertina-like springs at the heel, that they give themselves without shock to every inequality of ground. I can see why the beduin love their camels: it is the only beast of burden whose constant wish is truly to oblige. Like one of those unselfish people who are always gently moaning, the camel does all that is asked of it with a constantly negative mind: but it does try to do it, and when the bedu shouts "tariq" from behind, will leave the morsel of green leaves hanging on a branch in mid-air and find obediently the track from which it strayed. Only sometimes, when another caravan comes by, you will hear a vague, individual rumble from a male as he passes, while the lady whom he will never meet again turns to look distantly at him, as if through invisible lorgnettes.

To my ignorance there are only two sorts of camel, those with comfortable saddles and those without. Ours were without. But now, in the middle of the kaut, we saw a creature advancing in tassels, sent with a letter of welcome from 'Azzan, and a sayyid and two donkeys beside it. The 'Azzani boy had run ahead through the night with news of us and now came with the three newcomers—which made ten instead of seven for supper. I am sorry for anyone who organizes commissariats in Arabia.

All together we reached the western edge of the kaut and entered by a long winding defile the range of the pointed hills. Dinshale was on our left, Surba' straight above us; the round moon hung in a violet sky between their dusky walls; and far behind us the hills we had come from showed like a coronet of amethysts washed up to by the sand. In a windless corner of this unwatered range we pitched our camp at seven and watched our fire burning. My new donkey, with hennaed legs, came in a friendly way and sat beside me, like a dog, rubbing its head in the sand. The prejudice engendered by Robin began to evaporate. I offered rye vita biscuits, but it got up, spitting, only when Qasim, passing by, put chocolate in its mouth.

I had promised a present if we reached 'Azzan before ten the morning after, and the result was that Salih's small brother tried to rouse us at four. This we resisted passively, and set off in earliest daylight, pale as a sea-shell, and rounded the bastions of Surba', and followed a small wadi called Thire down from the watershed, till we came to a main highway, where the Wadi Salmūn flows with perennial water, from the town of Hauta to 'Azzan. Here, between broad beds of gravel, the village of Lahdzan stands screened in palms: seven towers are on the hill-tops about it, all within shooting distance and at enmity one with another till the coming of the "English peace" a few months ago. The river thence flows shallow and brown with fish in it, between villages, shadowed here and there with trees; the months of peace have already brought fields of lucerne and millet to its banks. No sight can be more restful than to come from the wilderness to see men and women knee-deep in their crops: unless perhaps it is to leave men and women and return again to the wilderness. But at this time, with a week of empty jōl behind us, the sight of man was pleasant in his labours. They are done here almost entirely by slaves, for the land belongs to the beduin who scorn to work with their hands and treat their people roughly, with scanty food and beating, and grudge them even the decent gift of clothes, so that the Arabs of the towns are loud in blame. The general rumour that the R.A.F. were coming to liberate these poor people brought them in droves across the field to greet me, welcoming me as they stooped in their rags to kiss my knees and garments as I passed.

I was now again riding a donkey, and the sayyid, its master, a big rough man, rode on a white female ass before me, which he made to go by pulling at a rope under its demure and shrinking tail. When this happened, it would give an irritated twist, and set off, very knock-kneed, small, and feminine, at an incompetent gallop over any boulder that happened to lie before it, while my donkey rushed amorously after. The sayyid, three sizes too large for his mount, sat loose and light-hearted; but I had a pack-saddle that went round and no stirrups, and—what is far worse—no initiative; villagers too were now crowding upon us, seizing my bridle right and left to lead me to their homes.

Slowly we made our way, in and out of reeds and shallow water, down the river, while the crowd gathered from the fields behind us: until we left the garden lands (called Ghail) and came to where, on either hand, low cliffs enclose the stream. Here on the left, a long ledge is inscribed with words and pictures notched into the gritty sandstone—a varied collection of Arabic[1] and pre-Islamic, jumbled together— a saddled horse, a man and lion fighting, and men shooting with bows standing on the necks of camels. Greetings and words are scratched there, and the feeling of the place is in its lesser way like that of the Dog River in Syria where the armies of antiquity passed and left, inscribed in stone, words more permanent than themselves.

This, too, through many centuries, must have been a passageway for the great frankincense route up into the hills. No one can travel, as I did, from the enclosed eastern lands into this open basin and not realize that Geography herself has made of the Wadi Meifa'a a highway to the sea. The great wadis of the north come down here and open the rich uplands of Nisab and Yeshbum and Habban; and lead without obstacle to the coast and the port of Cana. Even now the caravans from the coast go to Shabwa by this road through the Wadi Jardan, and the fortress of 'Azzan commands them

[1]These have kindly been described by Mr. J. Walker in *Museion*, LII.

as once the fortress of Naqb al-Hajr close below it commanded
the caravans of their ancestors; only the riches and the volume
have diminished—the skeleton of the great highroad remains.

And the place called Wād in the Quran, which was the
home of the sons of Thamud, is still the name given to
Meifa'a beneath the walls of Naqb and 'Azzan. (See
page 200.)

In spite of worried looks from 'Ali and my beduin, I stopped
to photograph the drawings of the ledge, while the fortunate
arrival of the uncle of the headman of Ghail brought a certain
quiet among the crowd. He was a handsome man with dark
eyes and short grey curls tied round him with a band, and
carried on the wooden butt of his gun a tuft of ibex caught by
himself in the hills; and he had served in the Levies in Aden.
He sat down on the rocks to watch me at my work, while
the men around, divided into parts like a Greek chorus, spoke
for me and against in low voices: at every halt, unless one
happens to have a friend already there, this chorus takes
place—and the traveller's most important business is to see
that the party *for* him remains in the ascendant. Now,
however, a woman, standing in the wadi bed below, began to
shout angry reproaches to the men on the ledge who let the
Unbeliever take pictures in their land. Uneasiness began to
be felt; the headman's uncle looked angrily down; I had to
take some notice.

"One thing," I remarked, "is ever the same in your land
and in mine."

"And what is that?" said they.

"The excessive talk of women." The delighted audience
rushed to the edge of the ledge to shout this remark down
with embellishments, and with a last vindictive snap the

female voice was silent. But I lingered as little as I could; demands for money began to be heard; 'Ali, mounting me on my donkey, asked me to hurry. The sayyid on the white ass had disappeared, and my animal seemed to respond to no stimulus except that of love alone, until a bedu soldier appeared and whacked it with a rifle from behind. We got away slowly, shedding the crowd over hot white distances of stones. Near ten of the morning we reached the point where the cliffs die down, and the six or seven high towers of 'Azzan with battlements whitewashed in the sun stand grouped on the open hill-ringed space of Meifa'a. The Sultan's new landing-ground, marked with white cairns, lies just below their walls.

The Sultan himself was away with Harold, carried off like Elijah in the fiery chariot under the fascinated eyes of his people and harim. But all his relatives were drawn up in a line to receive us with their body-guard behind them.

"Go first," murmured the headman's uncle to 'Ali. "The camel must not go behind the donkey."

The sayyid, who had now reappeared, pushed on too, so as not to be seen behind a woman.

But 'Ali solved the matter tactfully by dismounting and let me ride on alone, until, near the group, I too dismounted and shook hands.

They were handsome people—their hair tied back with bands of yellow leather, their eyes straight and fearless like the beduin. They had grace and colour about them; the Sultan's brother Ahmed might well have been a Malatesta of Rimini, so aquiline was his profile, so fine his thin-lipped mouth. He wore a purple silk turban, folded in a point on the forehead, and falling down his back; his European shirt, striped green and white, was covered by a yellow-and-black-striped coat of silk, his skirt was purple and his smile like that of the Gioconda. Beside him were two uncles; Husain, dim and tired with flat and straggly hair, and an old deaf man called the Wolf, full of spirit, with two handsome sons beside him. At the head of this little procession, varied and gay, we turned and entered the high, dust-coloured doorway of the fort.

Chapter XIII

NAQB AL HAJR

"Qui, dentro ad una gabbia
Fere selvaggie e mansueto gregge
S'annidan si che sempre il miglior geme."

(PETRARCH.)

THEY TOOK ME TO A WIDE ROOM WITH MANY LATTICED windows. There were two carved columns on a magenta matted floor and niches all around, and a table and two chairs which no one ever used. Here I rested for some days, visited at intervals by the Sultan's uncles and by the two young men, Nasir and Mutlaq, Sons of the Wolf, who more particularly looked after me. I was glad to rest; and wondered what new disease approaching made me feel so tired, but it was only the heat, pouring full upon us in that low wadi open to the sea.

In the cool of sunset we strolled down into the Wad below, where a great boulder scrawled over with Arabic letters lies in the dry bed of the stream. And I sat peacefully through the evenings, sewing at my embroidery, with the Sultans and a few old servants of the fort around me, listening to the troubles of that weary land.

It was perhaps like some rough little court of the early Carlovingians, helpless among their turbulent unlettered men. So the Sultans of 'Azzan lived, holding the beduin precariously

269

at bay, paying out blackmail and clinging, with desperate and unsuccessful effort, to the safety of their only remaining source of income, their trade-route to the sea. That too for many months had been endangered, and merchants took the long way round by eastern foothills, through the unbuilt lands of the Beni Nu'man under the range of Aswad, since the tribes on the main road were raiding, just as they had been doing twenty years ago when Colonel Lake came riding by that way.

Harold now with his visit had brought new hopes, all centred on the R.A.F., but as yet little good had come of them; truces had been made, but no means were at hand to enforce them; the raiding continued. Four tribes were busy at the moment: and the lawful beduin suffered, disarmed by the truce. When I returned to Aden I asked if it would not be possible to punish at least one of these plunderers of peaceful caravans, so that the land, now restive and doubtful, might settle down to a reality of peace: but though everyone agreed with the necessity, there was a great reluctance—after the Se'ar and Humumi troubles of the winter—to send out another R.A.F. police force, owing to the constant burden of criticism at home. And I could not help thinking how strange it is that a twist of sentimental ignorance in England should cause so much misery in Arabia, should keep the quiet labourer from his fields and wells and the peaceful merchant from the road of his traffic, and encourage the reckless beduin to trample on their slaves. Despite setbacks this is at present being gradually altered; the Wadi Meifa'a is now within government range; but when one compares the firm safety of Saudi Arabia or Yemen with the recent precariousness of life in British South Arabia, one should remember that the chief, indeed the only cause of it, has lain in the ignorant dogmatism of uninformed critics at home.

Not the fear of the beduin alone hung like a shadow in the fortress of 'Azzan. All sorts of domestic dramas hovered there. There was jealousy, I soon discovered, between the house of the Sultan and that of his cousins, the Sons of the Wolf. Ahmed, the handsome brother, never asked anything for himself; he had indeed the manners of a prince; but his cousin Nasir was twice as clever as anyone else there, it was he alone who could manage the unruly bodyguard and the beduin, who could mend a lamp or a saddle if they collapsed, and whom I found sitting on the floor sewing at my embroidery with tolerable success one day when I entered my room. He wanted to learn English and to travel, and had one of those adventurous minds that rise naturally to the top of circumstance wherever they may be.

These young men, brought up in their sociable hard life together, were, in spite of all, friendly with each other, in and out of each other's houses all day long. But there was another brother who "had taken sides with the beduin," and who had been "hidden" in a tower in Bal Haf for two and a half years, and his small son of ten wandered about in the house of his uncles, a sad little air of exile about him. I made friends with him by the present of a penknife, and he would come with the servants, hovering silent and aloof, until, one day, he cried suddenly: "I would like to fly, to fly away with my father," with all the agony of hidden feelings that filled his childish years. His father had tried to shoot the old Wolf, my host, through a window; the bullet had been intercepted by a daughter, who caught it in her arm, which hung now withered and useless from the wound.

Naqb al Hajr

I went to call on these ladies, and on the Sultan's harim, who lived in the tallest of the fortresses, beside whose ibex-decorated doorway the single cannon of the kingdom stands. Having asked 'Ali what he thought I should wear for the occasion, he pitched without hesitation on my dressing-gown, a flimsy yellow silk garment in which I sallied under the battlements in the wind and dust. The ladies too had dressed to receive me—they had indeed taken several hours about it and sat in a sphinx-like row, with yellow faces, and busts encased from head to waist over the shoulders in silver necklaces and bells. They wore the kadida of 'Amd, the coral head-dress with its crown of amulets and tinkling mane. The front of their heads were shaved, and the empty space decorated with a beading of black and scarlet lacquer, one line down nose and eyebrows (also shaved), and patterns on the temples, with a star made of sequins bought in Aden, or even a piece of tin-foil stuck in the middle of the forehead every day. The Sultan's wife wore thirty necklaces from chin to waist, silver and amulets, with coral in between. Her forearms were hidden in bracelets, and the first joint of every finger was made immovable with rings. And on their heads they wore, above the coral and bells and the broad ribbon of silver that hung on each side of their face—a wide-meshed net of black stiffened with scarlet lacquer, charming to look at. Having so decorated themselves, they sat and made no other effort at conversation, while we sipped glasses of spiced tea, until I asked to see the babies, whose heads, completely shaved, give a wonderful scope for decorative zigzag patterns, red and black, with red nostrils and a star on their brows. I believe that these patterns are very ancient, for an alabaster pre-Islamic head I bought in Shibam has runnels cut in the cheek and forehead, to be filled, I think, with coloured material representing the female decoration of that time.

On the second day of my stay I asked to see the fortress of Naqb al Hajr, the greatest of all pre-Islamic ruins in this land. It is little more than an hour's ride down the valley on a low rise of the western bank of the Wād. 'Ali, of course, was nowhere to be seen when wanted, so I started off on his camel with the sun low already in the afternoon. An old man, wrinkled like the bark of a tree, with white and straggly hair, held the rope. He was one of the Beni Himyar from whom the beduin suppose that the English are descended. "I am your maternal uncle," said he. He said it as a joke, but I took him at his word and called him Uncle, amid the cheers of his friends, and this small matter stood me in good stead a day or two later.

We trotted to arrive before the sunset, with the saw-like edges of the Dhila' range distantly parallel beside us, glowing flame-like and smothered to their last steepness in a wind-blown blanket of sand; all this wide Meifa'a valley is persecuted by sea-winds that seem to blow, hot and tiring, throughout the afternoons. The bodyguard of 'Azzan had turned out behind me, indistinguishable to all outward appearance from the enemies they were supposed to deal with: in these beduin crowds it was always difficult to tell one's own protectors from one's foes. They gave unexpected whacks to my camel with their rifles, which sent it hurrying with an out-raged expression, while the beduin of the district came running towards us from all the small villages that lay on our left hand. Across the flat wadi-bed they poured in dark-blue companies, hand in hand, cheerful and determined to get money if they could; a crowd of three hundred or so were soon upon us, clutching to draw attention, pressing questions and blackmail in one continuous stream. To lose one's temper or gaiety is fatal on these occasions; I was thankful to be among them alone; and even 'Ali, who now had come up, did little good. Over the ruins they rolled like smoke, parting reluctantly when I asked to take a picture, anxious above all to be told where the buried treasure lay. I realized why, with the visit of four parties here before me, no photograph had yet been taken of the inscription of Naqb and its walls.

It is a huge citadel, nearly a mile in length I should guess, on a low and stony ridge going east and west, and the town was once upon its eastern end. A deep ditch cuts the western isthmus, and another ditch, now filled in, ran down outside the wall which there is ruined. To north and south, where the two gates are, and to the east, where the peninsula ends, the walls remain sufficiently to show the good blocks of their building, and the shallow square buttresses that flank them all around. They are cut in yellow stone, a little darker than the landscape. Within the northern gate in a hollow was a well, and an Arab town must have been built on the earlier site, for it has used the pre-Islamic stone promiscuously, and left bits of glazed medieval ware lying about the ground. But pieces of pre-Islamic building remain here and there, carefully dressed and smooth outside and rough within—and on the highest point are the blocks of a square foundation laid with huge boulders. The inscription is inside the southern gateway and tells how the governor of the fortress rebuilt the wall with stone and wood and binding (mortar), and calls it by the name of Meifa'a, which has not changed. I sat and copied and kept a running flow of conversation to hold my crowd in hand, telling them the Arabic names of the letters as I wrote them down. Various travellers had been here before me: the young lieutenants, Wellsted and Cruttenden, who rode up, roughly handled by their beduin, from the Palinurus in 1839 and first discovered the fortress to the world; and Captain Miles in 1870, who continued overland to Aden, with less trouble than anyone else before or after; and in 1896 Count Landberg with the South Arabian Expedition from Vienna to collect inscriptions; he too was harassed by the beduin who prevented his progress from 'Azzan and extorted enormous sums. No one, as far as I know, came after him except Colonel Lake from Aden, who is still remembered affectionately here, as he is indeed wherever he has been.

With the exercise of a very exhausting amount of tact I kept my crowd friendly for an hour and twenty minutes, with 'Ali, unhappy and anxious, champing to be off. There is no doubt that 'Ali is not nearly so successful with beduin as I am. We had a moment of slight scuffle at departure; I handed my notebook quickly to one of the bodyguard before the beduin snatched it; my old Uncle gave a whack to the camel, and the crowd seeing me well away and out of reach above them, made up their minds to the loss of bakhshish and shouted the most amiable farewells; they had had a good afternoon; it was they, I said over and over again, who ought to pay me and not I them; and the bedu is civilized enough in his heart to prefer entertainment to money. The body-guard, now increased to about thirty volunteers, took me back at a trot, shooting rifles into the sunset. They sang alternate verses as they ran. One man gave the verse; it would be sung twice over by a line of men on the right hand, then twice by an equal number on the left, and so on till another verse was given. In the centre, Uncle, pulling the camel rope, his white hair flying, trotted and sang and changed his heavy gun from one shoulder to the other, to shift the camel rope to his other hand. They sang one verse a hundred and fifty times, and repeated the next eighty times with never a pause in their running or their breath, and they call this a Zamil. When we reached the palace door I took my Uncle and the head of the bodyguard in with me and gave them some dollars to divide among their beduin and their men; a foolish thing to do, for, needless to say, they went quietly away with it all, and Nasir had to struggle next day from six in the morning onward with a besieging crowd. A European visitor is no joke for these Sultans: it means a continuous series of small popular tumults to quell.

Chapter XIV

JEBEL KADUR

"Then what a rough and riotous charge have you
To rule those whom the Devil cannot rule?"
(SIR THOMAS MORE, M.S.)

THE SULTANS OF 'AZZAN, SITTING OVER THEIR HOOKAHS IN unending family consultations, determined to make the best use they could of my presence by showing me off to their rebellious subjects as a visible symbol of the friendship of Britain behind them. So they said they would take me down to the coast themselves by the dangerous but inhabited way in a strongly-guarded caravan.

I was pleased, for I hoped to find traces of antiquity if I travelled by the main road to the sea. But the plan began to show every symptom of delay and I grew impatient; and it was chiefly, I believe, to keep me quiet, that they drew my attention to some ruins in the heart of the country of the Beni Himyar, and offered Sultan Husain's own camel and silver-pommelled saddle to take me to the mountains of Kadur.

Nobody knew how far these mountains were; they were in the west, some said three hours, some said two days. Times vary according to whether you travel on a donkey, a camel or your own feet, and no one ever seemed to know to which of these methods of progression they were referring when they talked of a distance in hours. But I was now used to this; and set off in a faintly pessimistic spirit with a last recommendation from Sultan Husain to keep away from villages if I wished to be safe. He gave me four of his soldiers and a donkey for restful riding, and we started at seven-forty in the morning.

All went pleasantly for two hours. We followed a wadi that divides in the north and leads by forked ways to Amaqin and Habban. Water flowed in its bed, sparse villages screened in palms lay safely on the other side, across our way a ruined narrow channel, carved in the red sandstone, still showed the ancient labours of the land. But at ten we came to where our tracks turned left towards the mountains, where the village of Lamater—a few houses with minaret and palm trees— lies in a hollow near the stream. If we had turned here, few would have noticed our going; but 'Ali, deaf to expostulation, now pushed on and in no time forced us, with a crowd about us, into the headman's house. 'Ali had, he explained, forgotten the dates and rice in 'Azzan: he hated lunching out among the beduin: why not sit in the pleasant crowded darkness of the headman's room while his women cooked a meal?

This was just what I had been telling him to avoid; an angry feeling, like suffocation, seized me, and the four soldiers, and the Sultan's warning, were this time on my side. No sooner had the dates arrived, wrapped in plaited palm leaves, than—without further argument—we set off.

But it was too late. The whole village swarmed about us, and the goal of our journey, which we had been told to conceal, was perfectly obvious to all, since the left-hand track led solely to the mountains of Kadur. These, the people

shouted, are the strongholds of Himyar; they had no wish to
see a stranger there. The headman was friendly, but not so
his flock. They surged with waving arms round 'Ali, and I
was beginning to despair of the whole attempt when my
maternal Uncle of the day before appeared and took my
donkey by the rein. He too belonged, he said, to the village,
and promised to lead me by a secluded pathway to the jōl.
We slipped away; in the turmoil no one noticed our departure,
and we had climbed a small 'aqaba and already saw the level
lands before us and the foot-hills beyond, when 'Ali and the
soldiers appeared, emerging by the regular pathway. Eight
or ten of the villagers were behind them, and—seeing us—
made straight for my old man.

He went down like a swimmer, struggling, with floating
white locks and scrabbling arms, and

> "Old Coligny's hoary hair
> All dabbled with his blood,"

came, unpleasantly vivid, to my mind; but the group, like a
football scrum, was too close-packed for shooting, or even
for the effective use of knives. I reflected that when there
is trouble the nearest woman is generally the cause of it;
the best thing she can do is to remove herself—and I
continued to ride towards the hills.

'Ali, the origin of all this vexation, now came up in a
demented manner and begged me to return. He seized
my donkey; "We must go back," was all that he could say.
I slipped out of my saddle and tried to continue in my direction,
but he caught my wrists. I was so angry by this time that a
whole army of the Sons of Himyar would not have persuaded
me to stop but I could not disengage myself from the delirious

'Ali. One of the bodyguard, a tall man with a silver armlet, came up to say that things would be bad if we turned round.

"By God then, get me out of the hands of this man," said I.

He pulled, 'Ali pulled: released but lacerated, I finally walked on hand in hand with the soldier, while the noise of the battle grew loud and then fainter behind us. I avoided looking back. A panting blue bedu presently came up.

"There was something of a fuss (rabsha)?" I said.

"A little rabsha," said he, casually, and let the subject drop.

I longed to ask after my old Uncle but thought it wiser not to speak.

The donkey was brought, I mounted and rode in silence, listening to 'Ali, now recovered, indulging in an oration to the crowd behind me.

"She will go on," I heard him say, "until you kill her. And then the aeroplanes will kill us all, and what would be the good of that? Did you not hear how, when I begged her to return, she answered: "There is but one hour of death?"

This was pure invention but it sounded well.

We now rode over the jōl in pensive silence, with about thirty of the beduin behind us, and a rather doubtful future before, until we came to a basin where water poured over white rocks into jade-green pools in the sun. There in the shade of an overhanging boulder we settled to a tacit truce to eat.

Luckily there were dates enough now, and—regardless of 'Ali's feelings—I told him to deal them in handfuls among the thirty men. My old Uncle had reappeared, jaunty and apparently rejuvenated by the events of the morning. Under the divine influence of food, friendliness grew. I am quite convinced that to share food, either his or yours, is the quickest way to make the beduin friendly: I have tried both ways now, and have noticed the difference every time; and the fact that the town Arab never shares is no proof to the contrary, for he is, on the whole, far more disliked than a stranger by the beduin of his land.

When we had eaten our dates I showed the Beni Himyar how to make powdered milk, which they none of them dared to drink, and then asked them to rest out of sight in the shade of their rock while I bathed in the stream. No greater sign of trustfulness could be given, and it acted in a kindly way.

To me also it was soothing to lie in the sunlit water and hear its small noise in the noonday silence of the hills, solitary as Paradise except for the thirty beduin behind their rock. Frogs and newts and fishes, and a yellow and black barred butterfly darted among the reeds: in that coolness I lay thinking of the baby Dart in summer on the moors. All sudden sweetness, the call of a bird at sunset, the kitten-soft blossom of the samr, the voice of water, touch one with a knife-like sharpness in this hard land; and how should man also not be hard, living from year to year on the bare surface of his rocks? When I returned I found that 'Ali was getting rid of most of the beduin by sending them with a letter to 'Azzan: he did not tell me that he lured them to go with promises of bakhshish from the Sultans, a fraud I would not have allowed; but it was pleasant all the same to have a lesser number to deal with. Only eight and our escort of four soldiers remained: I sent back the donkey and mounted Sultan Husain's good trotting camel instead.

We now rode at a swinging pace across the jōl and watched the wall of Kadur draw near like a breaking wave, until, at the base of its enormous cliff, we came to pre-Islamic names, scratched in rude large letters on a face of rock, where the track becomes alpine in its steepness. Even these camels of the Beni Himyar, incredibly clever as they are at climbing, stumble and groan here as they mount. I got off and puffed up slowly; over the landscape beneath me our cliff trailed its shadow like a gown. 'Azzan and its white towers showed in the east with the Kaut small and flat as a mirror behind them; to north and north-west were wrinkled, rusty hills picked out with shadows; white boulders of streams of Kadur wound into Wadi Habban. The long wadis in the north coiled, in the south they died in mists and sands of the sea. A great longing came over me to follow the old incense road, to go to Shabwa, through Wadi Jardan—Ptolemy's Gorda— which must, I do not doubt, have been the ancient highway. Inscriptions are there, the beduin said, and pointed to small villages in sight. They laughed at my slowness and sat waiting on ledges with bunches of scented gummar in their hair, their guns against their knees; they ran with the same elastic ease up hill or down; at intervals they let me drink from their water-skin, a saffron-tinted and distasteful water, trickling it out into the palm of my hand, which they taught me to use as a funnel. It took us one hour and three quarters to climb from the base of the cliff. Then, by a slope of rubble with the drop on either side, we reached the remains of a gate, and a wall of small stones, narrowing to the top, which, the beduin said, runs, breached and ruined, round Kadur,

282

The home of the Beni Himyar

It must have been not a fortress, but a great fortified enclosure, dominating the Meifa'a roads, and there are many ways up to it, the beduin say, both from the east and from Habban. Through the few remaining rectangular blocks of the gateway one steps into a new landscape of round shoulders and flat stony spaces, and deep clefts filled with trees and water-holes, and finds the whole area scattered with flakes and flints of prehistoric men. Ibex must have been abundant, for their outline is frequent, notched on flat limestones polished by the wind. But the ruins themselves for which we had come so far were scarcely worth the trouble, for they were but shells of rough stone houses, impossible, I should think, to date, built along the edge of a ravine. We left them till the morning and descended to camp in a valley, under a tree they call labakh (*ficus sp.*), with edible pointed nuts and bright green leaves. I collected a branch of it but 'Ali lost it, for he took no interest in botany and thought it unnecessary for others to do so.

It must not be supposed for a moment that he was dejected by our tussle of the morning. Far from it. So pleased was he at my success that he continued to congratulate me, dwelling with joy on passages that any normal man would have been delighted to forget. To bear a grudge to one so unself-conscious would be impossible, and we spent an amiable evening, though the beduin came at intervals in private to ask why I did not send away my sayyid and go exclusively with them.

There were twelve of them now. The heights of Kadur are scattered with the children of Himyar. Into these hidden valleys, they said, no foreigner had come, and they made us just as welcome as if they had always wished for our presence, and built three fires, in the bottom, on the boulders, and brought a sheep and a goat and roasted them on stones. There was any amount of dry dead timber lying about. The night was cold. The little chirping creatures that sing on the jōl, were here also. "Like locusts," said 'Ali, "they hang on trees by their hind-legs and are so frightened that they chirp all night. Only the monkey is as full of fear as they are and moves always from place to place and wakes quite far from where he went to sleep." I found myself doing this in my sleeping-sack, trying to find comfortable hollows on the ground. The under-branches of the trees were fire-lit against the stars. 'Ali brought two small naked children who had appeared out of the landscape, and laid them in the warmth to sleep under a cloth beside me. In this place, so stony, so secret and so ancient, there was a friendly feeling of high remoteness, cold and still. The pole star shone down the valley, and the only sign of Time was the swinging of the Plough about it from the right-hand slope to the left.

Next morning we saw the ruins of the village, we saw the ibex outlines and two lines of slabs on end, possibly a tomb, on the flat above us, drank a bowl of fresh milk brought from invisible flocks, and descended again to the everyday world below.

Here trouble began, for I had spent my last money, and had also promised half a dollar for each man who went with us to Kadur; they could only get this present by coming to 'Azzan, and none would trust the other to fetch it. So they hung about us like bulldogs—while 'Ali—feebly hoping to shake them off—said that we had no food. His methods with beduin were infelicitous; you would have thought he might have known by this time that a bedu can starve far better than we.

"Is there no food at all?" I asked.

"Hardly any," said he, reluctantly. But we had it out and it proved still to be tolerably sufficient for a meal, and the beduin—pleased to see this attempt against hospitality frustrated—squatted happily under the rock by the green water, to which we had returned. One old man only still stood grumbling before me, and presently—working himself to a frenzy—turned to his tribesmen and the listening hills and asked them why they let foreigners, dogs and sons of dogs, loose into their land. "Give me my money," he said.

But the audience was now mostly on the side of the stranger, who had no liking to be called the child of a dog. "My money," I said, "is a gift, and I give it to those who are pleasant in their speech." The Beni Himyar were rousing every arrogance of the West.

"Pleasant?" said the old man, whose face would by now have been purple if it had not been dark blue to begin with. "Never will I be pleasant to Unbelievers, the curse of Allah upon them."

"You have eaten my food," said I. "Now you can go. All these shall have their present when we reach 'Azzan; but the uncivil tongue gets no reward. What sort of behaviour is that to a stranger?"

The beduin looked down in an embarrassed circle, while 'Ali and a soldier led him off and pulled his white beard, a thing I had never seen done before. I learned afterwards that they quietly bribed him to go as soon as they were out of earshot. 'Ali's political ideals are those of appeasement. When I reproached him for pandering to a bully, he merely laughed and said that it was better; and it was only long after that I learned that he had never, till that last moment, paid for the dates which belonged to the old man, whose moroseness was therefore understandable though ill-directed—for how could I possibly guess that a complaint against my religion was really a demand for the payment of 'Ali's debts?

As I rode down the short 'aqaba from the jōl, already tolerably weary of continuous strife, I saw the whole male population of Lamater village drawn up with their guns to intercept us. 'Ali, riding pillion behind me, twittering with the conscience of his yesterday's fraud upon him, turned the camel's head and got a start, avoiding the village, down the wadi on the way to 'Azzan. But they soon came up with us, cheerfully anxious to extract blackmail if they could; they jogged alongside in small groups of eight or ten, and if we tried to trot away, banged the withers of the camel with their rifles, so that it jerked and bounded, and made me stop at last by telling me of an inscription at the turn of the wadi on a ledge.

'Ali showed every symptom of approaching intractability, and the thought of more trouble with him, and the fatigue of twenty-two hours of camel in two days with a saddle that rubbed, together with the nagging of the beduin renewed by fresh reserves in an unending stream, all so acted, that I suddenly felt tears rolling down my cheeks, a spectacle which sobered 'Ali in one instant. I was allowed to climb among a jubilant crowd to the ledge and photograph the inscription, which had been put there by the Himyarites who restored the walls and irrigation ditches of this wadi in the year A.D. 540 or thereabout. It is an unknown inscription, and escaped the notice both of the Landberg expedition (who were never able to wander far from 'Azzan) and of Capt. Miles who followed the Habban wadi in 1870 and was told, as he passed, of the ruins of Kadur on his left.

We now rode with, before us and behind us, an endless scattered stream of dark-blue figures in small groups hand in hand, swinging their skirts and rifles along the flat space that ends in the distance with the towers of 'Azzan. When we got there I slipped through my door and left Nasir to deal with the tumult and found the Sultans rejoicing over the success of our adventure at Kadur. To them in their day-to-day fight, it was a victory over the beduin; prestige, it appeared, had been maintained. "And if you had turned back," they said, "no one in this country would have believed you when you said that you belong to the nation of the English."

Chapter XV

THE SULTAN'S CARAVAN

" My feet upon the moonlit dust
Pursue the ceaseless way."

(SHROPSHIRE LAD.)

THE ORIENTAL IDEA EXPRESSED BY ST. JOHN THAT CHAOS IS the beginning of all things except Speech is true in a lesser way of Arab journeys. By the middle of next morning signs of bustle began like small waves to lap around us, a last effort to extract money was made by all who could force an entry to my room, and at two o'clock Sultan Husain saw me on to a camel which knelt in the dust, in sight of the roofs and battlements and ladies of 'Azzan. They all had gathered to watch the caravan depart. Sultan Husain paused to write the names of his four worst enemies on a scrap of paper, so that I might not forget them in Aden, then arm in arm affectionately with Qasim he walked before me to where, in a busy group of farewells, our seven camels stood together. No one yet seemed to know who was going and who was staying. Nasir and his brother came walking down, with rifles on their shoulders and sandals on their feet: Ahmed, the Sultan's brother also, dressed gaily in green and mauve and yellow, a bunch of scented mauve-tipped herbs tied with a yellow leather fillet in his hair. A handful of the bodyguard was there, some going and some staying, their cartridge-belts

288

replenished round their waists. And now the Old Wolf
arrived pushing all help aside and climbed on to his camel as
it stood; having settled himself well above the mattress,
saucepans and coffee-pots that made his luggage, he opened
a black umbrella and went on. Untidily we broke away and
followed, growing as we went, for the merchants of Hauta
(which is the trading town, 'Azzan being the fortress only) had
heard of the strong caravan, and their camels and slaves were
descending by the bend of the stream with bales of tobacco
to join us.

Down the wadi we went, under the northern gate of
Naqb, whose shallow buttresses looked from their mound
upon us as in their day they have looked on many a caravan.
Here indeed we were travelling as the ancient merchants
travelled, their bales wrapped probably in the same sort of
sheets of plaited palm leaf, desert coloured, as these that now
bulged one on each side of the bobbing camels, in a long
line that caught the sun.

Ruined villages on gentle rises across the low, ribbed sands
of the seil-bed also caught the light. All here was ruined
except the mud forts of the Ba Rasheid in the distance, who
make perpetual raids: small cairns on the mounds about us
marked the places where the law-abiding villagers try to
snipe them when they come. This stretch of Meifa'a should
be an area of rich and lovely gardens, and possibly was so in
the days of the Indian trade: the water is there for the asking,
at sixteen to twenty-five feet below the surface of the ground.
But now, of its 360 wells, nearly every one is fallen in and
ruined; the villages are shells of houses mostly empty and
dead enclosures of untended fields. Far on our left we passed
Jōl 'Aqil and Raida, and Mansura with a few more people

inside it on our right: rich with rak and samr trees, with uth'ub (*Pluchea Dioscoridis Dc*) and the long flowered qaf (*Prosopis Spicigera L*) and a'ta (*Calligonum comosum L'Herit*) fluffy with red seed balls, the landscape glowed in the quiet light of evening. But it was a stricken land, and its peace only the deceiving silence of countries desolate in war. No dogs barked near the villages; no children rushed to meet us; poverty and death hung in the solitary air. When we had ridden four hours we turned left from the wadi through sandy hillocks, and camped by a depopulated village called Dhaheri, where a few miserable peasants lingered and took the Sultans to sleep in a house.

The rest of us settled here round quickly-built fires in the darkness in a sandy hollow alive with camel-ticks, surrounded by trees. Qasim made my bed; Nasir came out of the house with a basket of rice and meat and sat to eat with me by the light of a lantern; and I slept till Qasim woke me with hot ovaltine at one-thirty under a high cold moon. We had a long and unsafe stage to go.

The caravan was gathered already when we joined it at two o'clock, waiting dimly under a moon that scudded through pale clouds. We were supposed to be quiet and show no lights, for the country of the Al Dhiyaib lay close at hand, but there is something beyond mere human unobtrusiveness in the silence of a camel caravan with its soft padded feet in the night. Among the waiting shadows Nasir came up to ask me how I felt, and bent to take a drink of milk from my naga (she camel), whose foal ran loose beside her, in and out among the head-ropes like a dog. The Old Wolf had started; word was passed from one to another; the caravan like a snake uncoiling shook out its silhouette against the moonlit sand, and every camel-man tied his rope to the tail of the animal before him, like one of those long lines of fishing boats you see ploughing up the straits of Euboea into the early dawn.

So we too walked through the sand-dunes and bushes, drawing away from the stream-bed of Meifa'a towards the left. From the derelict houses one dog only barked as we passed. Dhaheri is the last village, we had sixteen hours of uninhabited country before us. Those who rode settled in to their baggage as you settle on your deck-chair for a day's cruising, arranging their shawls and soft objects around them, and resting on arms slightly bent like springs to break the constant jerking of the road; the bodyguard, twelve of them, walked with rifles here and there beside us; the camel-men, with their heads down, went crooning to themselves. As the morning light began to show faintly, ripples of talk would waken, up and down the caravan; it is a creature that has moods cheerful or morose of its own, apart from the beings who compose it, and feels sleepy or tired or hopeful according to the moments of its day. At five-thirty, after three and a half hours, word came that the Old Wolf had stopped. We too swiftly dismounted, gathered thorns for a fire, and were drinking tea in a few moments, for all knew that the time of rest was short before us. I slept on my sheepskin and woke at eight to find that we were starting already. The young Sultans had bought the day's meat from some beduin and were handing it round, freshly roasted, in rations to be eaten as we rode.

That was the last rest we had. We were now a large concourse of people, twenty-seven camels in all, and with our promiscuous parcels, paraffin lamps swinging, and the cooking-pot that always clattered from the Sultan's saddle, looked rather like a collection of tinkers than an expedition prepared for war. My old Uncle was there, striding gallantly through the morning, with a lizard (*dhabb*) about a foot long with a scaly tail, tied in his loincloth as a present for me. I came to love this little creature later on and called it Himyar, after the tribe and the hills from which it came.

Talk now grew lively through the early hours, a crackle of laughter and repartee running up and down. Beduin, falling into step below me, told me they meant to keep the motors that kill their camel traffic from 'Azzan. "One of them tried to come," they said, "last year, and followed the coast from Shuqra and would have run up the stretches of Meifa'a which are easy, but we threatened it, and the travellers refused the risk, though the chauffeur would have come. But we will kill whoever does so,"[1] they said unanimously. And I replied with the story of King Canute, who, like them, tried to keep out the waves of the sea.

In spite of our slow unvarying pace, we covered much more ground than when we rode alone. Now and then I would put out my feet and rest them in the teddy-bear thickness of the foal's back as it trotted alongside, with soft eyes and pretty lashes, rubbing affectionately against its mother. Sometimes it strayed and the two would call to each other with deep mooing voices, as if, amid the fussiness of our human chatter, they lived aloof in their remote primeval world.

The morning grew hot. We plodded across rivers of

[1] The tragic murder of three R.A.F. men who, unable to speak Arabic, were forced to land a little to the west of Meifa'a in November 1939, has since come to prove the difficulties of intercourse with these tribes.

Old Wolf

gravel among small limestone knolls, seeing no human being, though the Al Dhiyaib might be expected in these wastes :[1] only on the far right, across the invisible Meifa'a the oasis of Radhun could be seen in the distance, dark green and dim in the blaze of the sun.

The men on foot now began to come with water for the thirsty; a continual business of such little services ran up and down the line. If they wanted to walk, people slipped down the camels' legs and only clumsy ones like me had to make it kneel to climb up again. At intervals the Old Wolf, jolting beneath his black umbrella, gave presents of oil; from the goatskin that swayed at his saddle, men poured it over their heads and naked shoulders in the sun.

The slate-coloured plains of gravel shone satiny like the backs of well-groomed horses. Behind them ridges of "kaut" began to show against the range of Jebel Aswad on our left, and stole in front of it and hid it slowly with a pale, smooth wall. As we went south the sand increased in great two-coloured dunes, tawny and pale yellow; at noon we got a far glimpse of the sea. But we turned east, away from the estuary of Meifa'a, among even taller dunes, pure yellow now like islands on the limestone floor. The hills that look so white from the sea are "kaut"; they run in a long ridge about ten miles inland and mask harder mountains whose invisible presence is shown only by flints and pebbles that lie in a gay incredible variety of qualities and colours, brought down by torrent across our path.

The camels here had difficulties; the caravan floundered

[1] Professor Pike, who came down by this way a few weeks later, had an alarm among the sand-dunes and found the beduin well able to deal with marauders if they came.

293

and stumbled and broke into straggling ends. Anyone, you would have thought, could have attacked it, and the men pointed to a hollow close beneath us where nine on each side had been killed twenty years ago. The familiar wadi plants we knew had disappeared now, harmal and tzafar (*Tephrosia apollinea link*) and samr; new things—reedy grass and small white flowers, duweila (*Pulicaria glutinosa Jaub*) and sharh (*Odyssea mucronata Forsk*) and a sticky-leaved herb I had not seen, clung on to the hummocks of the sand, with rak and tamarisk in the hollows. On our right the dunes hid from us the sight of the sea, and looked in the heat like a line of immovable breakers.

You would have supposed, from the comforting words of the caravan, that we were just turning to our oasis at noon; but it took us four and a half hours to reach it, a smudge on the stubble-coloured slopes of sand. Nasir, who had walked these twelve hours with his gun upon his shoulder, was still ready to organize a dance as we approached, but first turned aside amiably to look at what seemed in the distance an artificial breakwater towards the sea. It was nothing but a natural outcrop, and there is, I think, no vestige of human labour on the flat stretch that lies eastward between Meifa'a and the volcanic hills. Having ascertained this in spite of weariness, we made for our oasis, beating tunes on my saucepan for the men, who danced their zamil divided in two wings. My old Uncle, with the lizard at his waist, joined in, apparently as fresh as when he started. Even at the end of such a day these men walk with their springy freedom, often hand in hand, and I noticed, looking down upon them, that their hair is not usually black, but has brown streaks in its slight curls that catch the light.

Methods old and new

This art of theirs of the caravan is the one thing the Arab has learned by endless repetition to do supremely well. One after one all my modern gadgets failed me; the thermos broke, the lunch basket was far too complicated, only the Mansab's quilt stood me in good stead. But the bedu's waterskin, with one hand used as a cup and a funnel, is economical and light; his coffee-pot, brass and unbreakable, hangs under the saddle over the camel's tail; his cotton shawl can be used for everything in the world that cloth is ever used for. He has all that is necessary and nothing superfluous; and if his rope were of the kind that did not break whenever you pull at it, one might say that his equipment was perfect of its kind.

At four-thirty we came to the oasis where palms grow rich and sudden round hot springs on the slope. The azure water runs in pools in their shade, delicious to bathe in if modesty allowed; but I could not rely on the villagers of 'Ain ba Ma'bad as I could on my beduin behind their rock. The people here were indeed mostly slaves who work for beduin owners and long for freedom and the Royal Air Force; while the thought of British interference is correspondingly unpopular with their masters. An old slave who crept up for medicine after dark, was tortured and twisted with beatings.

There are but a tiny mosque and a few low rooms, and pens of thorns for goats at 'Ain ba Ma'bad, and in the biggest of the rooms we sat and were received. When the chief Elder came briskly along with handshakes and, reaching me, saw that I was a woman, he started backwards and fled.

I was their first European female, and the British were anyway unpopular, because Harold was pressing for payment

The Sultan's Caravan

for some theft or murder. Chiefly however they were
annoyed with their own Sultans who had taken away from
them the guardianship of the track: "And now you see how
the Al Dhiyaib come and levy blackmail on camels. Two
of our men were made to pay a dollar each, only the day
before yesterday, at the place where you turned to the east."

"Perhaps you did not keep the ways safe enough. Are
you the people who let Colonel Lake be shot at along this
road?"

"Colonel Lake?" said they in genuine surprise. "He is
not a Moslem. It does not matter if he is shot at." And
though I argued the point, with quotations from the Quran
and the support of my companions, the atmosphere of 'Ain
ba Ma'bad remained unfriendly, and I was too tired to sit
and try to alter it with talk after food.

Qasim found a secluded goat-pen with a low door by
which one could creep in; and I had just settled for a long
night when Nasir appeared and said, regretfully, that we were
starting at 2 a.m. again next morning. The camel-men, he
explained, having heard that a dhow had just called at Bal Haf
were anxious to pick up a load and return the selfsame day.
The comfort of twenty-seven camel-men was obviously
more important than mine, though it seemed hard to realize
it at the moment, but nothing, I told Nasir, short of the Day
of Judgement would make me move before four in the morning,
and he departed, obviously relieved to get off so easily. The
affairs of every single man in the caravan devolved on Nasir's
shoulders, from the mending of a lamp to the milking of a
goat; he alone saw to it all, and was as cheerful and competent
at the end as at the beginning of the long string of crises that
the travelling Arab calls a day. He was good-looking too,

296

and sturdy as an oak tree, and had a smile that lifted the corners of his eyes.

In the morning, under a sky painted with high moonlit clouds like some baroque church ceiling, we once more padded darkling on the sand, and came, as the light broke, to the springs of Juwairi, that run hot through turf-green runnels into palm groves. Here the camels drank, stooping snake necks in decorative patterns, while mountains opened in the eastern distance under the wakening sky. Nasir dragged my quilt to a quiet place and I slept for two and a half hours, and we then rode inland again among sand-dunes, with only rak and shahr and the grass qalila and 'andam, the reed-like grass eaten by cattle, about us, and on the sands a glitter in sheltered places, shining "like eyes of locusts" the beduin said. This glittering powder comes from the sea, and lies in patterns where the waves end on black volcanic sand and even the fluted scallop shells are black. Far in the east, when one comes out on to the shore an hour from 'Ain Juwairi, one sees the long snout headland of Bal Haf.

It took us four more hours to go there, but no one minded in the delight of the waves and the fresh sea-wind. The breakers came rolling in in four long rows towards the shrinking camels; armies of crabs scuttled under their feet —like beduin, I thought, so numerous and active, round the hermit crabs, peaceful citizens, hampered by their shells. There were gulls, but not many; and shells pink and yellow lying among the black; and no cultivation in all this distance, and only one house, at Qal'a, where soldiers guard the water on which Bal Hal depends. Every two days they take it over by boat in goatskins.

As we drew near we saw how Bal Hal is built on a stream

of solidified craters that must have rolled once, liquid and convulsed, towards the sea. They are black, duller than night, and the sea shines strangely brilliant below them, and three white towers and a few palm huts are all the buildings that encircle a little harbour lined with dazzling sand. In the middle of it, a dhow rode at anchor, and bales of merchandise were lying on the shore. Indigo, sugar, rice, and chief of all, sesame, called *dijil*, both for eating and for oil—they lay there as the bales of Phoenician traders must have lain on the earliest Greek or Cornish beaches; and our camel-men hastily untied our own bales of tobacco and began to load, so as to return with the daylight to the oasis from which we came.

The Old Wolf stopped outside Bal Haf to say his prayers. My camel was stopped too, so that I should not enter before him, and by the time we proceeded, dismounted, towards the middle tower, the little garrison and all stray inhabitants were gathered in two rows to shake hands. Here too there were signs of reluctance at the sight of me; there were strangers, chiefly merchants from Hauta, who had already sent messages to say they had no wish to see me in their town; and while the Old Wolf and his retinue went up to sit in their tower, Nasir hurried me unobtrusively to a small and sunny room above the sea.

The last inhabitants had left smudges of indigo and other more animated traces which Nasir recognized, but—seeing my distress—pretended to be mistaken, till I produced two bodies. We thereupon gave up the tactful fiction with a smile. They were the first I had ever seen in the Hadhramaut, and a little thing like that was quite insufficient to damp the pleasures of washing in a room to oneself. I had done this and was sitting alone at my window watching the loading of bales, when a

tall man with his shawl like a toga about him entered un-
announced behind me and wished me peace.

"And upon you be peace," said I.

"Have you no mercy," said he, "you and your people?"
I looked at him in surprise.

"There," said he, pointing to the last of the small white
towers, square on the tongue of rocks, "there lies the Sultan's
brother, bound in that room three years, and dying."

I looked at him with a sort of horror. The tower stands
alone, one room to each story and three tiny windows on
each side; it looks out over a blankness of lava and sea. And
I thought of the prisoner's little son in 'Azzan, and his
cry.

"I have waited long by your door," the stranger continued,
"so that no one should see me come in."

"I will do what I can," said I.

Without a word, with a sort of dignified and manly haste,
he turned and left me. And I was able to speak for the
prisoner so that he was freed from Aden.

In the late afternoon our camel-men departed leading
their camels like a frieze below my window, against the shining
background of the sea. My own man was ill and lay groaning
for an hour or so under a rug in my room, and I could not
think what to do for him. He was a friendly youth, unhappy
because the beduin girl he loved had jilted him, and I pre-
vailed on the reluctant 'Ali, who does not believe in superstition and is honest in these matters, to write him a charm;
and now he had to go off writhing with pain, through the
lonely Hadhina, under Jebel Aswad a four-days' journey,
to avoid the danger of the road by which we came, for they
had no escort of soldiers. With the departure of the caravan,

299

our little harbour sank back into its sun-baked quiet; the Sultans and the garrison shut themselves in their tower; and only the passengers of the dhow, let loose on this unfortunate shore and unable to get any water, raised a small dust of chatter under my window till far into the night.

Chapter XVI

THE SITE OF CANA

"Sed nox atra caput tristi circumvolat umbra."
(*Aeneid.*)

IN THE DAWN I WAS AWAKENED BY VOICES AT PRAYER. IT WAS the garrison, led by Ahmed, the Sultan's brother, at the edge of the waves below. In the clear light, turning to Mekka, his charming and handsome face looked tranquil as the sea. His turban showed against the tower across the little bay in whose lonely whiteness his brother lay dying. Strangely, I thought, must that familiar voice of prayer rise to the prisoner's ears.

Nasir had told me that they would hold up the dhow for a day while he took me to visit the harbour of Bir Ali, the site of Cana, and that a boat in ease and comfort would replace the six-hours' camel ride along the coast. No boat however came. Except for the dhow, there was no boat in all the landscape, and by the time that the one sambuk of Bal Haf appeared in the distance bringing water, the wind had turned against us. I felt I could not cope with two things as capricious as the wind and the Arabs together and gave up the thought of going by sea. The dawn had turned into daylight, and it was eight o'clock when Nasir finally produced two camels, and said that we would get a boat from the men of Bir Ali to bring us back safely in the arms of the monsoon.

The Site of Cana

Apart from the endless indispensable condition of keeping one's temper, success on an expedition in Arabia depends, I think, chiefly on the amount of local information one has been able to collect. In Hureidha, where our excavations depended on it, I had been careful before I went to find out the ins and outs of all the chief affairs, and the winter had gone without a hitch. But here I was, so to say, on holiday; I had 'Ali as my only precaution, and he had made things easy everywhere except among the beduin—but otherwise I took no trouble and did not know the elementary fact that the two little harbours of Bal Haf and Bir Ali are chronically at war. Peace at this very moment was being laboriously engineered by Harold in Mukalla; this did not alter the fact that Bir Ali was a hereditary enemy; and if its inhabitants would make themselves sufficiently unpleasant to me, there was the chance that the R.A.F. might bomb them, or so my Sultans hoped. Nasir, with one camel-driver called Rupee and five soldiers, took me happily eastward on what I looked upon as an archæological expedition, while he looked upon it as something of a raid.

"There is a *little* difficulty sometimes between us and our cousins," he said in his understating way, and led me unsuspecting over the slag-heap coast of dead volcanoes, pitted with craters, whose only beauty is when their dusty blackness dips into the jewel-green of the sea.

Of all the visitors to Cana, Von Wrede alone, I think, has approached by land; and he took the inland road. So that it was a good thing to follow the coast and look there for any possible alternative sites where ruins might be found. Bal Haf I had carefully examined the night before, and had eliminated it from among the possible harbours because of its want of water now and in the past. The present trade is due chiefly to the fact that customs there are about two-thirds per cent compared to ten per cent at Mukalla. As we rode eastward, one only harbour looked promising, formed by the crater of Kaidi or Rotl, that stands out in the sea; but here too there is no water—only a rain-hole in the rocks long since dry—and there was no sign of building about it, either on its flanks, whose natural steepness looks like walls hung over by stalactites of the limestone, or on top, where a hollow cone is sunk in the circle of the crater. All these rocks have a flat sort of coral gallery, running round them at the water's edge; heaps of oyster-shells left by the beduin remind one of the Fish-Eaters' Bay.

Here, says the Periplus, just "beyond the cape projecting from this bay lies Cana of the Frankincense Country." As you round the black precipitous shoulder of Rotl you see it, Husn al Ghurab, a crater flattened and solitary, far off, beyond a sweep of sand. The sand of the intervening shore is here so white and shining that the foam of waves looks grey as it breaks. Crocodile black snouts of lava, half submerged, push through it everywhere. Beyond, in a sea misty with sunlight, are the islands as the Periplus describes them, white with the droppings of birds, and one on either hand. They lie, like pebbles, in the luminous lap of water and of sky. So graphically had the old mariner written that for a moment the centuries vanished, I heard him speaking, I saw the landmarks as he saw them, hugging in his small vessel that inhospitable shore.

Behind the crater is a bay, white-green with sand that shines through the deep water, and across it the small town of Bir Ali with walls, a single palm beside it. Eastward the land rounds to the black snout of Mijdaha, the only other possible site for Cana.

The whole bay, in a great wing-like curve, rises on every side to a semi-circle of dead volcanoes, twelve or twenty of them, that look down like spectators, observant from their thrones. Down their easy ridges caravans can journey by a dozen different ways. There, on the road to Hajr, is Obne,[1] or Libne, seen by Von Wrede, and another ruin of which they told me, called Mubna al-Kafiri, a day's distance from Bal Haf; the very geography of the wide amphitheatre shows how it must once have been a meeting-place of caravans.

Captain Miles, in 1870, found the ruins of the town and its houses in the flat ground between the crater and Bir Ali, and Count Landberg saw them, nearly buried and with no important buildings among them when he landed here in 1896. Built in the black lava stone that lies about, they are not visible to the casual eye; the fortified important places were on the rock above.

One can still climb there by the easy remains of a causeway, above the open shaft of what looks like a grave in the north of the hill. Great black blocks, roughly cut, show the sea-wall protecting the citadel's approach; and on a ledge east of the causeway the two inscriptions in the rock are clear as on the day that they were cut. Count Landberg photographed only the smaller of them, and I could see why, for the larger is difficult to get into the lens; but he copied them both, as I did again, not knowing for certain that he had done so.

---

[1] This is Bana, now (in 1939) visited by Harold Ingrams who followed and found many traces of one of the main incense routes from Bir Ali by Hajr—Wadi Irma—to Shabwa. He came upon a large causeway and ruins, and is I hope publishing an account of this journey.

Records of Cana

As through a rift in clouds, they show for a moment the history of Cana in the past. The citadel itself was called Mawiya, and the Governor of Cana here, in the shorter inscription, recorded his presence. The longer one is dated and tells how the tribes of Himyar, having made an expedition into Abyssinia, were harassed by the Abyssinians in their turn; with their lands invaded, their king killed, they shut themselves up in this fortress, and restored its single gateway, its cisterns and walls in the year A.D. 625 or thereabout, many centuries after the Periplus speaks of the ancient harbour. Of its later history under Islam, little news can be gleaned. Such as there is is taken from Ibn al Mujawir and Maqrizi and seems apocryphal. The old Wolf told me there had been a king here called Samana ibn adh-Dhubian and a village on the flat low-lying island of Hallani just below, but could not tell me where he got this news. With the decay of the trade-route, the strength that had kept the roads open and secure no doubt also decayed, and the natural advantages of the harbour and its wide approaches were counteracted as they are now by the wildness of the tribes. Nothing is left but the records of old labours, cut in volcanic rock. Four great cisterns, arranged with shallow slopes around them, to catch all rain that falls upon the crater; the ruins of buildings with glazed medieval potsherds and more ancient walls, and on the very summit the scattered traces of a serai or keep. From the height and wide area of the crater, several acres in extent, one looks out to a sea-horizon and to the semi-circle of the watching volcanoes: it is all desert now and wind-blown sand, but once there must have been oases and gardens, and Ptolemy's map shows various little harbours, where dhows would choose their anchorage according as the monsoon blew east or west. Count Landberg thinks that Mijdaha was the actual site of Cana, but my own opinion is that the town that gave its name to the harbour would lie beneath the walls of the fortress where the custom-houses and store-houses of frankincense and other merchandise would naturally stand: nor—having paced those cindery wastes by camel—do I think that caravans from the Meifa'a highway would go for anchorage and water one mile farther out of their way than they needed. Bir Ali is the first place they would come to where these two essentials are combined; and at Bir Ali any sensible caravan would stay.

These things I turned idly over while copying out the inscriptions through the quiet solitary hours of the afternoon, happy in the thought of ample time before us; for Sayyid 'Ali was to go east to Mukalla and as he passed through Bir Ali would send a boat to race us with the north-east wind behind it to Bal Haf.

So we proposed, and, towards four o'clock, sent Sayyid 'Ali walking round the little bay. I had finished my inscriptions and was resting, longing for water, which we had run out of, and dreaming of the harbour, my head against the roughened lava-blocks of the ruined sea-wall; and I listened in a pleasant vacuum to the small gay chatter of the sea. A noise and commotion seemed to be greeting 'Ali at the gate across the water. I paid no attention and time passed, until Nasir, squatting suddenly beside me with two strangers, remarked in a pleasant way that the townsmen wished to shoot.

I was very tired. I thought he meant that they were disappointed because we had not gone near them to enjoy a formal reception: I sat up and told the two envoys that I should be delighted on another occasion but had no time to-day. No answer could have been more fortunate. The envoys gazed blankly at their first experience of a female European enigma and Nasir looked delighted. I felt that I had adopted the correct attitude, but that something was wrong.

"They meant to shoot *us*," Nasir explained.

"And why didn't they?"

"The Elders persuaded them not to."

I was beyond anything else thirsty. "Are they sending the boat and the water?" I asked.

"They are sending the water, but no boat." Their methods of warfare, I could not help feeling, compared favourably with those of Europe.

It was time to attend to the bewildered envoys. Diplomatically speaking, we had the situation in hand. "Welcome and ease," I said. "When are you coming to shoot us?"

Outraged to see the matter treated with this levity, one of the ambassadors explained that they were not natives at all of the regrettable little town yonder, but inhabitants of 'Azzan who happened to be living there and had volunteered to come to their countrymen with a message. The message was that we should be attacked unless we went off instantly by the way that we had come. It was just upon sunset.

Sayyid 'Ali now re-appeared very twittery, and a little white-veiled huri with two waterskins behind him in the bay. 'Ali, because of his holiness, could enter the enemy walls. I counted out his money on the ground in the ebbing light and half expected trouble, for he had, I noticed, in an unobtrusive moment helped himself to what he considered a suitable amount, so that I gave less than I had intended; but

all he did was to burst into tears and kiss my hands, unable
to speak, and walked off sobbing with the envoys beside him,
a small forlorn figure with flapping skirts against the vast
arena of the darkening bay.

The shore of Cana grew forbidding in the twilight.

Our little band collected itself together, two camels, two
waterskins, a few packets of sticky sweets thoughtfully
brought by 'Ali, and a plank which one of the soldiers had
apparently (very ungratefully) looted from the huri. The
men, in a nonchalant way, took out their cartridges and
cleaned their rifles.

"They may cut us off at the pass," Nasir remarked, looking
over his small forces—six in all. "Now," he said suddenly,
"let us dance a zamil."

"Why?" asked the dejected soldiers.

"Why?" said Nasir with eyes so dancing with gaiety that
I shall ever comfort myself with the remembrance of them
when a fight is on hand. "Why? To annoy the town!"

Fatigue vanished in a moment: the six were off in a line
made uneven by the buried ruins, green flames from their
rifles scattering towards the hostile unresponsive walls, while
Rupee led my frightened camel after. There seemed to be
no path, and from a cloudy sky the dark was falling among
the sharp teeth of the lava: everyone spread out of sight. I
resisted a western passion for giving advice and waited, and
just as the night really fell the path was found. The squat
crater, the ghost of Cana, loomed behind us, a shadow
pursuing far into the night. We climbed, slowly and steadily,
into a blackness of lava unlit by any stars; the path, for some
strange reason, showed vaguely in a blind world; nothing
else was visible, except the dim silhouettes of volcanoes.

A journey by night

We rode and walked for hour after hour in a blank of time. I had no proper saddle and every limb was aching, but Nasir, in his useless sandals, walked cheerfully, leaving the other camel for his men. "A *little* fatiguing," he would say when pressed; and when asked how his feet were on the sharp invisible cinders: "They are all blood," he answered truly, in the same even tone. The camel too grew weary, and stumbled over the rough unseen way: "Wogar," Rupee would call, or "tariq" if it strayed from the path, or "leil," that is "the night is coming," to make it hurry, though it was an inapposite remark. In very bad places he sang " oh-ho, oh-oh-oh-*ho*," and I held on, for he was too tired to warn me of bad bits ahead, and I, for greater ease, was riding with one leg up in the insecure Arab way.

At some moment in the darkness we dismounted and saw by the light of a flare of thorns that it was only nine-fifteen —so strange and long are the hours of the night. We ate our sweet stuff and rested for ten minutes, and Nasir, who became in this adventure the gentlest and most thoughtful of companions, held the waterskin and showed me how to use it with one hand, pressing it against the ground, so that the water rises like a spring. He was never impatient. What is the use of being impatient in Arabia? People whose tempers break can never stand the strain. But when two of his men with nerves on edge quarrelled over a box of matches, he instantly leaped and seized the aggressor's rifle, wrestling with him for it in the light of the fire, and, as the two settled like growling dogs each on an opposite side, said unperturbed: "They will be friends to-morrow." The soldiers of his small garrison look up to him and take his hand and call him affectionately and intimately by his name. In readiness of wit, in cheerfulness and quickness of decision, in the unselfish bearing of hardship, he was a leader of his men.

After this we settled down again to one dark trudge of hours. The Southern Cross moved above our heads, the clouds had cleared away, but nothing could give beauty to our night, and whenever we passed from one shallow dip to another, new shapes of volcanoes, similar to the last ones, stood blacker than death on either hand. There must come a time, I reflected, when one can bear no more, and then I suppose one dies. Till then the spirit carries, strange and undefeatable, the unknown sustainer of men. But we were at last descending, a steep and long descent; there were no more craters before us; we stepped off the lava on to sand. Without a word Rupee hitched off the camel that followed and dropped asleep in the path as he lay, leaving me in the hands of the soldiers. We soon reached the sea: it was 2 a.m.; a moon, old and green, appeared over the ridges we had left, now shining, black and dead. We had been out for eighteen hours, thirteen and a half on a camel and two and a half on our feet, and there had been an average of nine hours a day on camel for a week before. When we reached the sleeping harbour I found that Qasim had packed my bed on the dhow; but the Mansab's quilt was there in a corner and I can remember the blankness of sleep falling like dew as I touched it with my cheek.

Chapter XVII

A DHOW TO ADEN

"*What spell, what enchantment allures thee*
Over the rim of the world
With the sails of the sea-going ships?"

(SAPPHO BLISS CARMAN.)

THE NEXT DAY BEING FRIDAY, THE DHOW WAITED FOR THE midday prayer and I was able to sleep. Nasir came in, cheerful with bandaged feet, and all the Sultans gathered to try to turn the day before into an Incident wherewith to bother the Sultan of Bir Ali. There was a last attempt to extract money; I did not grudge it, for it is a hard load to carry on a little kingdom with the beduin all around; the harbour, with its twenty-five soldiers, is all the source of income that there is. But it makes one feel rather like a sheep among wolves. I said to Nasir that I had meant to send a present from Aden.

"Presents are nice," said he, "but money is more useful." One has perhaps found that out oneself. I therefore sent an offering to the Old Wolf, and Nasir came back with a brightly coloured dilapidated basket and a goat cooked inside it to sustain us on our way. The old man was reluctant to be seen by the merchants of Hauta in public farewells to a woman, and was for staying in his tower. This, however, I would not have, and waited till he came. There was a shaking of

hands on the sand and a packing into huris, a climbing by
rope ladders up the side of the dhow. Farewell to Nasir in
his boat, farewell to the beach and its towers, the freedom,
lightheartedness and hardness, the courage, the fierce
merciless gaiety of Arabia.

The crew of eighteen, all from Dis in Oman and all related,
amid a welter of ropes, hoist up the double sail. How lucky
I was, everyone said, to get so big a boat; I wondered what the
size of a small one would have been. She was 120 feet long
and cost 8,000 rupees all complete. She had a tall tree from
Malabar as mast and a deck at the stern above the hollow
thwarts; here was the steering-wheel, and the compass in a
brass pagoda with a lantern inside it: and here the skipper
and I had sofas one on either side. The skipper, the old
Nakhuda, with hennaed beard cut short with scissors, makes
tea and tells of his yearly traffic between Calicut, Bombay,
Basra, Jedda and Zanzibar—over this wide range he roves
wherever his merchandise takes him. When the monsoon
blows too hard, between July and September, he shelters with
other dhows behind Ras Burum. He and his crew there
leave their craft with a single watchman, and go overland for
the date harvest in their homes of Oman, and stay till mid-
September, when they sail to buy dates in Basra. He is
related to the Sultan of Zanzibar, and has a brother, a judge,
in Oman, and has been since childhood the friend of his
employer, a rich merchant of Aden, where his dhow was
built thirty-two years ago.

As we left the harbour we nearly ran into the headland of
Bal Haf, for the chain broke that joins the steering-wheel and
rudder; three men came running to save it and tie the broken
ends with knotted oddments of cord.

At sea

The sails flap, their cordage makes a pattern against them. The edges are bound with thick rope that twists like a snake in the breeze. The hoisting is done to a chant, melodious and gentle like the voice of waves, ages of simple sea-faring are in it; when the hoisting is done the crew stand and admire, clapping their hands, with any able-bodied passenger who has helped because he happened to be there.

We have little cargo but thirty-two passengers, who pay three rupees each to be taken a hundred miles to Shuqra. They are mostly beduin and are sick decently over the side. The Sultans have sent eighteen people gratis, to the skipper's annoyance. Nearly all have done the journey by land, which takes ten days; and lying on the deck and thwarts, a thick carpet of bodies wrapped in *futahs* with naked shoulders, they make a running commentary on the landmarks of the shore where, far away in the haze, the familiar and for the moment unattractive shapes of volcanoes appear. The hours go peacefully. The crew sit about, plaiting ropes of palm leaf to sell in Aden for the making of seats. The skipper is pounding henna to dye his beard. At intervals they catch fish on a hook baited with wuzifs, trailed at the end of a long line. They are pulled, swishing like silver firework, through the water, and cooked on a primus stove among the cordage, and divided fairly between us all. The skipper feeds his passengers altogether on rice. There is a cheerful gong sound too on the deck, of ginger beaten in a mortar, to flavour the coffee which at intervals goes round. For me he has brought out his only tin of figs preserved in syrup, given him, he says, by the Italians, and pours out glasses of tea with a sailor's neatness, stirring with the handle of the teaspoon, so as to keep the other end dry for sugar, a thing no land Arab would bother to do.

A Dhow to Aden

It must be indelicate to eat in public. When the moment comes, a sail is brought and arranged like a curtain around me. But there are other moments for which no provision is made. The only sanitation are two small wooden cages, tied with rope to the outside of the dhow; here at intervals travellers stay meditating, their lower halves decently hidden, but the rest all exposed to the general view. This publicity I could not face and at last put the problem to the Nakhuda, who looked as if he had been a family man many times over. He saw my point and sent for three oars and a sail; these were draped like a tent, and there I could retire precariously over an ocean that rushed with great speed below, and with some reluctance, since, as I could not monopolize one-half of the sanitation altogether, the tent had to be erected afresh every time. There are inherent difficulties in the situation of a solitary female on a boat.

In the afternoon of the second day we anchored off Shuqra, a little town with mosque and palace against a pointed background of high hills. Here we dropped most of our crowd and continued for Aden with a few only, a soldier and a beduin or two from 'Azzan, servants of merchants in Hauta, who take bales of tobacco to sell for their masters and return after a week or two with different merchandise. These, in the sunset, lined themselves up for prayer with the crew in two long rows, swaying with the monsoon swell. There is ever a heartfelt accent in prayers at sea, but more so here, for we are very small, we creak in all sorts of places differently from a big boat, as if we were jointed and alive, and are alone too and have seen no craft on this ocean except a dhow far off whose high uplifted sail above the mast-top proclaims it from Sur in Oman.

Civilisation and the second rate

When the night has fallen and I can see only the cordage and sail against the stars, I listen to the steersman behind me singing softly over and over the ninety names of God to keep awake.

At three in the morning the lighthouse of Aden first appeared, a dim shaft on the hungry ridges, blossoming like civilization in recurrent intervals, with darkness large between. Only from the outer ocean and the night can you know how small a light it is, how vast the currents through which it beckons, how indomitable in his perpetual ventures the spirit of man.

As I lay there, drawing nearer, I thought of this civilization and of the beduin who is so happy without it. Perhaps it is because he need never choose the *second best*. Poor as his best may be, he can follow it when he sees it, and that is freedom. We, too often compelled to see two roads and take the worse one, are by that fact enslaved. Our lesser road may in itself be better than the wild man's best one; but that is neither here nor there, it is our *choice* of the second that makes us second-rate. The second-best for security in finance, the second-best for stability in marriage, the second-best for conformity in thought—it is our civilization, though not that of Hellas nor of the City of God; and every time we consciously accept it our stature is diminished. It would be pleasant, I reflected, to look back on a life that has never given its soul for money, its time to a purpose not believed in, its body to anything but love. The Arab can still say this, unconscious of alternatives. He will take a bribe gladly but will then do what he likes notwithstanding; his servitude does not penetrate far. Even 'Ali, regardless of the rules of property to an inconvenient degree, keeps his inner self free of them in an original way, which the materialist will never understand. The materialist too often is civilized man. Perhaps it is to get away from him, that so many quiet people like to travel in Arabia.

At nine the next morning we had already been sitting for hours at anchor in Aden harbour when the M.O., visiting from dhow to dhow, discovered me with surprise. Three beduin from 'Azzan, very naked with shaggy hair, leaped into his launch hoping to pass free of dues as my retainers; they were not mistaken; the port officer waved them kindly through among pleased pink-looking tourists landing from the P. and O., who looked upon us gratefully as Local Colour.

APPENDIX I

List of plants with Arabic names and uses, kindly identified at the Royal Botanic Gardens, Kew.

ADENIUM sp. *Madhadh.*

ADIANTUM CAPILLUS-VENERIS L. *Tulhub.* Maidenhair fern.

AERUA JAVANICA JUSS. *Rà.* Feathery seed used to stuff pillows.

ANOGEISSUS BENTII BAKER. *Misht.* Tree; leaf eaten by cattle.

BLUMEA GARIEPINA DC. *Sakab* and *Haugh.*

CALLIGONUM COMOSUM L'HERIT. *A'ta* . Tree; leaf eaten by camels.

CAMPYLANTHUS JUNCEUS EDGEW. *'Alat al-Jebel.*

CAPPARIS GALEATA FRES. *Lasaf.* A Caper plant. Eaten by camels.

,, SPINOSA L. *'Alas.* A Caper. Leaf pounded to scrape hair off water-skins.

CASSIA ACUTIFOLIA DEL. *Sene.* True Senna. Purgative. Leaves are beaten with water for wounds.

,, HOLOSERICEA FRES. *'Ishriq.* A Senna. Seeds edible.

CLEOME ARABICA L.

,, DROSERIFOLIA DEL. *Shajarat ad-Dib* or *Huwaim.*

,, MACRODENIA SCHWEINF.

CONVOLVULUS GLOMERATUS CH. A Bindweed.

CORCHORUS ANTICHORUS RAENSCH. *Saghrab.* A Jew's Mallow.

CROTALARIA AEGYPTIACA BENTH. A Castanet plant or rattle pea.

CYMBOPOGON SCHOENANTHUS (L). SPRENG. *Sakhbar* or *Tza'a.* Powdered for soap.

EUPHORBIA aff. DENDROIDES L. *Deni.* A spurge. Latex used as glue, for sandals.

FAGONIA CRETICA L. *Durma* or *Dureima.* Eaten by cattle.

Appendix I.

FICUS SALICIFOLIA VAHL. *Lithab.* Flavour for sesame oil. Said to poison camels.

FICUS sp. *Tzaraf.* Tree; eaten by cattle.

„ „ *Labah.* Fruit edible when cooked.

„ SYCAMORUS L. *Suqum.* Mulberry fig. Edible.

„ VASTA FORSK. *Tolak.* Bark cooked for fevers; makes tea.

FORSKALEA TENACISSIMA L.

GRANTIA SENECIONOIDES BAKER. *'Amkir.* Not edible.

GYMNOSPORIA SENEGALENSES (LAM.) LOES. *Tharar.*

HELIOTROPIUM ARBAINENSE FRES.

„ STRIGOSUM WILLD. *Tagrūm.*

„ UNDULATUM VAHL. *Rumran; ribla.* Used to draw out sores; the leaves are applied semi-dried.

INDIGOFERA ARGENTEA L. *Hawir.* Wild indigo. Used for dyeing.

„ ARGENTEA. *Hawarwar.* Small tree; eaten by camels.

„ SPINOSA FORSK. *Natsh.* Eaten by camels.

„ sp. *Hisar.* An indigo.

JATROPHA sp. aff. SPINOSA (FORSK.) VAHL. *Dumma'.*

KALANCHOE BENTII HOOK. F.? *Qurn adh-Dhabi.*

LASIOSIPHON SPHAEROCEPHALUS BAKER.

LEPTADENIA PYROTECHNICA (FORSK.) DECNE. *Marikh.* Eaten by camels.

LITHOSPERMUM sp. *Lubeine.* Eaten by goats.

MAERUA CRASSIFOLIA FORSK. *Sarh.* Leaf used for eye trouble.

„ „ „ *Sanawar.*

„ sp. *Himra.*

MORINGA APTERA (FORSK) GAERTN. *Ban.* Ben tree. Against snake-bite. Eaten by cattle. Seed soaked in water subdues swellings.

ODYSSEA MUCRONATA FORSK. *Sharh.*

PAVETTA aff P. LONGIFLORA VAHL.

PENTATROPIS SPIRALIS (FORSK.) DCNE. *'Akoka* or *Saqlul.*

Appendix I

PLUCHEA DIOSCORIDIS DC. *Uth'ub.* Tree; eaten by camels. A Marsh Fleabane.

POINCIANA ELATAL. *'Aradh.*

PROSOPIS SPICIGERA L. *Qaf.* A Mesquite. Tree; eaten by camels.

PULICARIA CRISPA (FORSK.) BENTH. ET HOOK. *Jithiath.* A Fleabane.

„ GLUTINOSA JAUB. *Duwaila.* A Fleabane.

RHAZYA STRICTA DCNE. *Harmal.* Root purgative. Leaves used as eye-lotion or beaten with water for wounds.

SALSOLA BOTTAE BOISS. *Rishi.* A Saltwort. Fattening for goats.

SALVIA sp. A Sage.

SAMOLUS VALERANDI L. Brook weed.

SCHWEINFURTHIA LATIFOLIA BAKER.

„ SPHAEROCARPA BENTH.

SCIRPUS LITTORALIS SCHRAD. *'Ais.*

SENRA INCANA GAV. *Sabata.*

SOLANUM PUBESCENS WILLD.

STATICE AXILLARIS FORSK. *Fashfish.* A Sea Lavender.

TAMARIX sp. *Ithl.*

TAVERNIA LAPPACEA DC.

TEPHROSIA APOLLINEA LINK. *Tzafar.* A Goat's Rue. Eaten by camels.

TRIBULUS MOLLIS EHR. *Shersher.* A Caltrops. Eaten by camels.

WENDLANDIA ARABICA DEFL. *Tzaraf* or *Dharaf.*

ZIZYPHUS HAMUR ENGL. *Habadh.* A Jujube. Lote-bush. Eaten by cattle.

„ SPINA CHRISTI (L.) WILLD. *'Ilb* or *Nebk* tree. Eaten by cattle. Berries edible. Used for timber.

ZYGOPHYLLUM ALBUM L. *Ruz Ribhan.* A Bean Caper.

APPENDIX II

List of distances in hours on the journey to 'Azzan; from the last point marked on this route in Von Wissmann's map.

Radhhain to Khurje (top of 'aqaba)	1 hr.	50 min.
Khurje to Zarub	3 ,,	40 ,,
Zarub to Suwaidat	3 ,,	—
Suwaidat to Madhun		50 ,,
Madhun to Ba Taraiq	2 ,,	—
Ba Taraiq to 'Aqaba Mothab ..	4 ,,	45 ,,
Mothab to 'Aqaba Medla'	5 ,,	20 ,,
Yeb'eth to 'Aqaba Mughaidifa ..	3 ,,	10 ,,
Detour in Wadi Rahbe	5 ,,	35 ,,
Rahbe to top of 'Aqaba	2 ,,	30 ,,
Rahbe jol to Dzera' pass	3 ,,	10 ,,
Dzera' pass to Lijlij	4 ,,	50 ,,
Lijlij to Naid pass	1 ,,	—
Naid pass to Mesfala	2 ,,	50 ,,
Mesfala to foot of Dhila' range ..	2 ,,	30 ,,
E. of Dhila' range to 'Azzan ..	3 ,,	30 ,,

INDEX

INDEX

Index

Index

Index

Index